SO-BYR-765

Renu

901
H77s

814
Em³p

WITHDRAWN

WITHDRAWN

DREAMERS OF DREAMS

by the same author

THE READING OF BOOKS
BOOKMAN'S HOLIDAY
THE ANATOMY OF BIBLIOMANIA
THE EIGHTEEN NINETIES
THE FEAR OF BOOKS
MAXIMS OF BOOKS AND READING
THE PRINTING OF BOOKS
OCCASIONS
ALL MANNER OF FOLK
ROMANCE AND REALITY
BERNARD SHAW
WILLIAM MORRIS

edited with an introduction

THE COMPLETE NONSENSE OF EDWARD LEAR

DREAMERS OF DREAMS

The Rise and Fall of 19th Century Idealism

by

HOLBROOK JACKSON

Dreamer of Dreams born out of my due time,
Why should I strive to set the crooked straight?
—WILLIAM MORRIS

FARRAR, STRAUS AND COMPANY

New York

820.9
J 13d

PR
469
I3
J3
1949

Made and printed in Great Britain

To
WILLIAM and CHLOE
PEAKE

91810

CONTENTS

INTRODUCTION   *page* 11

CARLYLE   55

RUSKIN   93

WILLIAM MORRIS   135

EMERSON   169

THOREAU   211

WHITMAN   253

INDEX   281

INTRODUCTION

I

The six nineteenth-century writers examined in the following pages were related to one another by sympathies and ideas. They all came under the influence of their times and in addition they influenced one another both directly or indirectly. Carlyle influenced Emerson and Ruskin; Emerson influenced Thoreau and Whitman; and Ruskin influenced William Morris. Nor were these influences merely partial or superficial. Directly or indirectly they were fundamental, inspiring loyalties and disciple-ships, altering or deflecting ideas and trends of thought, and determining for good or ill the attitude towards life in general, and, in some measure, towards their own individual way of living, of those who followed these teachers.

The most powerful influence and in other ways the most remarkable member of the group was Thomas Carlyle. Through Emerson and Ruskin he gave a new quality to the minds of the others by emphasizing the more obvious causes of nineteenth-century discontents, and the mystical element of his moral teaching had a wide if vague influence, under the name of Transcendentalism, especially among the New England writers of the first half of the century. Carlyle, himself, was not influenced by the other members of the group. His intellectual descent is from Goethe and Jean Paul Richter, and it was principally through him that nineteenth-century English thought was deflected from its Latin (largely French) to its Teutonic ancestry.

He was not without humility and reverence before the power and mystery of life, but he had pride, spiritual and intellectual, as well. That pride often prompted him to adopt the attitude of Emerson's nonconformist, as if everything were 'titular and ephemeral' but himself. Hence the numerous deprecatory criticisms and caricatures of contemporary writers and politicians which afford so much entertainment to readers of his letters and other occasional works. His own followers do not escape. Even Emerson and Ruskin, much as he respects both of them, are subjected to occasional slight and belittlement. He suspects Emerson's transcendentalism and Ruskin's volubility and enthusiasm, because these characteristics depart from his own ideals of practicability and seriousness.

Carlyle tries to keep his Pegasus near to earth and Emerson's celestial flights disturb him. Emerson is not sufficiently 'concrete' and he wishes he would 'write prose in the straightforward way'—which comes rather oddly from the author of *Sartor Resartus* and *Frederick the Great*! But strongly as he disapproves his friend's 'Gymnosophist view of Heaven and Earth' he finds 'an agreement that swallows up old conceivable dissents'. Earlier he had doubted the policy of *The Dial*, which was edited, he grumbles, by 'a Miss Margaret Fuller', a disciple of Emerson, 'who goes into very high flights about Art, Self-Sacrifice, Progress, etc., etc., it is all of a very ghostly (not *ghastly*) character, and cannot one would think have many readers,—though some of it has and ought to have'. When Emerson comes down to earth he has Carlyle's full approval, as in the famous lecture on *Man the Reformer* read at Boston in 1841 and printed by Carlyle's Lancashire friend, Thomas Ballantyne, at Bolton in the following year. He thought this essay one of the best, or almost the very best, he had ever seen of his, and he praises Ballantyne for getting it reprinted: 'everybody thinks it a favourable symptom of Lancashire Radicals that they have a sense for such ideas as these.' He may occasionally question Emerson's style, but he never doubts the quality of his mind, still less the integrity of his character. 'I do not know another man in all the world to whom I can speak with clear hope of getting adequate response from him,' is an opinion from 1847, which never changes. 'You are so companionable,' he tells him in another letter, that 'God has made you Man as well as Poet.' Higher praise could not come from Carlyle.

His attitude towards Ruskin has, perhaps, more affection than admiration. Ruskin's personal charm and generous nature touch the heart of Carlyle; his good intentions are appreciated, but his wisdom and steadiness are in doubt. Carlyle, in his old age, finds 'a real spiritual comfort in the noble fire, wrath, and inexorability with which he smites upon all base things and wide-spread public delusions', but 'for the rest I do not find him wise—headlong rather, and I might even say weak'. Yet there is 'nothing like him in England in these other respects'. And here, as in the criticism of Emerson, is the practical earnestness of the Carlylean attitude: 'I have seen Ruskin, these three Saturdays in punctual sequence . . . who promises to come weekly . . . I get real insight out of him, though he is full of friendliness and is aiming as if at the very stars; but his sensitive, flighty nature disqualifies him for earnest conversation and frank communication of his secret thoughts.' This opinion is neither new nor hastily formed; on the contrary, twenty years earlier, in the young days of their friendship, Ruskin, though pleasant company, is 'no more than a bottle of beautiful soda-water'. Ruskin's volatile nature puzzles Carlyle, but admiration for his genius ultimately triumphs, especially when he supports Carlyle's attack on Mammon. 'You go down through those dismal science people like a treble X of Senna, Glauber and Aloes, like a fit of British cholera threatening to be fatal!' He reads *Unto this Last* with exhilaration, laughter, and bravissimo, and 'marvels at the lynx-eyed sharpness' of Ruskin's logic, 'at the pincer-grip (red-hot pincers) you take of certain bloated cheeks and blown-up bellies'. 'More power to your elbow,' he concludes, 'though it is cruel in the extreme.'

In spite, however, of Carlyle's qualifications of his appreciation of Emerson and Ruskin, there is evidence that both occupy high places among those few of his contemporaries who stand the test of personal contact with him.

13

Charles Eliot Norton records that 'Emerson and Ruskin are the only distinguished living men of whom Carlyle spoke—in all the talk I ever had with him—with entire freedom from sarcasm or depreciation, with something like real tenderness'. And in the end all doubt of even Ruskin's instability disappears, and he is believed worthy to carry on the Carlylean torch.

2

Emerson has few doubts about Carlyle and his appreciation has a generosity of which Carlyle is incapable. 'What all men think, he thinks better', he records in his journal in 1848. 'Once read he is only half read', he says again, for he 'crowds meaning into all the nooks and corners of his sentences'. Curiously enough, he resents Carlyle's playfulness, but that is an act of worship: 'for why should an imagination such as never rejoiced before the face of God, since Shakespeare, be content to play?' For the rest Emerson is happy to play John the Baptist to Carlyle in America. It is through his practical enthusiasm that *Sartor Resartus* finds a publisher in the United States before it appears in England, and even when Carlyle is famous he arranges the American appearances of the *French Revolution* and *Cromwell*, and the Sage of Chelsea is very properly grateful. Proud as Emerson is of his high standing in both America and England, he is still happy to look to Carlyle as his Master and as the leader of the intellectual movement whose New England citadel was Concord. The inscription in the first edition of *Society and Solitude* which Emerson sends to Carlyle in 1870 is proof of this attitude. The words are, 'To the General in Chief from his Lieutenant'.

His relationship with Thoreau is much more intimate than that of any other of the personal associations of the group of writers. There is a considerable difference in age,

Emerson having reached middle age and literary distinction whilst Thoreau is a youth and unknown. Thoreau is a pupil as well as a disciple and a personal friend and housemate. To Emerson he is a marvellous boy, 'brave enough not to postpone his life but to live'. He admires the lad's simplicity and clear perception and his sense of humour. 'Everything that boy says makes merry with society, though nothing can be graver than his meaning.'

The relationship between the Sage of Concord and the Bard of Democracy is more ambiguous and includes one of those reversals of opinion which are characteristic of Emerson. This hesitancy is of special interest because, ten years before *Leaves of Grass* was published, Emerson himself had appealed for a true American poet in a passage which probably inspired Whitman: 'We have yet no genius in America, with tyrranous eye, which knew the value of our incomparable materials, and saw, in the barbarism and materialism of the times. . . . Banks and tariffs, the newspapers and caucus, methodism and unitarianism, are flat and dull to dull people, but rest on the same foundations of wonder as the town of Troy, and the temple of Delphos, and are as swiftly passing away. Our logrolling, our stumps and their politics, our fisheries, our Negroes and Indians, our boasts and our repudiations, the wrath of rogues and the pusillanimity of honest men, the northern trade, the southern planting, the western clearing, Oregon and Texas, are yet unsung. Yet America is a poem in our eyes; its ample geography dazzles the imagination, and it will not wait long for metres.'

When *Leaves of Grass* first appears Emerson seems instinctively to recognize the poet-child of his dreams, and sends Whitman a generous letter of appreciation. This opinion is not generally shared by the Concord circle. 'The New England crowd below stairs didn't like me,' Whitman writes with approval, for he could only have 'commanded their approval by being false to the job' he had to do. When the letter is published by Whitman's friend William

O'Connor Emerson gets into trouble. His praise is taken literally and *Leaves of Grass* is read aloud to ladies. Emerson does not exactly recant but he makes it known that if he had realized that his letter would have been published, he might have modified his praise. 'There are parts of the book', he says, 'where I hold my nose as I read.'

Whitman talks about the incident for the rest of his life, but always seeks to excuse Emerson. He comes to believe, finally, that Emerson's objections 'were neither moral nor literary, but were given with an eye to my worldly success'. Emerson believed the book would sell 'but for its sex handicap'. 'He did not see', Whitman concludes, 'that if I cut sex out I might just as well have cut everything out—the full scheme would no longer exist—it would have been violated in its most sensitive spot.' The fact is that Emerson is bewildered by Whitman, and not without reason, for they are as wide apart in methods as they are in habits.

He feels that something new and irresistible has happened but he does not trust his feelings. This bewilderment is summed up in a letter to Carlyle a few months after *Leaves of Grass* has made its appearance: 'One book, last Summer, came out in New York, a nondescript monster which yet had terrible eyes and buffalo strength, and was indisputably American—which I thought to send you; but the book throve so badly with the few to whom I showed it, and wanted good morals so much, that I never did. Yet I believe now again, I shall. It is called *Leaves of Grass*, was written and printed by a journeyman printer in Brooklyn, New York, named Walter Whitman; and after you have looked into it, if you think as you may, that it is only an auctioneer's inventory of a warehouse, you can light your pipe with it.' Emerson may qualify his earlier enthusiasm, for much of *Leaves of Grass* must have offended his taste, but he never underestimates Whitman's genius, or fails to recognize his originality. 'I know', Bronson Alcott tells Whitman in 1868, 'how fully he shares in my appreciation of yourself and your works.'

3

Thoreau is a genuine but qualified admirer of both Emerson and Carlyle. He looks upon them as the twin prophets of his time. They are the complement of each other, Emerson dealing with men of action, Carlyle with thinkers. Carlyle is the only intellectual export from England worth the attention of the American reader. He is more even than that. 'It is the best apology for all the bustle and the sin of commerce, that it has made us acquainted with the thoughts of this man,' he says in the first long article written on Carlyle by an American. Carlyle's wisdom startles and provokes rather than informs us. 'A rare preacher, with prayer, and psalm, and sermon, and benediction, but no contemplation of man's life from the serene oriental ground, nor yet from the stirring occidental.' But in his gospel there is an 'entire absence of cant and dogma'. He sweeps away 'many cart-loads of rubbish' leaving a 'broad highway' to 'the future and the possible'. And if he does not show us the way into the Promised Land he affirms a new idea of kingship which is not beyond even the consideration of a republican such as Thoreau.

Whitman, whom he meets the year after the publication of *Leaves of Grass*, puzzles Thoreau. He does not fit into any of the categories of great men according to the Concord standard. The New England coteries are democratic, but here comes a bard in the questionable shape of a superbly common fellow who is 'apparently the greatest democrat the world has ever seen'. He is strong and coarse, but 'of a sweet disposition' and 'essentially a gentleman'. His poetry is egoistic, sensual, rude: he is sometimes ineffectual and a braggart. 'He does not celebrate love at all. It is as if the beasts spoke.' No wonder Thoreau is 'somewhat in a quandary about him'. He reserves judgment, but is not dismayed by the portent. And after a few days' experience of the man and his poem Thoreau is convinced that even in his most criticized passages, Whitman 'has spoken the truth more than any American or modern' that he has known. After 'all deductions' these poems are 'very brave and American', better than all the sermons 'that have been preached in this land'. Whitman may even turn out 'the least of a braggart of all, having a better right to be confident'. But whatever his own objections he thinks so highly of the bard that he challenges the objections of others. On Emerson's authority we know that he carries *Leaves of Grass* around Concord 'like a red flag—defiantly, challenging the plentiful current opposition there'.

He feels that he ought to like Ruskin but stumbles, as Emerson does, at Ruskin's preoccupation with life from the point of view of art. He is disappointed because he finds *Modern Painters* less of an 'out-of-door book' than he has been led to believe. Ruskin 'does not describe nature as nature, but as Turner painted her. Although the work betrays that he has given close attention to nature, it appears to have been with an artist's and critic's design.' That approach appears shallow to Thoreau, and he attributes Ruskin's failure 'to the common infidelity of his age and race'. In the first place, he 'has not implicitly surrendered himself to nature. . . . He does not speak to the condition of foxes that have more spring in their legs', and, in the second, Thoreau thinks it is 'the Church of England, questioning whether that relation to nature' is of any real value. 'The love of nature and fullest perception of the revelation which she is to man', he concludes, 'is not compatible with belief in the peculiar revelation of the Bible which Ruskin entertains.' He is obviously disturbed by the novel turn given by Ruskin to the relationship between nature and art, for he returns to the subject several times. He is too much interested in aesthetics to wish for a complete separation between art and nature, so, he says, 'it has come to this, that the lover of art is one, and the lover of nature another', but 'true art is the expression of our love of nature'.

At the same time, 'it is monstrous when one cares but little about trees, and much about Corinthian columns'.

Thoreau and Ruskin would have had some difficulty in understanding one another, yet they are not so far apart in idea and method as might be supposed. Thoreau despises Ruskin's artistic approach to nature, but even here the difference is not fundamental, Thoreau being a keen but not a disinterested observer, and often more literary than precise. Both he and Ruskin, however, revere exact observation. Thoreau has been labelled 'poet-naturalist' by his admirers: they doubtless mean literary-naturalist, although philosopher-naturalist would be a better description, and, if so, he is brought still closer to Ruskin. The real affinity between them is not an interest in nature, but a common concern for the technique of living, and both of them seek and find support for their theories from natural objects—though not solely from these, and not always in the same way. Thoreau's understanding of Ruskin improves upon acquaintance. In 1857 he is reading the fourth volume of *Modern Painters*, having lately read 'most of his other books' and though he still finds that he is 'not without crudeness and bigotry' his books are 'singularly good and encouraging'. *The Seven Lamps of Architecture* is 'made of good stuff—but there is too much about art in it for me and the Hottentots. We want to know about matters and things in general. Our house is yet a hut.' It must be remembered, however, that Thoreau's opinion was formulated before Ruskin had abandoned his Evangelical attitude towards nature and art in later works like *Munera Pulveris*, *Unto this Last*, and *Fors Clavigera*.

4

Whitman hails Emerson as his Master, but the men and their methods are so different that the association, after early enthusiasms have calmed down, is rather uncomfortable

on both sides. Their contacts are broad generalizations like
Freedom, Democracy, and America. And they share an
independence of outlook and a concrete method of expression
which is America's chief contribution to the literature of
those times. For the rest the Atlantic might have separated
them, and they know it: at least, Whitman knows it and
Emerson feels it. Emerson feels that he has been hit but he
doesn't quite know where.

The thing which stands between these two great
Americans is the 'barbaric yawp'. Emerson represents the
old European culture Americanized, Whitman and Thoreau,
a return to the wild. Whitman contends that 'Emerson
possesses a singularly dandified theory of manners. He seems
to have no notion at all that manners are simply the signs by
which the chemist or metallurgist knows his metals. To the
profound scientist, all metals are profound, as they really
are. The little one, like the conventional world, will make
much of gold and silver only. Then to the real artist in
humanity, what are called bad manners are often the most
picturesque and significant. Suppose these books becoming
absorb'd, the permanent chyle of American general and
particular character—what a well-wash'd and grammatical,
but bloodless and helpless, race we should turn out!' But
Whitman's main objection to Emerson's teaching is that it
is 'based on artificial scholarships and decorums at third
or fourth removes'. It is a built up thing, never an 'unconscious growth . . . the porcelain figure or statuette of lion, or
stag, or Indian hunter—and a very choice statuette too—
appropriate for the rosewood or marble bracket of parlor or
library; never the animal itself, or the hunter himself.' The
appearance of the real animal or Indian would put to flight
all those ladies and gentlemen 'talking in subdued tones of
Browning and Longfellow and art'. The final influence of
such a teacher is 'to make his students cease to worship
anything—almost cease to believe in anything, outside of
themselves'.

This opinion is an afterthought and it does not preclude

respect for Emerson, whose life affords 'one of the few perfect and flawless excuses for being, of the entire literary
class'. Throughout his own life Whitman requires very little
prompting to set him off explaining away his early enthusiasm for Emerson. The attitude is summed up in the
penultimate paragraph of the note on Emerson's books from
which I have already quoted: 'The reminiscence that years
ago I began like most youngsters to have a touch (though it
came late and was only on the surface) of Emerson-on-the-
brain—that I read his writing reverently, and address'd him
as "Master", and for a month or so thought of him as such
—I retain not only with composure, but with positive satisfaction. I have noticed that most young people of eager
minds pass through this stage of exercise.' This looks like
an ungenerous attempt to bolster up his own originality, a
criticism supported by the paragraph which concludes the
note: 'The best part of Emersonianism is, it breeds the giant
that destroys itself. Who wants to be any man's follower?
lurks behind every page. No teacher ever taught, that has so
provided for his pupil's setting up independently—no truer
evolutionist.' This may be taken two ways. It may be a
compliment to a teacher of personal independence; or it may
be an oblique way of saying that Emerson's works fortunately
contain the seeds which finally destroy their baneful influence. In support of the former it should be recalled that
Whitman himself asserts that they are his own best disciples who learn from him how to destroy the master. But
from the general attitude of the note the latter interpretation
is probably the correct one. Whitman was jealous of Emerson.

Whitman's attitude to Carlyle who influences him not at
all is, probably for that reason, much more tolerant. He forgives him his literary origins, his bookishness, his 'college
point of view', his anti-democratic politics, and the dyspepsia
which is to be traced in every one of his pages and sometimes fills the page. 'Not for his merely literary merit
(though that was great)—not as a "maker of books", but

as launching into the self-complacent atmosphere of our days a rasping, questioning, dislocating agitation and shock, is Carlyle's final value.' He likes, as might be expected of the advocate of a 'world primal again', to remind himself of Carlyle's ruggedness—'Rugged, mountainous, volcanic . . . more a French Revolution than any of his volumes.' And he even forgives his criticism of the United States: 'I doubt', he says magnanimously, 'if he ever thought or said half as bad words about us as we deserve.' He tries to picture 'British thought' during fifty years with 'Carlyle left out' and concludes that 'it would be like an army with no artillery'.

Carlyle, the British Hamlet from Cheyne Row, more puzzling than the Danish one, 'the most erudite and sincere mind in Europe', is none the less a reactionary, the literary product of a decadent society. 'He was curiously antique.' It was his 'grim fate to live and dwell in, and largely embody, the parturition agony and qualms of the old order, amid crowded accumulations of ghastly morbidity, giving birth to the new'. The results might have been different if Carlyle had gone to America and been 'recuperated by the cheering realities and activity of our people and country—growing up and delving face-to-face resolutely with us here, specially at the West—inhaling and exhaling our limitless air and eligibilities'. He never recovers from his sophisticated environment and the 'books, and all those quiddities and mere reports in the libraries, upon which the man . . . almost wholly fed, and which even his sturdy and vital mind but reflected at best'. The fundamental difference between them is that of optimism and pessimism. Whitman is the uncompromising optimist of America as Browning is of England. He has no doubt that all's right with the World. Carlyle is haunted by 'the spectre of world-destructions'. He is a 'marked illustration' of the malady he diagnoses.

With Thoreau, as might be expected, Whitman is on better terms, although he also is bookish, but that disadvantage is negatived by the practical adjustment of his life to nature, his non-compromising attitude towards re-spectability and convention, his conscientious objection to authority, and his general go-as-you-please attitude towards men and manners. 'Thoreau's great fault was disdain—disdain for me (for Tom, Dick, and Harry): inability to appreciate the average life.' Whitman puts it down to a lack of imagination, and he is surprised and disappointed that so promising and practical a philosopher should afford 'such a very aggravated case of superciliousness'. Whitman thinks Thoreau has this failing of disdain in common with Carlyle. They both 'stood about with a wall around them'. Next to this aloofness Whitman places the charge of bookishness which he also brings against Carlyle and Emerson. 'Even his love of nature seems of the intellectual order—the book-ish, library, fireside—rather than smacking of out of doors.' At the same time he does not distrust Thoreau's intellectual-ism as he does that of the others. He even admits with satisfaction that he often finds himself 'catching a literary scent off his phrases'.

Whitman feels that there is some sort of affinity between himself and Thoreau, but he is obviously puzzled. It comes out pleasantly in a conversation at the little house in Mickle Street, Camden, when Thomas B. Harned asks him whether he thinks 'Emerson will size up in history eventually bigger than Thoreau?' Whitman replies: 'Tom, you've a hell of a habit of putting the most difficult questions to me when I'm least prepared for them.' Tom insists: 'Do you?' Whitman takes his glasses off his nose and says: 'I'm not dead sure on that point either way; my prejudices, if I may call them that, are all with Emerson; but Thoreau was a surprising fellow—he is not easily grasped—is elusive: yet he is one of the native forces—stands for a fact, for a movement, an upheaval: Thoreau belongs to America, to the trans-cendental, to the poetasters: then he is an outdoor man: all outdoor men, everything else being equal, appeal to me. Thoreau was not so precious, tender, a personality as Emerson: but he was a force—he looms up bigger and bigger: his dying does not seem to have hurt him a bit: every year has added to his fame. One thing about Thoreau keeps him very near to me: I refer to his lawless-ness—his dissent—his going his absolute own road let hell blaze all it chooses.'

It is not surprising to learn that he wavers in his appreciation of Ruskin. His attitude towards Emerson and Thoreau would prepare us for that. Horace Traubel once remarked that he never heard him quote Ruskin. Whitman replies: 'I don't like him—I don't care for him, don't read him— don't find he appeals to me. I've tried Ruskin on every way, but he don't fit.' It should be remembered that although Whitman criticizes modern civilization his teaching is inclusive and affirmative, and on those grounds alone he would have differed from such a master of exclusions and negations as John Ruskin. On one occasion the conversation at Mickle Street turns on the report of an objection raised by Tennyson against the constructions of a railway near his home in the Isle of Wight. Whitman has no sympathy with such 'sensitiveness' nor does he fear the 'age of steam'. 'There is Ruskin,' he says, 'Ruskin seems to think himself constituted to protest against all modern improvements.' Whitman welcomes them all. Yet he feels that 'Ruskin's notions of professional integrity—in art, literature—were noble, admirable, no doubt productive of vast moral educative benefits'. His knowledge of William Morris seems to have been limited. He has not read the *Earthly Paradise*—not because he does not honour Morris, but because 'I am not a constitutional reader: I do not apply myself to reading in the usual way. I have read, to be sure— read a great deal since I have been tied up indoors—but after all that has never been the chief thing with me.'

5

Ruskin even more than Emerson looks upon Carlyle as his Master. Emerson is aware of the relation: 'Carlyle was the revered Master: Ruskin the beloved disciple.' But Ruskin is not oblivious of the Master's faults, particularly his perpetual grumbling about his health. 'What . . . I chiefly regret and wonder at in him is, the perception in all nature of nothing between the stars and his stomach.' He is aware that his own diaries and letters are 'full of a mewing and moaning' but persuades himself that he keeps such things to himself and out of his letters to his friends where he 'tries to be pleasant'. Apart from such 'personal' remarks his appreciation of Carlyle is unlimited, and there are numerous acknowledgments of his influence. Carlyle is 'the only man in England to whom I can look for guidance', he says in *Fors Clavigera* (No. 37); and, in the Preface to the 1871 edition of *Munera Pulveris*, he pays a noble tribute to 'the friend and guide who has urged me to all chief labour', to whom the edition is inscribed: 'I would that some better means were in my power of showing reverence to the man who alone, of all our masters of literature, has written, without thought of himself, what he knew is for the people of his time to hear, if the will to hear were in them: whom, therefore, as the time draws near when his task must be ended, Republican and Free-thoughted England assaults with impatient reproach; and out of the abyss of her cowardice in policy and dishonour in trade, sets the hacks of her literature to speak evil, grateful to her ears, of the Solitary Teacher who has asked her to be brave for the help of Man, and just, for the love of God.'[1] After the death of Carlyle, Ruskin feels that there is nothing left for him to do but to throw himself into the 'fulfilment of Carlyle's work'.

[1] Elsewhere he calls Carlyle 'the greatest of our English thinkers'. *The Crown of Wild Olive*, 99.

Ruskin sets considerable value upon Emerson's ideas but seems to mistrust his sprightly style. He places him among 'our great teachers', second only to Carlyle. That opinion was expressed in 1867, and he still holds it in 1873, when 'no modern person has truer instinct for heroism than he'. Ten years later the opinion becomes confused. In a letter to Alexander Ireland he says, 'I have never cared much for Emerson; he is little more than a clever gossip, and his egoism reiterates itself to provocation'—a clear case of pot calling kettle black! One month later he tells Charles Eliot Norton that Emerson is often unintelligible but 'infinitely sweet and wise'. There are obvious incompatibilities between both philosophers. Ruskin often finds Emerson ambiguous and intangible, and Emerson's American optimism is revolted by Ruskin's gloomy view of life and the world, but their high regard for each other is unimpaired by differences which are largely temperamental.

I can find no evidence that Ruskin is acquainted with the works of Thoreau, but he reads Whitman, acknowledges his power, regrets his lack of humour, and helps to make him known in England, believing as he does that Whitman's poems excite hostile criticism because 'they are deadly true —in the sense of rifles—against all our deadliest sins'.

6

The two great influences in the life of William Morris are Carlyle and Ruskin, but Ruskin is the more abiding. *Sartor Resartus* and *Past and Present* fire his imagination at Oxford and the impression those works make upon him endured through his life. Ruskin also is read at Oxford where 'the earlier volumes of *Modern Painters* had been received by him with admiration akin to worship', although 'he was heard to describe the fifth volume, when it appeared in 1860, as "mostly gammon!" ' Nevertheless he shares with Burne-Jones the opinion that 'Ruskin rose like a Luther of the Arts'. The most profound influence however comes from the chapter in *The Stones of Venice* called 'The Nature of Gothic', and *Unto this Last*, both of which he reverently prints on the Kelmscott Press. 'My father's affection for Ruskin never altered as the years passed,' says May Morris, and he never tired of expressing it.

There is no ambiguity about the influence of Ruskin on Morris. It is so clear that it would be no exaggeration to say that William Morris the Craftsman-Socialist is Ruskin's greatest work. Ruskin in turn has unqualified approval for his disciple. He refers publicly to him as 'the great conceiver and doer, the man at once a poet, an artist, and a workman', as well as his 'old and dear friend'. Morris himself, who was always frank and never mean, acknowledges his indebtedness in the Preface to the Kelmscott Edition to 'The Nature of Gothic' (1892). 'To some of us when we first read it, now many years ago,' he says, 'it seemed to point out a new road on which the world should travel. And in spite of all the disappointments of forty years, and although some of us, John Ruskin amongst others, have since learned what the equipment for that journey must be, and how many things must be changed before we are equipped, we can still see no other way out of the folly and degradation of Civilization.' He believes the chapter 'one of the most important things written by the author', and that 'in future days it will be considered as one of the very few necessary and inevitable utterances of the century'.

7

The plan of this book has made it necessary to confine my interpretations to those ideas which are common to each of the six writers, and to refer briefly to special attitudes and ideas held by one author or one of the two groups. The most considerable omission is the engagement of the three American dreamers with the idea of a national literature, then as now an active theme with countries which are new or still evolving towards a characteristic form. The subject does not arise with the British dreamers, who are members of a community with an established national convention, but with the Americans it is so important that it cannot be wholly ignored, and will therefore form a part of this introduction.

The beginning of this conscious relation of mind and place may be traced in several American writers of the early nineteenth century, but in none more clearly than in Emerson, Whitman, and Thoreau. Each is an ardent advocate of Americanism because he believes that the influence of Britain and Europe, both spiritually and materially, is unsuitable to a 'new' and democratic people. They are American by anticipation: Americans born out of their due time, and like many converts they are addicted to excess of zeal, and occasionally wear their new-found faith a little awkwardly. The earliest advocates of Americanism, such as Charles J. Ingersoll, are uncompromising utilitarians emphasising material well-being as a national ideal. It is in fact, his *Discourse concerning the Influence of America on the Mind*, delivered originally before a Philadelphian audience in 1823, which provokes William Ellery Channing to make what is perhaps the first approach towards a genuine American culture. He advocates a closer relation between literature and life and that the human mind in the 'new continent' should 'move with a new freedom, should frame new social institutions, should explore new paths, and reap new harvests'. To do so will need a new attitude: 'We shall blush for our country', he says, 'if, in circumstances so peculiar, original, and creative, it shall satisfy itself with a passive reception and mechanical reiteration of the thoughts of strangers.'

8

The idea is given further emphasis and definition, in 1837, when Emerson, then the finest American flower of European culture, and one of the earliest advocates of intellectual nationalism, lamenting the absence of native writing, makes an impassioned appeal for spiritual national-ism in his famous oration delivered before the Phi Beta Kappa Society, at Cambridge (U.S.A.). 'We have listened too long', he says, 'to the courtly muses of Europe. The spirit of American freemen is already suspected to be timid, imitative, tame.' 'We all lean on England,' he insists, 'scarce a verse, a page, a newspaper, but is writ in imitation of English forms.' He is thinking as much of the influence of Coleridge, Wordsworth, and Carlyle upon himself, as of the more popular influences, and he knows that America can never achieve a national literature until she has acquired a native idiom. 'Our conventional style of writing', he says in 1839, 'is now so trite and poor, so little idiomatic, that we have several foreigners who write in our journals in a style not to be distinguished from their native colleagues.' The remedy is reversion to the colloquial for 'whatever draws on the language of conversation will not be so easily imitated, but will speak as the stream flows'.

Some years later the situation had so little changed that he seems to resign himself to America's fate as a literary dependency of Europe: 'We have our culture . . . from Europe, and are Europeans.' That is truer than even Emerson imagined, and so much truer to-day than it was then, that America, which had the chance of being the birthplace of a New World, may yet be the death-bed of the Old World. Emerson is not happy in the conviction that America prefers to be European rather than to be herself, and asks, 'can we never extract this maggot of Europe out of the brains of our countrymen?' But he can do no more than

29

make the best of a bad job, for 'the first thing we have to say respecting what are called *new views* here in New England, at the present time 1842, is, that they are not new, but the very oldest of thoughts cast into the mould of these new times'.

Emerson speaks with authority as the leader of the new movement. Americans must therefore be content, until the 'Great Yankee' comes. Curiously enough, however, 'there shall be no Great Yankee, until, in the unfolding of our population and power, England kicks the beam, and English authors write to America; which must happen ere long'. In the meantime he concludes, in a typically Emersonian somersault, 'he who first reads Homer in America is its Cadmus and Numa, and a subtle but unlimited benefactor'. For himself he says, 'I am thankful that I am an American as I am that I am a man,' and the chief merit of England is that 'it is the most resembling country to America which the world contains'. He is fully aware of his own affinity with England. Whilst trying to look upon himself as 'the total New Englander', he probably knows that he might just as easily have been a total Old Englander. His scholarship, shorn of its audacity, would have needed little acclimatization at Oxford if Harvard had not coddled and confused him. Another throw of the dice and he might have been a Matthew Arnold instead of the American scholar-saint.

9

Thoreau is more confidently American than Emerson, consequently his Old World intellect is more acutely at loggerheads with his New World sympathies. 'His aversion from England and European manners and tastes almost reaches contempt', and for that insufficient reason Emerson

believes that 'no truer American ever existed'. But he is
something more than contemptuous, he strives to be American and his contempt for imported ideas and things is the
measure of his failure to realize his ideal. It is not his
Americanism so much as his own national backsliding which
is the cause of the anti-European outburst which runs like
a chorus through his works, for try as he will he can neither
live up to his American ideal nor feel quite at home in the
land of his birth. 'My countrymen to me are foreigners', is
the burden of a plaint which takes a variety of forms and
indicates a faulty adjustment to his American environment
and that nostalgia which is the spiritual malady of trans-
planted peoples.

Thoreau, though of French descent, could easily have
been English. He was eccentric and England specializes in
eccentricity, but, more significantly, he was a field-naturalist, and England is the home of the field-naturalist and
nature-lover. The English may be said to have discovered
Nature. But whether that is an exaggeration or not, we
abound in bird-watchers and botanists. Our flora and fauna
are always under the eye of a Gilbert White, a Richard
Jefferies, or a W. H. Hudson. But no field-naturalist,
before Thoreau, has looked upon his hobby as a demonstration of nationalism. It could be argued that he is a naturalist
because he is a nationalist. When he is getting closer to
Nature he is getting closest to what is essentially American.
'Natural objects are the original symbols or types which
express our thoughts and feelings.' These objects should
be the source of literary inspiration. 'When I really know
that our river pursues a serpentine course to the Merrimack,
shall I continue to describe it by referring to some other
river, no older than itself, which is like it, and call it a
meander? It is no more meandering than the Meander is
musket quiding.'[1] The hooting of the owl, for instance, is
significant, because it was heard by his 'red predecessors

---

[1] *Journal: Autumn*, 116–17. Musketaquid is the Indian name of the
Merrimack.

. . . more than a thousand years ago', it is therefore a 'grand, primeval, aboriginal sound'. Even the grass on which he walks depresses him unless grown from native seed. He loves to get out of the cultivated fields, where he walks on 'an imported sod of English grass' and to 'walk on the fine sedge of woodland hollows on an American sward'. His interest in the Red Indian is nationalist. The aboriginal belongs to America, he is as indigenous as the moose-elk and the muskrat. As American as the prairies with their vast herds of buffaloes. But unlike his brother-nationalist, Emerson, Thoreau is not content with talk and advocacy, he strives to become what he preaches. His pilgrimage is a prolonged effort to merge himself with the *genius loci* of his native town. He is constantly making amends for the accident that made him a colonial and not an aboriginal.

I O

Walt Whitman might easily have remained a fine workman in any other land. In England he might even have been no better than a bounder. At one time it was a toss-up whether he became a 'Babbitt' or the Bard of Democracy. It is no mere assumption to say that something American gives him the twist which illuminates him with prophecy, and authorizes him to sound his barbaric yawp over the roofs of the world, recalling men to a new nonchalance towards life and a novel friendliness towards one another, towards which America is still striving.

His Americanism is a logical development of an early enthusiasm for Emerson, and a practical demonstration of literary nationalism. Walt Whitman sets out deliberately to be the first hundred per cent American poet. Emerson points the way, Whitman takes it—and he knows precisely what he is doing, and why. No writer has left such carefully stated memoranda of his aim and object. The whole of Whitman's active literary life is devoted to writing, expounding, and revising *Leaves of Grass*. His letters, diaries, conversation, and prose works generally, are commentaries on his poetry.

There are differences in complexion between Emerson's and Whitman's Americanism, as might be expected when the differences in their culture and habits are considered. Emerson always takes the scholar's point of view. He may occasionally let himself go to the extent of waving a hand to what is wild and free, but he soon recovers his habitual caution. He shrinks from the rough and tumble of commercial and industrial activities, and American heartiness does not affect his heart. Whitman, on the other hand, loudly welcomes all manifestations of national vitality. Vulgarity has no place in his vocabulary. For him, more than for any other poet, everything is for the best in the best of all possible worlds, and the crown of civilization is America.

He shares with Emerson a confusing habit of sitting on the fence, or of seeing two, or even more, sides to every question. With him, however, it is not due to intellectual hesitancy, but to his idea of a democracy which has no exclusions. But it is always possible to segregate his main trend of thought. He believes, for instance, that 'the ferment and germination even of the United States' of his day 'dated back . . . to the Elizabethan age in England', and that American literature remains in that tradition whilst American democracy is leaping ahead of it, and he decides to adjust the literary balance. It is in that capacity that he is unique and remains significant.

Whitman not only tirelessly advocates a national literature, he insists that without the development of a local imaginative literature the material achievements of the United States will avail little. He is convinced that 'America has yet morally and artistically originated nothing', and as Washington freed America from political dependence upon England, so Whitman will rescue America from dependence upon European ideals. He is an optimist and believes that a new literature will be born for the inspiration of the new and splendid state, but being also a democrat he believes that men must in the long run save themselves:

> *I lead no man to a dinner-table, library, exchange,*
> *But each man and each woman of you I lead upon a knoll,*
> *My left hand hooking you round the waist,*
> *My right hand pointing to landscapes of continents and the*
> *public road.*
> *Not I, nor anyone else can travel that road but you,*
> *You must travel it for yourself.*

I I

These dreamers and idealists have the habit of intellectualizing their emotions, but much as they revel in thought and imagination, none of them wishes to abide in those realms. The aim is always an act, however profound or complicated the thought and whatever its origin. They are, or would be, practical idealists, seeking by reform or revolution or personal example to realize their dreams. On the negative side their idealism is a protest against the materialistic (i.e. the commercial) trend of civilization; on the positive side it is an attempt to discover practical methods of reasserting and reinforcing spiritual values. The method adopted is the enlightened one of education and persuasion, but all, even Thoreau, who advocates occasional civil disobedience, would have agreed that persuasion ultimately requires the support of law, and Carlyle, Ruskin, and, to a less extent, Morris, are ready to add force.

They agree on the external causes of their discontents, but differ about the cure. Individual differences are dealt with in my chapters devoted to individual authors, but apart from them there are general differences as well as agreements between the English and the American group. The main difference is one of attitude towards the social problems of each country. The British idealists are pessimists. They look upon the Industrial Revolution and the doctrine of *laissez-faire* as a calamity. 'The great conversions of the nineteenth century', says Bernard Shaw, 'were not convictions of individual, but of social sin. The first half of the nineteenth century considered itself the greatest of all centuries. The second discovered that it was the wickedest of all the centuries. The second half saw no hope for mankind except in the recovery of the faith, the art, the humanity of the Middle Ages.'

The American idealists regret the growth of commerce with a materialistic aim but believe that the new movement can be spiritualized: 'since', as Thoreau puts it, 'the problem is not merely nor mainly to get life for our bodies, but by this or a similar discipline to get life for our souls.' The reason for these differences is obvious. England is the battleground of the Industrial Revolution and great wealth and world commerce have been achieved at the cost of hard labour for the members of the working class who are employed, and destitution and even starvation for those who are unemployed. Many of the English settlers in America at that time are refugees from the Industrial Revolution. In America there is work for all and hope for a full and free life. Emerson, Thoreau, and Whitman are advocates of a simple life and even of voluntary poverty to counteract the dangers of a commercial system which looks as though it would produce, not povery, but a vulgar prosperity.

All of them, with the possible exception of William Morris who calls himself a social-democrat, doubt or else are opposed to democratic rule. And even Morris, the only one of them who has any practical knowledge of democratic organizations, is disheartened by the experience, and falls back upon the revivalist idea of a 'new-birth' for society, and he would have supported a revived Guild System under the control of Master Craftsmen. Whitman is the bard of

Democracy, but he plays for safety, and puts his faith in great and powerful persons. Carlyle, Emerson, and Ruskin believe in leadership rather than the counting of votes. Ruskin makes many precise references to the necessity of some sort of mastership, and, like Carlyle, is a convinced opponent of the popular idea of liberty which the nineteenth century inherits from the French Revolution. 'My own teaching', he says, 'has been and is that Liberty, whether in the body, soul, or political estate of man, is only another word for Death, and the final issue of Death—Putrefaction; the body, spirit, and political estate being healthy only by their bone and laws.' Thoreau believes that all individuals should save themselves. Carlyle is an individualist who would rather rely on salvation by dictatorship.

Their opinions are important because they have had considerable indirect influence, largely in the direction of confusion, upon the reform and revolutionary movements of our time. In so far as we have an element of enlightened individualism it is due to the teachings of men like Emerson, Thoreau, and Ruskin. The ideas of Morris and Whitman, without being responsible for Acts of Parliament, have coloured the thoughts of Socialists in many parts of the world. The American and the British dreamers fall politically into two fairly distinct categories. Emerson, Thoreau, and Whitman are libertarian-individualists, with faith in the regeneration of the social system by practical goodwill and virtue. Carlyle, Ruskin, and Morris are authoritarians in revolt against forces which are destroying the remnants of a benevolent feudal system which had received its death-blow in the French Revolution, but which they think could be revived in an improved version.

I 2

Carlyle starts a set of ideas based upon hero-worship which have had a disturbing renaissance in our time. This doctrine has had perhaps a more general approval than any of the phases of his philosophy of life. It is popular because easy. Most people prefer to be ruled especially if they are encouraged to believe that they are ruling themselves. Even democrats like Whitman anticipate with gusto the coming of the great man who shall lead the herd into the promised land. Our heroes are reflections of ourselves in our heroic moments—which are generally reveries and day-dreams. The more ineffectual we are the more powerful and ruthless our hero-projection. Thus Carlyle, most frustrate of all modern prophets, gloats on tyrants like Cromwell and bullies like Frederick the Great. Thoreau, who succeeds in living many of his ideas, but achieves only a local, almost a private, boldness, is not much of a hero-worshipper. He admires John Brown of Harper's Ferry, for his 'civil disobedience' in the cause of slave-emancipation, and his Indian guide, Joe Pulvis, for his closeness to nature. Whitman gets even more of his own way, and his hero is a 'large flowing personality', like himself, tolerant, competent, American, and his name is Abraham Lincoln.

The authoritarian bias of Carlyle is evident throughout his work. It is the idea upon which his political theories are based. He is often inconsistent, confused, and ambiguous, but always clear and firm about autocracy. 'Great men', he says in his essay on 'Schiller' (1831), 'are the Fire-pillars in the dark pilgrimage of mankind'. Those words might have been taken for the text of *Heroes and Hero-worship* (1841). But the idea appears earlier in a more general form, indicating that it pervades his mind. In the essay on 'Goethe' (1828) he says, 'any given age can have but one first man' but many ages have to be content with 'a crowd of secondary men, each of whom is first in his own eyes'. The idea is dominant in *Sartor Resartus* (1831) where he sees in hero-worship a 'true religious loyalty' which 'exists, has existed, and will forever exist, universally among Mankind', and it must again become 'the corner-stone of living rock, whereon all Politics for the remotest time may stand secure'. Carlyle believes that 'the history of what man has accomplished in this world, is at bottom the History of the Great Men who have worked here. They were the leaders . . . the modellers, patterns, and in a wide sense creators, of whatsoever the general mass of men contrived to do or to attain.' These words are from the opening paragraph of the series of lectures 'On Heroes' which he delivers in London during the summer of 1840, and the remaining lectures are a repetition and amplification of this theme. It is never quite clear, however, whether greatness is right or right greatness, although it is a fair conclusion that with such a moralist as Carlyle, goodness and greatness are to be united. He has a sentimental love of power for its own sake,[1] and can excuse for that reason alone some of the more atrocious actions of a Cromwell or a Frederick, though he prefers a moral explanation. A hero, for instance, is not merely a 'great soul' he must be a 'God-created soul which will be true to its origin'.

There would have been nothing remarkable in his politics if he had gone no further than that, but he opposes his ideal of the hero as God-ordained man, and the only means of implementing man-power with God-power, to the growing dominance and confusion of democracy. He foresees, with an intense dislike, what Amiel calls the coming of the 'era of the ant hill', and attributes, sometimes unfairly, the evils of the Industrial Revolution as much to the low standard of life accepted by the masses as the lust for money-power of the masters. He realizes, in fact, that the difference between the two is not one of taste but of opportunity, yet he is unable to realize that lack of opportunity is an inherent defect of the

---

[1] 'The strong thing is the just thing.' *Chartism* (1839).

38

commercial system and not the result of defective morals on the part of masters or men. His aim is to correct abuses, not to alter an accepted and powerful system, based though it is upon what he feels to be false economics.

13

The American background of Emerson, Thoreau, and Whitman has marked and far-reaching characteristics of its own although it is more under British as distinct from European influence than it is to-day. The immigrations from Europe are growing yearly but as yet the newcomer has not altered the Colonial balance of thought or habit. When Emerson publishes his first book (*Nature*, 1836) the United States are still in the post-revolutionary period which does not end until the Civil War (1861–6). It is a period of growth and adaptation to new conditions in intellectual, industrial, and political affairs. Culture, prosperity, and unity have all to be re-considered from a new point of view and re-established on a new basis. The country is rich in natural resources, but it is largely unsettled and in some parts only partially explored: Indians and buffaloes, it must be remembered, still roam the plains.

Agriculture is the chief industry, but commerce is rapidly growing although the demand for manufactured goods is still dependent upon foreign supplies. Immigration creates an ever growing spending power and the home market is soon promising enough to encourage manufacturing enterprise, and commerce and industry develop at an unprecedented rate. There is little difficulty in earning a living and many opportunities of making fortunes. This vigorous transition from an agricultural to an industrial society is expedited by the application of steam to transport. It has been said that civilization is transport and few Americans of the first half of the nineteenth century would have contested the statement. Side by side with this material energy and in spite of the constant influx of foreign elements, national consciousness grows, and the foundation of an American culture is laid. It is obvious, however, to those who look below the surface of an ebullient patriotism, that material, rather than spiritual or even intellectual, forces are making the more rapid advances.

The Industrial Revolution then raging in England has its repercussions in America but there are marked differences due in the main to the existence of a more fluid and generous spending power and the slower development of the factory system. America pays for her imports of manufactured goods by the export of raw material, particularly cotton. Poverty and destitution as understood in England are unknown. That immunity gives a different character to the intellectual revolt against commercialism as represented by Emerson, Thoreau, and Whitman, from that of Carlyle, Ruskin, and Morris. The Americans, as we shall see, attack the materialism of commerce rather than its backwash of poverty, and the attitude is part of an impulsion which aims at the creation of a native culture based upon the spiritual and moral concepts of the early settlers in the Eastern States. Politically and socially it is based on the Declaration of Independence and in the main it is Liberal and individualist. Widespread opportunity of obtaining the means of livelihood, and absence of destitution, eliminated any such insistence upon the control of industry as that which the abuse of *laissez-faire* has produced in England.

It is on this problem that the prophets of both countries unite. Emerson, Thoreau, and Whitman represent a turn of the American conscience against itself. But they also join with Carlyle, Ruskin, and Morris in an attack upon the material success which the nineteenth century worships under the names of progress and prosperity. They fear material prosperity and demand that men should seek wealth, either within themselves or by merging themselves and their interests in the common human stock; and when all the ambiguities and subtleties, all the fine phrases and cleverness, are stripped from their works, this remains clear. America is exhorted to beware of that emphasis on possessions which these idealists believe is undermining the heroic spirit of the colonist. The mania of owning things is the burden of Whitman's message. Thoreau knows that money cannot buy what is best worth possessing. They are all convinced that what is commonest and cheapest is best, and, even in the salad days of Americanism, they fear with Emerson that

> *Things are in the saddle,*
> *And ride mankind.*

They are convinced also that their country is at the crossroads and that the quality of their civilization depends upon the turning then being taken. The same problem looms in England and the voice of our local Jeremiah, Thomas Carlyle, booms across the Atlantic, and, so far as Emerson is concerned, to some effect. Even before Carlyle, the red light is seen by Wordsworth, who sounds his warning in words which Emerson must have approved and might have written:

> *The world is too much with us; late and soon,*
> *Getting and spending, we lay waste our powers:*
> *Little we see in Nature that is ours;*
> *We have given our hearts away, a sordid boon!*

The specific danger which they see and seek to avert is the growing desire for possessions as symbolized by the pursuit of money, and much of the fear of English influences is stimulated by their dislike of that commercial civilization which England begat, and which is then in the first arrogant vigour of its ruthless and irresponsible youth. They see the evil which Wordsworth is one of the first to condemn in England, and which Carlyle later tries to arrest with his rhetoric, and later still John Ruskin and William Morris strive to supplant with utopian economics and aesthetics.

Stripped to the skin the philosophies of these three sages come to this: Life is to be lived for itself and the joy of living is the reward. That joy can best be obtained by each individual living his own life with the minimum of interference with and from others. The chief hindrance to such a code of living is the tendency to place getting before being, things before actions. They see possessions and mechanical conventions standing between men and the true life, and frankly, honestly, clearly, each according to his means, spends his genius in a vain endeavour to arrest material progress solely with spiritual and intellectual weapons.

14

Emerson is the inspirer of this protest. He sees the material trend perhaps more clearly than either Whitman or Thoreau, and suffers for his clear vision more than they do, if they can be said to suffer at all, for they have fewer doubts than their Master and fewer self-imposed responsibilities. Whitman saves himself by non-resistance. He says what he has to say, then sits and watches the results whilst his friends take care that his simple wants are satisfied. He turns his protests into affirmations and allies himself with all that is disinterested, heroic and friendly in an acquisitive world. Thoreau frankly runs, or rather saunters away. He says his say, and lives his own life, despising possessions of any kind and renouncing most of them. Emerson, on the contrary, compromises with the philistines by living among them and according to their code. He makes the best of a bad job in the hope of saving them and himself. He believes that all may yet be well and the world well saved if men could only see the soul of goodness in things evil and act in accordance with that vision.

These differences neither augment nor invalidate the

doctrines of either of the three sages. They do not externalize their philosophies and neither of them has much faith in reform. They are benevolent individualists, lovers of liberty (when it is well-behaved), and convinced believers in personal salvation. It is significant that neither Emerson nor Thoreau join the Brook Farm Socialist experiment. Emerson says, 'I do not wish to remove from my present prison to a prison a little larger. I wish to break all prisons. I have not yet conquered my own house. It irks and repents me. Shall I raise the siege of this hencoop, and march baffled away to a pretended siege of Babylon? It seems to me that so to do were to dodge the problem I am set to solve, and to hide my impotency in the thick of a crowd. . . . Moreover, to join this body would be to traverse all my long trumpeted theory, and the instinct which spoke from it, that one man is a counterpoise to a city, that a man is stronger than a city, that his solitude is more prevalent and beneficent than the concert of crowds.' What these American dreamers do is what they are, for each is conditioned in his actions by what he believes. Their teachings would be intact even if they had behaved otherwise; as it is, nothing they do can be interpreted as recantation. They try to live their philosophies, to hammer out their ideas on the anvils of their own lives, and for that reason alone, although their cause has yet to be won, they still command a place in the foreground of the panorama of American thought. No American thinkers, before or since, have thought deeper or more courageously, or seen further— or, indeed, been more American.

15

What they oppose can be stated in their own words. As far back as 1836 Emerson sees two causes operating against the 'intellectual performances' or what we might call the social progress of the time. They are devotion to property and to the influence of European ideas and traditions. What art they have is not 'enlisted in the service of Patriotism and Religion . . . the mind of the race has taken another direction—Property, Patriotism, none. Religion has no enthusiasm. It is external, prudential.' 'The age will be characterized as the era of Trade, for everything is made subservient to that agency', everything gives way to it save 'avarice'. The danger is that these material forces have a disintegrating effect upon character:

> *There are two laws discrete,*
> *Not reconciled,—*
> *Law for man, and law for thing:*
> *The last builds town and fleet,*
> *But it runs wild,*
> *And doth the man unking.*

Yet at its inception, this trade which has become the evil genius of America, was not in itself evil. The 'new and antifeudal power of commerce . . . the political fact of most significance to the American at this hour', might have created a democracy which would have satisfied the romantic aspirations even of Whitman. America is, in fact, suffering from a shortage of the right sort of human material. 'Yes, it is true there are no men. Men hang upon things. They are over-crowded by their own creation. A man is not able to subdue the world. He is a Greek Grammar. He is a money machine. He is an appendage to a great fortune, or to a legislative majority . . . or to some barking and bellowing institution, association, or church. But the deep and high and entire man, not parasitic upon time and space, upon traditions, upon his senses, or his organs, but who utters out of a central hope an eternal voice of sovereignty, we are not, and when he comes, we hoot at him "Behold this dreamer cometh!" '

Emerson shares Mackay's belief that 'there's a good time coming, boys, so wait a little longer', as most people did in

those days. He believes that the time will pass when
Americans will be content to take their 'intellectual culture
from one country and their duties from another'. But he is
disturbed and puzzled, because he fears that all is not well
and he is not certain of the remedy. 'Our people are sur-
rounded with greater external prosperity and general well-
being than Indians or Saxons: more resources, outlets,
asylums: yet we are sad, and these were not. Why should
it be?' The answer is vague enough; sadness is inevitable
when there is disequilibrium between ideas and actions.
He sees some good in the feverish new commerce which
is being grafted upon the culture of his country, but he is
conscious as well of the seeds of degeneration in this new
thing. Prosperity and success bring evils in their train. They
dominate where they should serve. The only hope is that
progress will find a way out, for 'trade is but for a time, and
must give way to something broader and better, whose
signs are already dawning in the sky'.

The preoccupation of people with the getting of money
disturbs him: 'O what a wailing tragedy is this world, considered in reference to money-matters.' He knows that money
which cannot spend itself is of no value and we have lived to
witness the irony of America facing poverty in the midst of
undreamt-of possessions. In the year 1844 he realizes that
'the currency threatens to fall entirely into private hands'.
The threat has been consummated in a manner unimagined
even by Emerson. He fears also, what the whole of Western
Civilization has since experienced, the establishment of 'a
public mind so preoccupied with the love of gain, that the
common sentiment of indignation at fraud does not act with
its natural force'.

The New World is even compared unfavourably with
'that old rotten country Germany', where there would seem
to be more spontaneity of character than in 'this country,
called new and free'. 'We are the most timid crippled old
uncles and aunts that ever hobbled along the highways without daring to quit the sidewalk.' His essay on 'Self-Reliance'

protests against that condition, and he prophesies that 'A great genius must come and preach self-reliance', because 'our people are timid, desponding, recreant whimperers'. In his most courageous moments he advises his people to 'cut the traces' of a life which has grown so ponderous that 'the poor spirit' cannot drag any longer 'this unnecessary baggage-train'; and he hopes the 'sluggard intellect' of America will 'look from under its iron lids, and fill the postponed expectation of the work with something better than the exertions of mechanical skill'.

He has faith enough to look forward into a future less grasping in industry, less conventional socially, and morally of greater heart and culture; but he has little faith in the institutions of his day, still less in politicians, and little in the churches. In such a mood he exhorts the youth of America to come to the rescue of their degenerate country. 'I call upon you, young men,' he says, 'to obey your heart, and be the nobility of this land. In every age of the world, there has been a leading nation, one of the more generous sentiment, whose eminent citizens were willing to stand for the interests of general justice and humanity, at the risk of being called, by the men of the moment, chimerical and fantastic. Which should be that nation but these States? Which should lead that movement if not New England? Who should lead the leaders, but the Young American?' But Young America takes no notice.

16

In these views Emerson is aided and abetted by his disciples, Thoreau and Whitman, each in his own way, independent of the Master in form of expression but charged with the fervour of his idea, and lit with his fire. But they both differ from him in that they call neither upon God nor

46

man for aid. They believe that revolutions should begin at home, in the only realm they are entitled in some measure to rule—themselves. It is true that, under the influence of Carlyle and Emerson, they salute the idea of salvation by heroes and supermen, but they do not allow that to interfere with the real business of being themselves. 'If', says Thoreau, 'we would restore mankind by truly Indian, botanic, magnetic, or natural means, let us first be as simple and well as Nature ourselves, dispel the clouds which hang over our own brows, and take up a little life into our pores. Do not stay to be an overseer of the poor, but endeavour to become one of the worthies of the world.'

The worthies are not those who have achieved success by accumulating material possessions. 'The poor rich man! all he has is what he has bought. What I see is mine. . . . He is a rich man, and enjoys the fruit of his riches, who summer and winter for ever can find delight in his own thoughts.' *Walden* is not only the account of an experiment in simple living, it is a demonstration of the advantages of voluntary poverty. The practical philosopher must face poverty, for in that condition only can he keep close to the essentials of life. 'It is life near the bone that is sweetest. . . . Superfluous wealth can buy superfluities only. Money is not required to buy one necessary for the soul.' You actually make a man richer, he argues, 'in proportion as you rob him of earthly luxuries and comforts'. Thoreau looks upon America's business enthusiasm as trivial and dangerous, and the worship of prosperity as illusion-hunting. Trade is artificial and impermanent, going against the grain and postponing life. 'If the first generation does not die of it, the third or fourth does.' He asserts in the face of statistics that it is not the descendents of tradesmen that keep the state alive, but of simple yeomen and labourers. He dislikes the commercial system with its competition for money and its reliance on banks and prophesies that it will not last.

He compares the frailty of finance with the permanence of inward riches, the 'commonsense' of the philistine with the 'moonshine' of the transcendentalist; and is able to crow a little when, in 1857, one of those periodical financial crises looks like wrecking the whole system. 'If there was any institution which was presumed to rest on a solid and secure basis, and more than any other represented this boasted common sense, prudence and practical talent, it was the bank; and now those very banks are found to be mere reeds shaken by the wind. Scarcely one in the land has kept its promise. It would seem as if you only need live for forty years in any age of this world, to see its most promising government become the government of Kansas, and banks nowhere.' He is unaffected by those still more familiar operations which reduce financial blood-pressure, and consoles himself characteristically: 'this general failure . . . is rather occasion for rejoicing, as reminding us whom we have at the helm—that justice is always done.' If merchants and banks did not fail his 'faith in the old laws of the world would be staggered. The statement that ninety-six in a hundred doing such business surely break down is perhaps the sweetest fact that statistics have revealed—exhilarating as the fragrance of sallows in spring.' He believes that hard times are valuable because they show us what financial promises are worth and 'where the *sure* banks are'.[1]

Thoreau's life is an effort to dodge the commercial system. 'Farming and shopkeeping and working at a trade or profession are all odious to me. I should relish getting my living in a simple primitive fashion. The life which society proposes to me to live is so artificial and complex, bolstered up on many weak supports, and sure to topple down at last, that no man surely can ever be inspired to live it, and only "old fogies" ever praise it. At best some think it their duty to live it.' And he suspects even his own aim to live simply, 'raising what you eat, making what you wear, building what

---

[1] *Familiar Letters* (1894), 371–2. There had been a similar 'crisis' in 1837. The latest and greatest came nearly a hundred years later (1929–30) when over six hundred banks in America defaulted and millions of people were ruined.

you inhabit, burning what you cut and dig, when those to whom you are allied outwardly, want and will have a thousand other things which neither you nor they can raise, and nobody else, perchance, will pay for. The fellow-man to whom you are yoked is a steer that is ever bolting right the other way'. Civilization is not making life but substitutes for life. 'It makes shoes, but it does not toughen the soles of the feet. It makes cloth of fine texture, but it does not touch the skin.' Inside the civilized man stands the savage still in the place of honour.

17

How far these idealists have influenced their American compatriots it is not easy to say. On the face of it their influence is so small that there is abundant evidence of America having progressed in the opposite direction to that indicated by them. The last fifty years have seen the world's biggest bid to make a success of materialism. The voice of the idealist has been drowned by ballyhoo. Success has beaten quietism. Argument has been superseded by advertisement, romance by security, patriotism by success, thrift by extravagance, religion by megalomania, and nationalism by an internationalism, which her opponents call imperialism. And now, as Emerson, Thoreau, and Whitman could have told, and did, in effect, tell them, the Tower of Babel has collapsed.

Yet this vast experiment in salvation by material success is not ending without a struggle for righteousness. America has never lacked, even within her boundaries, Jeremiahs and candid friends. No country in the world has produced so many would-be saviours. Whilst the whole nation is ostensibly building a business structure to give permanent material prosperity and a good time to all, other Americans are protesting that all is not well and advocating reform or flight. Reform by making business a service or flight towards the negation of business and international activities.

It is an ironical comment on recent American history both in ideas and affairs that much of it has been perversely influenced by the early idealists, and especially by Emerson. There are those even who have ventured to steal his thunder though none has had the temerity to tamper with his lightning. It may be, however, that at this point we come closest to an intellectual and perhaps a spiritual attitude which may be real rather than mimetic. There are reasons why Americans should react from European pessimism. They are in the main refugees from Europe and despite nostalgia America is still the Promised Land. Emerson and Thoreau, with all their disenchantment, launch the barque of optimism, and Whitman fills its sails with such a gale of hope as neither America nor any other country have felt before. Their optimism is so convinced, their faith in man so invincible, that each in his own manner is either a believer in *laissez-faire* or an unabashed anarchist.

All those American philosophies and theologies that have not been peculiar to a group, which are retreatist if not exactly defeatist, have played their various tunes upon the broken harp of hope. And, taking into account at its fullest value the national attitude recorded above, which has become temperamental, it is not stretching analogy too far to say that in Emerson you may find the origins of those diverse movements and modes of thought represented by the pragmatism of William James and the humanism of Irving Babbitt, as well as the mental therapy of Mary Baker Eddy and the business evangelism of Elbert Hubbard—to come no further forward.

Nothing more tangible than an intellectual and in some measure a spiritual striving is left of all that revolution of the spirit which made Concord the American 'home of lost causes and impossible ideals'; nothing of Emerson but an echo in human philosophy. Thoreau's experiment by Walden Pond, like Brook Farm, lives only in a book; Whitman and his curious circle of comrades have no successors, and the imitations of his chants and drum taps are curiosities of literature. Life goes on in America as though none of them had preached or sung, but the still small voice has, perhaps, been ignored, not silenced, for in the pages of the *Essays* and *Representative Men*, in *Walden* and the *Week on the Concord*, and in *Leaves of Grass* and *Democratic Vistas*, it repeats the message and will continue to do so until Western Civilization is ready to listen.

18

It should soon become obvious to the readers of this book that the six dreamers of dreams have been as much concerned with their own as with the world's salvation. William Morris asks, in the quotation I have used for my text—'why should I strive to set the crooked straight?' I have tried to answer that question by examining their lives in relation to their ideas. The conclusion is that they were all out to straighten what was crooked in themselves, that they were all geniuses of acute sensibility, endeavouring to adjust themselves to disagreeable or antagonistic conditions. Being lively observers of human behaviour they are aware of this egoistic tendency, sometimes even in themselves but more often in others. Emerson, himself a professed egoist and self-saver, recognizes with disapproval the egoism which prompted the aristocrats of the eighteenth century to believe that the world could not go on without them. He thinks the illusion amounts to insanity. 'Lord Bristol', he says, 'plainly believes that it is very good of him to exist.' Ruskin is often irritated by Carlyle's self-concern which permits him to spend two months in North Wales without seeing a 'Cambrian thing or event, but only increase of Carlylian bile'.

All of them would have been ready to admit with Sir

Thomas Browne that we carry the universe in the 'cosmography of ourselves', but such an admission would have had little or no effect upon them. The reforms or revolutions advocated are designed to promise better conditions for themselves, and acceptability by their fellow men is a secondary consideration. But as they are not only dreamers but men of moral ambition with highly developed social consciences, they feel it necessary to justify their self-willed demands, and they do so by using the familiar argument that what they advocate is good for others. All world-savers have done the same with varying degrees of frankness, but actually they have no more interest in humanity than a painter in pigments, a writer in words, or a violinist in his fiddle. Pigments, words, and fiddles are the media of their arts and tolerable only if they serve the artist's purpose. Human beings are the raw-material of artists in reform or revolution.

It is impossible for those who would save their fellows, no matter how disinterested they may seem to be, to disguise this fundamental egoism from any but the credulous acceptor of human phenomena at their face value. Saviours are usually more successful in disguising their motives from themselves, but some of them have moments of self-realization when they are frank enough, or indiscreet enough to reveal those motives to others. Thoreau, the *enfant terrible* of New England intelligentsia, takes a delight in giving the show away. 'I in my folly am the world I condemn.' This would be almost a trite remark if uttered by an ordinary man, but coming from such a self-analyst it demands more careful consideration, especially in the light of what follows, and of what he confesses elsewhere. He very rarely, 'indeed, if ever', feels 'any itching' to be 'what is called useful' to his fellow men. He has no 'designs on society, or nature, or God'. Sometimes when his thoughts have nothing better to do, he says, 'I have dreamed idly of stopping a man's horse that was running away; but, perchance, I wished that he might run, in order that I might stop him;—or of putting out a fire; but then, of course, it must have got well agoing. Now, to tell the truth, I do not dream much of acting upon horses before they run, or of preventing fires which are not yet kindled.' All of which is rather involved, but it is preliminary to the life-long reformer's confession that he has no desire to save his fellows. 'What a foul object is this of doing good!' he says, 'instead of minding one's own life, which should be his business; doing good as a dead carcass, which is only fit for manure, instead of as a living man—instead of taking care to flourish, and smell sweet, and refresh all mankind to the extent of your capacity and quality.'

● It might seem even now that he is thinking of an indirect influence upon his fellow men, but he is not. He is still thinking of himself and excusing himself. He knows instinctively that every man in the last resort is saving himself, but being a puritan with a conscience to placate, he must first persuade himself that he is doing good, bad as he believes that to be. This is evident from the remarks he makes about his acquaintances as well as about himself. 'They mistake', he says on one such occasion, 'their private ail for an infected atmosphere.' There are innumerable indications in his essays and letters that he is addressing himself, and at least one where he admits it: 'You will perceive that I am as often talking to myself, perhaps, as speaking to you.' Thoreau devotes most of his waking life to talking, writing, or thinking about himself, and his only prayer is a plea for help towards a satisfactory self-realization:

> Great God! I ask thee for no meaner pelf,
> Than that I may not disappoint myself.

Ruskin, as might have been expected, is as frank. He lives in a constant irritation at the appearance of the world and the behaviour of its inhabitants. 'I will put up with this state of things, passively, no longer,' he says in *Fors Clavigera*, and he goes on to admit that since he is not 'an unselfish person, nor an Evangelical one' he has 'no particular pleasure in doing good'. But he 'cannot paint, nor read, nor look at minerals, nor do anything else' that he likes, 'and the very light of the morning sky, when there is any—which is seldom, nowadays, near London—has become hateful' to him, because of the misery both seen and unseen which he knows to exist.

Parallel passages could be obtained from the other dreamers. They would not be so frank but they would all express the reactions of acute sensibilities against unsuitable environments and conditions, when they do not reveal, as in some few instances, notably in Thoreau and Ruskin, an instinctive wish to be in opposition to general opinion. •

THOMAS CARLYLE

Fantasy being the organ of the Godlike; Man thereby, though based, to all seeming, on the small Visible, does nevertheless extend down into the infinite deeps of the Invisible, of which Invisible, indeed, his Life is properly the bodying.

THOMAS CARLYLE

I

Of all the prophets who wrestled for the soul of an era
which seemed to be heading for destruction on the
rocks of materialism, Carlyle is the most Biblical. The
prophets of old are pessimists and so is he, and like them, he
believes that if his advice were only taken a mad world might
become sane. He looks with foreboding upon the break-up
of an old system which had its faults but was at least orderly,
and the oncoming of changes which seem to lead to confusion, or even to chaos. He tells Caroline Fox, in 1842,
that the social system 'seems all going wrong and tending
irresistibly to change—which can't but be for the worse'.
There is not, in fact, a single existing institution which is as
he would have it. His advice is not taken any more than that
of any other prophet. It must be recognized however, that
the advice would not have been easy to follow even if it had
been less negative than it was, for his mind is so fashioned
that he can denounce the disease and doubt the remedy
simultaneously. His negations are always more emphatic,
and numerically more formidable than his affirmations. He
has as little sympathy for the disjointed times as for those who
try to set them right, and seems to take a savage delight in
making the worst of a bad job.

The doctrines of the social reformers are 'windy shibboleths'. Mazzini's republicanism and progress are 'Rousseau
fanaticism' for which Mazzini has 'at no time the least
evidence'. 'Progress of the species' he can 'get no good of at
all'. He is a violent opponent of *laissez-faire* in all its aspects,
particularly Free Trade, and the economics of 'supply and
demand'. Reformers whether political or religious, are cranks
and faddists, or misguided fools. 'Sect-founders as a class I
do not like. No truly great man from Jesus downwards ever
founded a sect.' The idea of 'universal peace' is 'balderdash'.

Darwin's theory of evolution is 'wonderful' only 'as indicating the capricious stupidity of mankind'. He 'never could *read* a page of it, or waste the least thought upon it. There is no 'discernible Religion' in the land 'except a degraded species of Phallus-Worship, whose liturgy is in the Circulating Libraries!' Ten years earlier (1840) he announces that the Church of England is 'soon about to leave the world'. And for democracy, the still new political faith of Europe, he reserves his heaviest blows. Democracy is 'the gradual uprise, and rule in all things of roaring, million-headed, unreflecting, darkly suffering, darkly sinning Demos come to call its old superiors to account, at its maddest of tribunals'. Even the United States, 'which can do *without* governing—every man being able to live', falls under the threat of the democratic *débâcle*, with its 'speeches to Bunkum' and its 'constitutional battle of Kilkenny Cats' at Washington. The prospect of a democratic era arouses his wrath and fear, and the conception of Parliament with 'twenty-five millions mostly fools' listening to it, is the measure of his contempt for the constitution bequeathed to us by his hero, Cromwell.

2

There is much deliberate exaggeration here. Carlyle enjoys over-statement as much as he enjoys grumbling. Exaggeration is also one of his ways of being humorous. There is violence even in the look and sound of the Carlylean vocabulary. Such words as *footlicker, voiceful, fugle-worship, pococurantism, mumbo jumboism, potwalloper, dryasdust*, are irritable and provocative, but, at the same time, they are among the little jokes which Carlyle explodes like Chinese crackers for the amusement as well as the good of his friends and readers. He dislikes crowds, therefore London during the

Great Exhibition in 1851, witnesses 'such a Sanhedrin of windy fools from all countries of the Globe' as were 'never gathering together in one city before'. He dislikes Roman Catholics therefore he dislikes even the idea of one of Jane's nurses who 'was under the foul tutelage and guidance . . . of some dirty, muddy-minded, semi-felonious, proselytising Irish priest'. He is always dramatizing his emotions and takes a pleasure in living up to his own idiosyncrasies. Like Bernard Shaw, his nearest twentieth-century prototype, he cultivates shock-tactics. In the last of the *Latter-Day Pamphlets*, the most explosive chapter in one of his most explosive books, he seems to gloat on this form of attack: 'By way of finish to this offensive set of Pamphlets, I have still one crowning offence and alarm to try if I can give.' He is frequently like a termagant who is determined to give people a piece of her mind at the top of her voice.

. The objection to this habit of vituperation is that it tends to entertain rather than convince. I can imagine Carlyle's contemporaries waiting for these outbursts and missing the message, as opera audiences wait for the top-notes of a tenor or the bottom notes of a bass. The consequence for Carlyle is that he is remembered more widely for his crackers than for his profundities. Even his *potwallopers* and *blockheads* may congratulate themselves that they are exceptions to the 'twenty-five millions—mostly fools', and those who are aware of the march of superstition are stunned rather than outraged when told that the 'Human Species' has 'gone all to one Sodality of Jesuitism' and 'is in truth like death-in-life; a living criminal . . . with a *corpse* lashed fast to him'. By the time the psychologist has explained that these outbursts were not entirely pretty Fanny's way, but the attempted consolations of a frustrated but great-hearted man, the wisdom behind the words is forgotten. But without this intellectual brawling there would be no Thomas Carlyle. Invective acts upon him like adrenalin, and enables him to transmute his low spirits into the high endeavour of trying to save his Gadarene compatriots from destruction. He is so infatuated with his own rhetoric that one is not always certain whether he is overwhelmed by pity or anger, or simply and noisily enjoying himself. He is, says Emerson, 'like a drunken man who can run but cannot walk'. His thoughts are as tumultuous and as eccentric as his prose, having so much punch and so little direction that one is persuaded that cursing rather than curing has become a habit—or a hobby. Grumbling becomes his profession. Emerson again comes near the truth when he ventures to describe the Carlylean brand of vituperation as 'the rhetoric of a highly virtuous gentleman who *swears*'. Grumbling, like swearing, is a relief from some forms of frustration, and whether Carlyle was frustrated in his personal life or not, he was conscious, too conscious, of the general absence of enthusiasm for his gospel and so, he tells Emerson, 'for the years that remain, I suppose we must continue to grumble out some occasional utterance'. In addition to such legitimate causes he enjoys contemplating his own real or imaginary sorrows, shutting his lips 'with a kind of grim defiance, a kind of imperial sorrow which is almost like felicity'. He can even joke about his dyspepsia ('I enjoy bad health, too, considerably'), and if his letters continue to explode with such expression as *Ach Gott! Oh, dear me! Eheu!* and *Ay de mi!* the detonations are little more than a habit, or, as his wife ventures to remind him, a trick. But whether from anger or for amusement, he never ceases to grumble even when he shoves his 'paper-whirlpools aside' and growls, 'in pleased response' to the letters of his friends.

There is obviously something abnormal in anyone who wallows in woe,[1] even with such grim good humour, and whilst listening to his demands, one cannot help suspecting that to grant them might plunge him further into the Slough of Despond by robbing him of that right to grumble which fires his genius. Even after a lecture has been acclaimed by

[1] He is fond even of using the word, but, apparently, in order to make it more woful, he spells it 'wo'.

the public he 'is ready to hang himself . . . in the idea that he has made a horrible *pluister*[1] of it'. No demonstrations of satisfaction by his audience can convince him to the contrary.

3

This duality may also be observed in the special range of lamentations reserved for his literary work. He voluntarily wears the mantle of a prophet but complains bitterly of the resulting drudgery. Yet he knows that writing is a relief as well as a torture, though he stresses the painful side of it. He feels himself both a master and slave of letters. 'The business of writing has become contemptible to me,' he cries, 'and I am confirmed in the notion that nobody ought to write, unless sheer Fate force him to do it.' Writing is 'a terrible business and will not get on with me hitherto at all; so the whole soul of me is filled with a black confused lake, for which there is yet no outlet: a very unjoyful state of things'. He is in the 'birth-throes' as he calls it, of *Past and Present*. When he is writing *The French Revolution*, he tells his mother with more justification, that he 'often thinks it is a great malady and madness this poor Book of mine, which wears one so'. His 'thrice unfortunate book on Cromwell . . . is a real descent to Hades, to Golgotha and Chaos', and he feels that it 'were possibler to die one's self than bring it into life'. But, as might be expected, he reserves his loudest grumbles for *Frederick*, a masterpiece vast and complicated enough to tax any writer's health and patience. 'In my despair', he says, 'it often seems to me as if I should never write more; but be sunk here and perish miserably in the most undoable, least worthy, most disgusting and heartbreaking of all labours I ever had.'

[1] A mess.

In spite of all this he can also tell his mother during the progress of *The French Revolution* that the work is 'a great happiness, and gives me the completest undifference towards all fretting of fortune, towards much that has haunted me like pale spectres all my life long. With little in my purse, little in my hope, an no very fixed landmark in this Earth, I stand serene under the sky, and really have the peaceablest fearlessness towards all men and things. Such blessing I owe to the poor Book; and therefore will not abuse it, but speak well of it.' These words become heroic when it is recalled that they refer to the enforced rewriting of a whole volume, the manuscript of which had been used for lighting fires by a housemaid of John Stuart Mill.

4

Carlyle was undoubtedly misanthropic but he was not a complete misanthrope. His letters and pamphlets carelessly read, give an erroneous impression of invincible gloom and bad temper, of a prickly curmudgeon who shrinks from his fellows and curses them from afar. He may have helped to create this caricature of himself for purposes of advertisement or disguise, but once his spiritual as well as his physical doorstep had been crossed, a kindly and companionable man is revealed. And just as too much has been made of the legend of Carlyle and Tennyson enjoying an evening together silently smoking, so too much, also, has been made of the numerous depreciations of his fellow men which, individually as well as in the mass, are so characteristic of his work. His pity for men in general as well as his tenderness and affection for his friends, are well-established, although his habit of raillery, does not prevent him from making misleading remarks about them. He must have had a genius for friendship or he could not have maintained the affection of such men as Tennyson, Ruskin, and Edward FitzGerald, to name but three difficult members of a wide and distinguished circle. His *Life of John Sterling*, where in his own words, he flings 'down on paper some outline of what my recollections and reflections contain in reference to this most friendly, bright and beautiful human soul; who walked with me for a season in this world, and remains to me very memorable while I continue in it', is an elegy of friendship deeply felt and generously expressed.

Long ago Ruskin pointed out that when analysing the mind of Carlyle no one had succeeded in separating the pity from the anger. The feat would be as difficult even now because of Carlyle's querulous method of expression. It is not necessary, however, to attempt any serious segregation for, in spite of the habit of overlaying his sympathy with angry words, all who know him testify to his kindness and generosity. The essential tenderness of this bombastic preacher is revealed in his letters to his family, particularly those to his mother, and pity, always hiding somewhere in his works, often peeps through his noisy scoldings. *Sartor Resartus* ferments with self-pity, but it could not have been written without pity for humanity as well. The gentleness with which he handles character in *Heroes and Hero-Worship* is almost feminine, and *The French Revolution* is an epic of pity for his fellow men in their blindness and frenzy.

Carlyle is a man of feeling striving yet failing to translate his feelings into thought. This striving explains his irascibility and the fantastic rhetoric in which it finds expression. It has been suggested that these exaggerations, repetitions, verbal explosions, are means of relief. He may have found in such noises, as Nietzsche has suggested, respite from mental confusion. But more likely, his style is an unconscious bulwark against the perils of introspection, the 'scepticism: diseased self-listenings, self-questionings, impotently painful dubitations, all this fatal nosolgy of spiritual maladies, so rife in our day'.

5

More than usual even with egotistical writers the works of Carlyle are mainly about himself. 'To reduce matters to writing', he tells Emerson, 'means that you shall know them, see then in their origins and sequences, in their essential lineaments, considerably better than you ever did before.' He is not interested in anything for its own sake. He is a romantic and cannot dodge himself even if he would. Emerson is quick to note this peculiarity and he has the courage and honesty to tell him: 'You are very wilful, and have made a covenant with your eyes that they shall not see anything you do not wish they should.' *The French Revolution* is a background for his broodings on life and destiny. He pays more legitimate attention to himself in the *Reminiscences*, where he exhibits himself to the world as an object of pity. Even in his comparatively objective works on Oliver Cromwell and Frederick the Great he often pays more attention to the propagation of his own taste for authoritarian principles than to the facts of history. He is, in fact, over-ridden by his own ego, and in lucid moments he knows it. His books are extracts of himself; he writes as he feels and feels as he writes and the end is exhaustion as well as relief.

6

Some of his peculiarities are now attributed to the still disputed evidence that he was wholly or partially impotent. 'Carlyle', says Geraldine Jewsbury, 'was one of those persons who ought never to have married.' That is vague and not sufficient evidence in itself, but it is the opinion of one of Jane Carlyle's closest friends, and quoted by Froude in such a way as to leave no ambiguity. The point, however, need not be pressed, for whether he was physically defective or not there can be little doubt that either through inhibitions or excessive absorption in intellectual work he was, like his brother John, physically reluctant, a condition not conducive to marital fulfilment. All might have been well if he had married a cold or indifferent woman who would have been content to function domestically, but in Jane he found a mate who was capable of giving more affection than he needed or could return. The incongruity must have been observed early, but as Froude points out, 'Carlyle did not know when he married what his condition was', and he sought relief from the distress of frustration in outbreaks of temper.

'The morning after his wedding-day', according to John Nichol, 'he tore to pieces the flower garden at Comely Bank in a fit of ungovernable fury'. Displays of temper were succeeded by fits of gloom. The habit of shutting himself up in 'interior solitude' began during that curious honeymoon. He 'seldom saw his wife from breakfast till 4 p.m., when they dined together and read *Don Quixote* in Spanish. The husband was half forgotten in the author beginning to prophesy: he wrote alone, walked alone, and for the most part talked alone, i.e. in monologue that did not wait or care for answer. There was respect, there was affection, but there was little companionship.'

The threatening storm, or series of storms, is observed by Jeffrey even in these early days. After a visit to Craigenpattock he advises Carlyle to leave the lonely farmstead and settle in Edinburgh, 'and in the meantime be gay and playful and foolish with her, at least as often as you require her to be wise and heroic with you'.

There can be no doubt that Jane had physical as well as social charm. Men are attracted to her, and she apparently resists temptation because she has no desire to do otherwise. Her heart she feels is capable of a love 'to which *no* deprivation would be a sacrifice—a love which would overleap that reverence for opinion with which education and weakness have begirt her sex'. The fact that Jane could rely upon her own natural prudence before and after marriage is not inconsistent with an appreciation of masculine attentions, an appreciation often but dimly veiled by humorous contempt. It must not be forgotten that Jane is a sociable woman with plenty of what we now call sex-appeal, and Carlyle a bilious philosopher with no time for love. Yet they are so necessary to each other that these and other incompatibilities cannot finally break the loyalty and admiration which bind them together, and although the relationship is often strained, it is saved from cleavage by a sense of humour on the part of Jane which is so rare in such circumstances as to be very nearly unique.

Neither Jane nor her more intimate friends and relations are ignorant of her effect upon men. Geraldine Jewsbury agrees with the opinion of a relative that 'every man who spoke to her for five minutes felt impelled to make her an offer of marriage'. This attractiveness continues after marriage, and although her fidelity is never questioned, she is a coquette and not above flirtation, which her husband seems to condone, perhaps as a penance for his own inadequacy. Jeffrey, for instance, becomes, 'in a sort, her would-be openly declared friend and quasi-love, as was his way in such cases'. Carlyle rightly concludes that 'suspicion of her nobleness would have been mad', and 'could I', he asks, 'grudge her the little bit of entertainment she might be able to extract from this poor harmless sport, in a life so grim as she cheerfully had with me?'

7

But if he is tolerant of Jane's innocent flirtations, Jane is not equally tolerant of the attentions he pays to Lady Harriet Baring, for although Froude has distorted the affair, there can be little doubt that the Sage of Chelsea takes a particular delight in the company of that lady, and that Jane is jealous. The intensity of his affection is not known, but it is certain that it does not trespass upon his love for his wife. She, in fact, is more disturbed by her own jealousy than by any real fear of an estrangement. 'O why cannot I believe it once for all,' she asks him, 'that with all my faults and follies, I *am* "dearer to you than any earthly creature".' At the same time even a more patient wife might reasonably have complained if a husband who is an inadequate bed-fellow and mewed up in his study for the best part of the day, should devote a disproportionate part of his leisure to the company of another woman, whatever the motive.

Here, in these purely sexual disparities, is sufficient explanation of a homelife which their own epistolary gifts expose to undue curiosity and remark, without emphasizing a not proven physical defect.[1] In spite of the legend that they were unsuited for married life, the letters prove that they are not always unhappy. And in spite of a warmth generated by absences, and expressed in letters of fervency, charm, and humour, there must have been innumerable hours of tranquillity when their lives blend in a harmony of content. Tennyson, who knows them well, thinks that, 'on the whole' they enjoy life together, 'else they would not have chaffed one another so heartily'. Emerson believes that they

[1] 'It was very good of God to let Carlyle and Mrs. Carlyle marry one another and so make only two people miserable instead of four, besides being very amusing.' Samuel Butler, *Letters between Samuel Butler and Miss E. M. Savage* (1935), 349–50.

'live on beautiful terms. Their ways', he writes in his Diary, 'are very engaging, and, in her bookcase, all his books are inscribed to her . . . each with some significant lines.' One such occasion is recorded for Emerson's delight in a letter of 1838, immediately following the unappreciated appearance of *Sartor Resartus*. Carlyle is recoiling from the blow, feeling 'forsaken, sad, sick' but 'not unhappy'. Life still seems beautiful and great were it never to be joyful any more, and, he says, 'I read books, my wife sewing by me, with the lightness of a sinumbra, in a little apartment made snug against the winter; and am happiest when all men leave me alone, or nearly all—though many men love me rather, ungrateful that I am'.

There is no doubt of their love for one another, but it is not a normal love. On her side it is admiring and protective. She knows his weaknesses, and is more often amused than annoyed by them. She is capable of admiring his genius and of liking his books. On the lecture platform she thinks that he 'really looked a surprisingly beautiful man'. She is convinced that he is incapable of taking care of himself, and proceeds to mother him. As he 'would almost have an affair with a mad dog as with a Cockney shopman', she has to do his shopping for him, even to ordering his coats and trousers. But she cures him of this shyness to some extent when she buys him a sky-blue coat with 'glorious yellow buttons' which would have made him 'an ornament to society'. The philosopher's faith in his wife's judgment is shaken 'at least so far as dressing him is concerned', and henceforward he buys his own clothes.

When he is absent from her and depressed she wants 'to kiss' him 'into something like cheerfulness'. And when he is in real sorrow, as, for instance, on the death of his father, she wraps him, he says, 'like the softest bandage'. She is even disturbed when he ceases to grumble, as he does when he goes on a jaunt to Wales while she gets on with the spring cleaning. 'I wish he would growl a bit,' she complains to a friend. On another occasion she compliments him on his faculty for travel, when 'you are fairly committed to it, and have not me at hand to complain to'. She is content if she can relieve his discontent, and is never happier than when she can perform the services of a buffer state between him and external annoyances, as, for instance, when he is in the throes with *Frederick*, he is so easily upset that she says, 'my life is spent in standing between him and the outer world'.

8

Carlyle never tires of extolling Jane. His admiration for her is unbounded. 'Not all the Sands and Eliots and babbling *cohue* of "celebrated scribbling women" that have strutted over the world, in my time, could, it seems to me, if all boiled down and distilled to essence, make one such woman.' These words are written in his later years after her death, but they would have been the same if expressed at any period of his married life. The *Reminiscences* are aflame with her praises. When he is writing the *French Revolution*, 'Jeannie, alone of beings, burnt like a steady lamp beside me'. And, in spite of his absorption in his work, and his 'sacred horror' of shopping, he celebrates many an anniversary with a small gift, and once, Jane records, 'he had the incredible audacity to buy *me* a cloak for a Christmas present! And 'a very well-cut coat . . . warm and sober, and a good shape', adds the surprised and delighted wife.

Yet if she retains her individuality, she cannot escape his influence, and her letters are full of indications, sometimes whimsical, of her resistance to his dominance. When the famous sound-proof study is being built on the roof of the house in Chelsea, she sends him away for the duration of the upheaval, and tells his brothers that it is amazing how little she cares about it 'now that I feel the noise and disorder with my own senses'. In the absence of 'Mr. C's' recognition of the disturbance 'with his overwhelming eloquence' she can 'regard the present earthquake as something almost laughable'. All these conflicts might have recurred even if there had not been the complication of ill health on both sides. There is even more disparity in their illnesses than in their tastes. What agrees with one disagrees with the other. Jane dines at two, 'Mr. C.' at seven. When she needs the hills he needs the sea. She 'grows better with the hot weather; he, always worse'. And although they give out that ill health forces them to occupy separate rooms at night, 'his nervous state' acts upon her until, she says, she is 'become more sleepless and agitated than himself'. It is certain also that her nervous moods react detrimentally upon him.

It is impossible, however, to judge them by any ordinary scale of happiness. They are not ordinary and what is happiness to them would not be happiness to most people. When Jane makes such remarks as 'there is everything here needed for happiness, but just one thing—the faculty of being happy', it would perhaps be unwise to take her literally, for it is possible that neither she nor her husband would have approved of what is usually meant by happiness if they had achieved it. 'Joy', he says, 'is unenjoyable, to be avoided like pain.'

In the light of this knowledge it is possible to understand his peculiarities. From the earliest time he feels that he is hindered by poverty and although he never faces destitution in his childhood, nor even indigence during his early days in London, he is conscious of the handicap of limited means, whilst upholding the discipline imposed. He is never destitute of means but for the first half of his life he is relatively poor, and he probably denounces riches for the same reason that he condemns hedonism. He never resents the peasant-poverty of the small lowland farmstead at Craigenputtock, and in old age he attributes many virtues to it. He blesses it because it has made the memory of his old home 'tenfold more dear and sacred' to him, and he is equally grateful to the struggles of his early married life, because they beautify his relations with Jane: 'My noble one, how beautiful has our poverty made thee to me.'

9

Carlyle suffers all his life from morbid introspection and its concomitant self-pity. He seeks peace and finds a sword with which he never ceases to prod himself, and he seeks relief from these self-inflicted wounds in lamentations and appeals for sympathy. 'Write to me,' he implores Emerson, 'were it again and over again—unweariable in pity.' He is always seeking himself and always running away from himself. He boasts of being a stay-at-home (which in the main he is) but ever longs for change. 'I must alter my habits, cost what it may . . . I cannot live all the year round in London, under pain of dying or going rabid . . . must learn to travel, as others do.' He has thoughts of 'raging and lecturing' in America 'like a very lion' or 'a frothy mountebank'; not this time for the sake of travel, but to gain 'a thousand pounds; therewith to retire to some small quiet cottage by the shore of the sea, at least three hundred miles from this, and sit silent there for ten years to come, or forever and a day perhaps'. But when he ventures away from Chelsea he is not happy until he gets back. His love of silence is mainly utilitarian, an aid to his work as a writer, for the rest of his life, like that of Dr. Johnson, is largely a conversation piece.

The living moment is rarely filled with content, and his happiness is ever retrospective. Life for him is a chain of lost opportunities. His affection for Jane develops in ratio to his distance from her, and it is not until after her death that he realizes many of her best qualities. He is restless and irritable during the early married period at Craigenputtock, but in old age those seem to have been their 'happiest days'. Such lamentations are common objects of his more intimate writings and it is no surprise to hear him admitting that 'the past grows even holier the farther we leave it'. The past grows even something more than holy. It becomes so real that reminiscence takes the place of experience. The past becomes more real than the present. Although, for instance, he suffers little from a poverty to which he and his race were inured, his outlook on social affairs is permanently distorted by his early difficulties in earning a living. His famous advocacy of work for its own sake, to be examined later, is adjusted to this dilemma when he tells Emerson that 'work and wages are the two prime necessities of man'. 'My *pride*, fierce and sore as it might be, was never hurt' by the simple but sound furniture 'in the house called mine' at Craigenputtock, yet he always resents the enforced economy of that establishment, and, nearly forty years after, the memory of it produces a characteristic apostrophe: 'Oh, shall not victory at last be to the Handful of Brave; in spite of the rotten multitudinous canaille, who *seem* to inherit all the world and its forces and steel-weapons and culinary and stage properties? Courage; and be true to one another!'

His attitude towards the present alternates between petty temper and acute loathing. He is never satisfied with what he is doing or with things as they are, and for the future he has nothing but fear. Social conditions as he sees them are bad enough, but the worst is yet to be. The lamentations of this nineteenth-century Jeremiah never cease. They moan through his youthful letters and essays and end only when he ends. 'Alas, the age of Substance and Solidity is gone (for the time); that of Show and hollow Superficiality (in all senses) is in full swing' (1832). 'It often painfully seems to me as if much were coming fast to a crisis here; as if the crown-wheel had given way, and the whole horologe were rushing rapidly down, to its end' (1835). The people are 'all staggering down to Gehenna and the everlasting Swine's-trough for want of Gospels' (1847), and in 1852 he is convinced that 'this distracted dog-kennel of a world' is 'about to have its throat cut'.

10

From this madhouse of modernity he takes refuge among dead heroes and lost causes, and bombards his age with books whose admonitory words fall upon a generation which pays him the dubious compliment of sentimental approval, but is determined to go its own way. Not even a Carlyle can disturb Victorian England's faith in Progress.

There is no doubt about his sincerity. He never trifles with himself or life. In his most explosive moments he is exalted with passionate reverence. 'You are so dreadfully in earnest!' Jeffrey complains. But his sincerity is cathartic rather than humane. When he thinks he is saving the world he is trying to save himself. A humour which he calls 'desperate hope' attends him all his life. At college he finds himself 'advancing towards huge instalments of bodily and spiritual wretchedness'. The condition is aggravated by a physical shyness which turns Edinburgh University into purgatory, and he has to 'purify himself in penal fires of various kinds for several years to come'. In middle life when he is in reasonably good health and comfort, and increasing fame, he moans: 'All my life has been black with care and toil, labour above board and far worse below; I have hardly had a heavier year (overloaded with a kind of "health" which may be called frightful); to "burn my own smoke" in some measure is all I was up to.' Even when writing his memoirs some fifty years afterwards, those experiences are still 'horrible to think of'. He explains that 'the bodily part of them was a kind of base agony (arising mainly in the want of any extant or discoverable *fence* between my coarser fellow-creatures and my more sensitive self), and might and could easily (had the age been pious and thoughtful) have been spared a poor creature like me. Those hideous disturbances to sleep, etc., a very little real care and goodness might prevent all that.' He looks back 'with a kind of angry protest' 'and would save his successors from it', except perhaps, that 'one needs suffering more than at first seems', and the spiritual agonies would not have been enough. His sufferings are 'wholly blessed in retrospect . . . infinitely worth suffering, with whatever addition was needful! God be thanked always.'

Such a passage, and it is only one of many, reveals the authentic hypersensitive whose moral protests are symptoms of his own neurosis. Self-torture and self-pity alternate with blame and vituperation throughout his life and works, the rumbles of the storm can be heard even in the more objective of his books, *Cromwell* and *Frederick*, as definitely if not as loudly as in *Sartor Resartus*, *Past and Present*, *Latter Day Pamphlets*, and *The French Revolution*. Carlyle is cast at birth for the part of Jeremiah and his lamentations never vary in essentials. In early manhood (he puts it at thirty-two, but it was much earlier, as his letters show) he 'had gotten really something' which he 'wished to say—and has 'ever since been saying the best way' he could. But he does not attribute this something so much to study or observation as to his 'bits of experiences'. He is destined for his mission from the first and it only requires someone to pull the trigger for the Carlylean howitzer to start firing. This act is performed by Goethe. Carlyle seeks in German literature solace for his own soul and for a counterblast to the imagined degeneration of the literature and the ideas of the England of Wordsworth, Coleridge, Shelley, and Keats.

I I

Carlyle is fundamentally a moralist. His watchwords are Character and Work. All his books from the slim *Sartor* to the portly *Frederick*, preach the doctrine of good behaviour safe-guarded by hard work. His praise is for those who support this doctrine, his condemnation for those who don't. This faith in the gospel of work is not of his own inventing; it is inherited from his lowland peasant forebears. 'We were all practically taught that work (temporal or spiritual) was the only thing we had to do; and incited always by precept and example to do it *well*'. It is not solely a moral precept although to Carlyle and his kind even a necessary function must be moralized before it is approved. Work for the peasantry of the Solway country, or any other peasantry at that or any place, is the first law of survival. And since the product of work is so meagre in those spare lands the next law is frugality. His ancestors are Spartans perforce and their hardihood also is welded into the Carlylean doctrine. At Ecclefechan character is born of work and thrift as Carlyle remembers and applauds. 'Mother and Father were assiduous, abstemious, frugal without stinginess. They shall not want their reward'. These hard conditions produce a stubborn quality which he also admires and associates with that 'Obstinacy as of ten mules' which has been among the 'manifold unspeakable blessings' of his life, and a 'real bower-anchor' for riding over 'rough seas'. And finally out of these frugal conditions he fashions that gospel of thrift and duty which is concentrated in one of his most familiar axioms: 'The Fraction of Life can be increased in value not so much by increasing your Numerator as by lessening your Denominator.'

What begins with an attempt, not unsuccessful, to justify hard conditions, ends in a general measure of social salvation. The process is nowhere so explicit as in the reminiscences of his early married life on the small farmstead at Craigenputtock. 'To me', he says, 'there is a *sacredness* of interest in it; consistent only with *silence*. It was the field of endless nobleness, and beautiful talent and virtue, in Her who is now gone; also of good industry, and many loving and blessed thoughts in myself, while living there by her side. Poverty and mean Obstruction had given origin to it, and continued to preside over it; but were transformed, by human valour of various sorts, into a kind of victory and royalty; something of high and great dwelt in it, though nothing could be smaller and lower than many of the details. How blessed might poor mortals be, in the straitest circumstances, *if* only their wisdom and fidelity to Heaven and to one another, were *adequately* great! It looks to me now like a kind of humble russet-coated *epic*, that seven years' settlement at Craigenputtock; very poor in this world's goods, but not without an intrinsic dignity greater and more important than appeared. Thanks mainly to Her, and her faculties and magnanimities; without whom it had not been possible . . . it is certain that for living in, and thinking in, I have never since found in the world a place so favourable.'

12

Carlyle is a haunted man, over-loaded with acquired and self-imposed anxieties which express themselves in his worship of obedience, duty, and work, as well as in the vituperations and scoldings of his books. Acute consciousness of the evanescence of life prompts some of these perturbations. He has something of Sir Thomas Browne's sense of the poetry of evanescence but, in spite of liberal influences he can never bring himself to complete calm when forced to think of the hereafter. It might even be argued from intrinsic rather than direct evidence that those Herculean literary tasks, self-imposed but pursued with groanings and anguish, were vain and clumsy attempts to anaesthetize himself against such painful thoughts. He is faced by two not unfamiliar difficulties: death and judgment and death and annihilation. If the one causes fear the other arouses his contempt. 'Death, and the *Judgment-Bar* of the Almighty following it', he says, 'may well be terrible to the bravest', but the idea of Death, with *nothing* of that kind following it, is possible only 'to very mean and silly creatures'.

Generally his fears express themselves in remorse for lost opportunities of doing well by himself or others, for, in spite of much practical benevolence to the members of his family and others, like most of us he leaves undone many of the things he ought to have done and the thought of it endangers his spiritual health. There is no more pathetic document among autobiographical writings than his reminiscences of his wife. He recalls Poe's 'unhappy master, whom unmerciful disaster, followed fast and followed faster' till his tune 'one burden bore, of never-never more!' That note is dominant throughout the memoirs. 'Alas, her love was never known completely to me, and how celestial it was, till I had lost her! . . . But all the minutes of time are irrevocably past:—be wise, all ye living and remember that time *passes* and does not return!' 'Oh, why do we delay so much,' he asks again and again, 'till Death makes it impossible?'

I 3

Anxieties are also provoked by his own physical disabilities. He is rarely free from the pains of the abdominal disorder which began in his twenty-third year and continues throughout his life. He and others call it dyspepsia or 'liver',[1] but it might have been diagnosed later as duodenal ulceration. It is not unnatural that his opponents should have made use of this defect, as when Nietzsche describes his method as 'Pessimism after undigested meals'. But he himself is conscious of looking upon the world through the green spectacles of his condition, and the habit is discussed and perpetuated among his friends and admirers.[2] Following Carlyle's lead too much stress has probably been laid on this condition. It was no doubt uncomfortable but the fact that he is rarely laid up and lives more than eighty years proves that it could not have been very serious. The creaking gate serves its purpose admirably for he is as vigorous mentally at the end of his life as at the beginning. Bending over his writing, as he himself is aware, increases the creak. He has one disease, he tells his brother, but it has a fifty years' record brought to a head by the writing of the 'unspeakable *Frederick*'. It is 'the utter inability to digest any kind of food —nothing that I swallow except spring water alone', he says, 'can be disposed of with impunity'. He is in fact, for the greater part of his life, so aware of what Emerson calls his 'hairy strength' that his work as a man of letters 'seems very contemptible to him'. Dyspepsia aggravates rather than creates despondency. We must look elsewhere for the real causes. They are to be found in certain deep-rooted inhibitions.

Carlyle never at any time feels that he is getting full value out of life. There is ever a sense of insufficiency, not the craving of shortage, but the faintness, the nausea, of incapacity. 'Dinners do nothing for me except hurt. . . . Work, thou poor Devil, I say to myself; there is good for thee nowhere in the Universe but there.' He fears leisure,

---

[1] 'I am myself very ill and miserable in the liver regions; very tough otherwise.' *Correspondence of Carlyle and Emerson* (1851), ii, 199.

[2] 'Carlyle's conversation and general views are curiously dyspeptic, his indigestion colouring everything.' Caroline Fox, June 1842, *Journals* (1882), 164. 'What I chiefly regret and wonder at in him is the perception in all nature of nothing between him and his stomach.' John Ruskin, 1883, *Letters of John Ruskin and Charles Eliot Norton* (1913), ii, 190.

therefore resents the bait of shorter working hours trailed before the voters by politicians. 'The Future is not to be made of *butter* . . . no noble age was ever a *soft* one'; 'it is *not* good always, or ever, to be "at ease in Zion"'. He is obviously encouraging himself when in *Sartor Resartus*, he, in the person of Herr Teufelsdröckh, says: 'With Stupidity and sound Digestion man may front much. But what, in these dull unimaginative days, are the terrors of Conscience to the diseases of the Liver! Not on Morality, but on Cookery, let us build our stronghold: there brandishing our frying-pan, as censer, let us offer sweet incense to the Devil, and live at ease on the fat things *he* has provided for his Elect!'

14

These defects also re-inforce the puritan fear of what is light, easy, and legitimately irresponsible, and, as with all men of the recessive type, happiness and pleasure are suspect. 'Love not pleasure' is the 'Everlasting Yea'. The French Revolution was precipitated by the luxurious habits and dilettantism of the old aristocrats, and he doubts the English nation of his own day because it is 'no longer an earnest Nation, but a light, sceptical, epicurean one'. At times he fears that he is overdoing this attitude. 'It is impossible', he tells his fellow-puritan Emerson, that 'you can be more Puritan than I; nay, I often feel as if I were far too much so', and he doubts if 'there will hardly ever live another man' who will believe as he does in his hero Cromwell's Puritanism.

The fine arts, being instruments of ease and pleasure, are deprecated. We 'are sent hither not to fib and dance, but to speak and work'. Poetry without purpose is anathema: 'Close thy *Byron*; open thy *Goethe*.' He sees little more in poetry than 'speech without meaning' and as such it becomes a 'mockery'. Fiction whether 'fine' or 'coarse', is condemned because it has an 'alarming cousinship' with lying. Men-of-letters should not concern themselves with 'the unspeakable glories and rewards' of pleasing a generation which they 'are not sent hither to please'. All writings which lack moral purpose are proscribed. Leave 'the thing called Literature' he commands 'to run through its rapid fermentations . . . and to fluff itself off into Nothing, in its own way—like a poor bottle of soda-water with the cork sprung'. He prophesies that the man-of-letters will sink 'to the rank of street-fiddling' with a chance perhaps of an 'endless increase of sixpences flung into the hat', but 'no higher rank'. So, once more, 'Of "Literature" keep well to windward, my serious friend!' Even Shakespeare 'the most divinely gifted; clear, all piercing like the sunlight, lovingly melodious; probably the noblest human Intellect in that kind', is tolerated not for the 'Fiction' but for the 'Fact'. What Carlyle most admires in him are 'the traces he shows of a talent that could have turned the *History of England* into a kind of *Iliad*, almost perhaps into a kind of *Bible*'. He believes the *Bible* to be the 'truest of all books' because it springs 'from intense conviction', and Homer's *Iliad* he 'almost' reckons 'next to the *Bible*, so stubbornly sincere is it too, though in a far different element, and a far shallower'.

Out of this tangle of whim and self-defence, there emerges nevertheless one of the most significant commentaries on the era of finance-commerce, then in its hearty and heartless youth. Carlyle's work has no outward meaning except as the reaction of a sensitive mind to the changes brought about by the final dissolution of the Feudal System then proceeding, and the indifference of the new industrial rulers, and indeed the whole nation, to the devastation being wrought by the change. His attitude is moral and political, chiefly moral, coloured by that transcendentalism which he imports from Germany, and which itself is more moral than mystical. He never even tries to be objective or impartial, and his works, from the *Miscellaneous Essays* to *Frederick the Great*, are, in the last resort, as personal as his autobiographical letters and reminiscences. *The French Revolution* is as much a commentary on post-revolutionary conditions in England as a history of the then greatest of social upheavals. He is talking at the England of his day from what happened in France the day before, and warning his countrymen of what he imagines will be the chaotic consequences of the growing demand for democratic institutions. *Cromwell* and *Frederick the Great* advocate a return to authoritarian government, which he believes is the only method of saving the social system from complete anarchy. Carlyle is first and last a pamphleteer, and next to Milton, the most inspired pamphleteer who has used the English language.

I5

He is a reformer rather than a revolutionary, except that, like Tolstoy, he advocates a revolution in the spirit of man. He has no utopian predilections such as those held vaguely by Ruskin and concretely by Morris: 'To shape the whole Future is not our problem; but only to shape faithfully a small part of it, according to rules already known.' He is an individualist and a believer in the efficacy of good-will as the basis of useful and wise action: 'It is perhaps possible for each of us, who will with due earnestness inquire, to ascertain clearly what he, for his own part, ought to do: this let him, with true heart, do, and continue doing. . . . The general issue will, as it has always done, rest well with a Higher Intelligence than ours.' By this means we may arrive at wisdom in government based on rule and obedience: sovereignty in control of democracy. This conception of a New Feudalism is to be the work of man for generations to come, if the evils of undue liberty and *laissez-faire* are to be cured: 'How, in conjunction with inevitable Democracy, indispensable Sovereignty is to exist: certainly it is the highest question ever hitherto propounded to mankind! The solution of which is work for long years and centuries. Years and centuries, of one knows not what complexion;—blessed or unblessed, according as they shall, with earnest valiant effort, make progress therein, or, in slothful unveracity and dilettantism, only talk of making progress. For either progress therein, or swift and ever swifter progress towards dissolution, is henceforth a necessity.'

The opinion that he is a complete reactionary is unsound. Carlyle is never completely anything but himself. He would put the clock back but only on his own terms. He cries for a strong man, but strength for its own sake will not do. His superman must be good, disinterested and competent: 'The tools to him that can handle them . . . is our ultimate Political Evangel.' He desires to rescue the old landed aristocracy from domination by the new aristocrats of money, but only if they will mend their ways and live for others rather than themselves: 'False Aristocracies are insupportable. . . . No-Aristocracies, Liberty-and-Equalities are impossible . . . true Aristocracies are at once indispensable and not easily attained.' As for the people he would save them from plutocracy and democracy, or what, in our day is called, 'pluto-democracy'—a word he might have invented. But again, he is not against wealth. He opposes 'Poverty and Vice' which are the 'Indictment . . . against lazy Wealth'. His opposition to democracy is equally relative and he apparently has no objection to 'the Toiling Millions of Mankind' taking the initiative in their search for 'Guidance' as distinct from 'False-Guidance'. He has in fact as great an objection to slaves as to their enslavers. He will permit the slave to recoil against his slavery: 'Let him shake-off such oppression, trample it indignantly under his feet: I blame him not, I pity and commend him. But', he warns, 'oppression by your Mock-Superiors well shaken off, the grand problem yet remains to solve: That of finding government by your Real-

Superiors.' Then follows a passage of that foreboding in which Carlyle specializes, and which has so much meaning for us to-day: 'Alas, how shall we ever learn the solution of that, benighted, bewildered, sniffing, sneering, God-forgetting unfortunates as we are? It is a work for centuries; to be taught us by tribulations, confusions, insurrections, obstructions; who knows if not by conflagration and despair! It is a lesson inclusive of all other lessons; the hardest of all lessons to learn'—at the same time 'This lesson will have to be learned,—under penalties! England will either learn it, or England also will cease to exist among nations.'

16

Carlyle has no ambiguities about the theory of rulership, and some of his sanest and clearest thinking is to be found in his famous lectures on *Heroes* which are a co-ordination of many scattered thoughts on the same subject in his earlier works—particularly *Sartor Resartus* (1831) and *The French Revolution* (1837). The lectures cover the hero in various capacities from Divinity to King but they are all contained in the latter. The King is 'practically the *summary* for us *all* of the various figures of Heroism; Priest, Teacher, whatsoever of earthly or of spiritual dignity we can fancy to reside in a man, embodies itself here, to *command* over us, furnish us with constant practical teaching, tell us for the day and hour what we are to do'. He recognizes Divine Rightness for the job rather than Divine Right— royalty evoking loyalty by fitness to rule. The ideal king must be 'The Ablest Man . . . the truest-hearted, justest, the Noblest Man: what he *tells us to do* must be precisely the wisest, fittest, that we could anywhere or anyhow learn;— the thing which it will in all ways behove us, with right loyal thankfulness, and nothing doubting, to do! Our *doing* and life were then, so far as government could regulate it, well regulated; that were the ideal of constitutions.' He is not blind to the elusive character of ideals, and he knows that they can never be completely embodied in practice, but it is a pivot of his doctrine that 'Ideals do exist' and 'that if they be not approximated to at all, the whole matter goes to wreck!' He names as the nearest modern approximations to this ideal, Cromwell and Napoleon.

His hope of the future 'lies not in the direction of reforming Parliament', but of 'reforming Downing Street', by which, I imagine, he means the control of Parliament by Cabinet or personal rule, or both. But he would prefer to 'find some sort of *King*, made in the image of God, who could a little achieve for the People, if not their spoken wishes, yet their dumb wants, and what they would at last find to have been their instinctive will'. He recognizes no such Hero-King of England since Cromwell, and no Parliament worthy the name since the Long Parliament which 'both in regard to its destinies in History, and to its intrinsic collective and individual worth among Deliberative Assemblies', he considers, 'the Acme of Parliaments . . . the consummation . . . and slow cactus-flowerage of the parliamentary tree among mankind, which blossoms only in thousands of years, and is seen only once by men: the Father, this, of all Congresses, National Conventions and sublunary Parliaments that have since been'. At the same time he has no regret that it was a 'transient phenomenon'.

In the place of a Long Parliament or some approximation to it, he sees an assembly degraded in function and warped in purpose. Such a 'National Palaver recognized as Sovereign, a solemn Convocation of all the Stump-Orators in the Nation to come and govern us, was not seen on earth till recently'. He looks upon debate as an obsolete function in Parliament and the Press Gallery as a menace to legislation. The conclusion is that although parliaments may be useful as advisory bodies, they are no use as 'Ruling or Sovereign bodies, but useless or worse'.

But whether we have a reformed 'Downing Street' or a 'New King' or both, 'Parliament will continue to be indispensable' and it is desired that all men see clearly that it functions correctly. Its 'real function' being the 'maximum of all we shall be able to get out of it'. How that is to be accomplished and what should constitute the maximum are not clear. Nor would he abolish the suffrage. 'Votes of men are worth collecting, if convenient', because, although their opinions are of 'little wisdom, and can on occasion reach to all conceivable and inconceivable degrees of folly', their instincts, where these can be deciphered, are wise and human . . . the unspoken sense of man's heart, and well deserve attending to. At the same time, he is violently opposed to any extension of the franchise and he has only contempt for the idea of Universal Suffrage. He will consult it about the quality of pork or the coarser kinds of butter, but on matters of importance it is likely to be wrong. Universal Suffrage is no more to him than the brawling of thousands of pot-wallopers and blockheads.

17

Carlyle is more preacher than teacher: a master of exhortation rather than explanation. He can tell you 'why' but not 'how'; or he can tell you 'how' only in broad generalization. His moral counters are right and wrong, beauty and truth, good and bad, duty and obedience, aristocracy and democracy. Sometimes he ventures to qualify and expound these abstractions. Aristocracy is not desirable in itself or even right in itself. There are good and bad aristocrats and he contrives to make clear which is which; but he does not succeed in teaching his age how to select the best aristocrats for the benefit of a democracy which is incapable of governing itself. He knows where he wants to go but does not know how to get there, and in the end he leaves it to God. Indeed, his vision of the struggle between good and bad is always on the point of becoming the battle of Heaven and Hell, of God and Devil.

In the midst of a political tirade, when you are expecting some practical conclusion, he will fall back on the 'commandment of Heaven' which can only be ignored at the risk of 'incurring Heaven's curse'. He may be discussing how to get the best out of a reformed Parliament, and, in answer to the voter's query, 'Who is to decide it?' he replies: 'We are all, and each of us for his own self, to decide it: and wo will befall us, each and all, if we don't decide *aright*; according as the Almighty has already "decided" it, as it has been appointed to be and to continue, before all human decidings and after them all!' Unless we obey the 'Commandments of Heaven' which also appear as the 'Laws of the Universe', the 'Eternal Law', and the 'Law of the Planets', we shall become (in fact, have become) victims of the 'Prince of Darkness' and 'Father of Delusions', not living but afloat upon the 'Pool of Erebus'—'now nameless in polite speech'. 'He that can ascertain, in England or elsewhere, what the laws of the Eternal are, and walk by them voted for or unvoted, with him it will be well; with him that misses said laws, and only gets himself voted for, not well.' That is the one thing needful and not 'to be dispensed with', and as for voting—'I value it little at any time, and almost at zero in this'.

18

Whenever he is faced with the problem of putting his theories into practice, Carlyle falls back upon loose generalization, or the mystical conception of right and wrong. It is not cowardice nor yet, altogether, the attitude of frustration or impotence, though both of these play their part. He is a transcendentalist and believes that 'there is an Infinite' in man 'which he cannot quite bury under the Finite', that there is a 'Higher than Love of Happiness' for which the martyrs, poets, and priests of all time have spoken and suffered, 'bearing testimony, through life and through death, of the Godlike that is in Man, and how in the Godlike only has he Strength and Freedom', therefore 'Love not Pleasure; love God. This is the Everlasting Yea, wherein all contradiction is solved: wherein whoso walks and works, it is well with him.'

Not only 'walks' but 'works'. Walking and working in the Inner Light are inseparable conditions of Carlyle's transcendentalism, which, whether it succeeds or not always aims at action. 'The end of Man is an Action, and not a Thought, though it were the noblest.' But, again, not any sort of action. Carlyle is the last man to advocate mere activity. The action he has in mind must be an extension of the infinite which every man carries within him. 'Do we not know that the name of the Infinite is Good, is God?' He calls it Duty, and it is a mystical faith in duty that helps him over the spiritual crisis which shatters his traditional belief. 'Perhaps at no era of his life was he more decisively the Servant of Goodness, the Servant of God,' he says of himself in the person of Herr Teufelsdröckh, 'than even now when doubting God's existence'. Thenceforth, love of God becomes love of Truth, and Duty is truthful conduct. 'Thus, in spite of all Motive-grinders, and Mechanical Profit-and-loss Philosophies, with the sick ophthalmia and hallucination they had brought on, was the Infinite nature of Duty still dimly present to me: living without God in the world, of God's light I was not wholly bereft; if my as yet sealed eyes, with their unspeakable longing, could nowhere see Him, nevertheless in my heart He was present, and his heaven-written Law still stood legible and sacred there.'

The ultimate destiny of truthful conduct is not merely good behaviour, but useful behaviour, which Carlyle visualizes as Work. Work and duty are closely related. 'A certain inarticulate self-consciousness dwells dimly within us; which only our Works can render articulate and decisively discernible. Our Works are the mirror wherein the spirit first sees its natural lineaments. Hence, too, 'the folly of that impossible Precept, *Know thyself*, till it be translated into this possible one, *Know what thou canst work at*'. Work is a means of unrolling, evolving, yourself: a means of light. Doubt can only be removed by dutiful action: 'Let him who gropes painfully in darkness or uncertain light, and prays vehemently that the dawn may ripen into day, lay this other precept well to heart . . . *Do the Duty which lies nearest thee*, which thou knowest to be a Duty! The second Duty will already have become clearer.' There is no cause to look about for a sphere of action. Your 'America is here or nowhere,' he quotes from *Wilhelm Meister*, 'here, in this poor, miserable, hampered, despicable Actual, wherein thou even standest, here or nowhere is thy Ideal: work it out therefrom; and working, believe, live, be free.' All his major books, from *Sartor Resartus* onwards are variations on this theme.

19

Carlyle is an original writer but not an original thinker. Nothing he has said is original, but he has an original way of saying it. Benjamin Disraeli, whom he despises, and the Chartists, whom he fears, are equally opposed to the industrial chaos, which he condemns; his religious ideas are German metaphysics moralized, his morals are inherited from a puritan ancestry or adapted from Calvin and John Knox, and his political concepts would have had the approval of both Bolingbroke and Horace Walpole. In his early days the novelty of his style is a hindrance to its acceptance.

Delayed recognition is due also to the fact that although his ideas are not new, they are unpopular because they deny the efficacy of the prevailing faith in material progress, the religion of the Nineteenth Century, so that when he achieves popularity and becomes one of the most distinguished men of letters of his time, acceptance is a compliment to his gifts as a historian, or even the sort of recognition given to a worthy character, rather than to any appreciation of his more reactionary doctrines. He might not have been acceptable even then but for his dogged insistence upon himself and the reiteration of his adopted ideas. Everything he has to say is said in his early books, the rest is repetition and amplification. Outside the class of zealous reformers his ideas receive no more than lip homage or sentimental distortion.

The chief difficulty in the way of a more profound acceptance is the personal conduct test of all his teachings. Carlyle believes in government, but suspects Parliament. Loyalty to the hero as leader is his ideal, and for the rank and file, duty and discipline. Do the duty which you know to be a duty; the next duty will then have become easier. Theoretically, this is acceptable to many, but always with reservations. There has never been a Carlylean 'whole-hogger', for there inevitably comes a point where his doctrine conflicts with self-interest, and for that reason alone he lacks the power to move men to action. Those of his readers who are convertible rarely overcome the clash between high-mindedness and self-interest. As soon as it is realized that Carlyle means that reform should begin at home revulsion sets in, and he is relegated to the shelf of the impossibilists. His advocacy of feudalism is appreciated by landed proprietors who have no impulse towards improving agricultural conditions. Members of the aristocracy favour his support of their class, but they have neither the will nor the taste to reassert their leadership with all its responsibilities. The idle rich applaud his gospel of work—for others. The yeoman farmers enjoy his attacks on the manufacturers and the Corn Law reformers—but are defeated by them. The manufacturers like him when he calls them 'Captains of Industry' but suspect him when he proposes to abolish Free Trade, whilst the working class, or that part of it which is literate and heading for Socialism, cannot understand why he condemns the commercial system and social democracy simultaneously.

20

These hindrances to practical acceptance do not interfere with Carlyle's popularity. No serious writer of his time, with the possible exception of Macaulay, stands so high in the estimation of the thoughtful among both classes and masses. It is possible for him to conclude his series of lectures on *Heroes and Hero-Worship* with the remark which is a compliment to himself as well as a gracious recognition of the distinguished company which had sat at his feet on six separate evenings: 'The accomplished and distinguished, the beautiful, the wise, something of what is best in England, have listened patiently to my rude words.' This rugged peasant-prophet, like his compatriot Burns, is a social lion, but without disastrous results. He is a welcome member of the brilliant circle at Holland House, and his own humbler dwelling in Cheyne Row, Chelsea, was a place of pilgrimage even whilst he was alive. And beyond these exalted circles he is so eagerly read by growing numbers of those to whom the higher realms of literature had been made accessible by voluntary and mutual cultural enterprise and later by the Education Acts, that popular editions of his works are absorbed in large quantities, and immediately after his death a complete edition appears, including the difficult *Frederick*, at one shilling a volume; whilst *Heroes and Hero-Worship* is sold for threepence in Cassell's National Library. Such a widespread readership had never been achieved by a writer of equal seriousness and distinction. That he should have become a best-seller, alongside Tennyson and Dickens, is a compliment to the age which produced him.

But his influence upon this wide body of readers is not so easily defined. Many of them are more interested in his personality than his philosophy. Carlyle is a legendary figure rather than a living force. But if he gets nothing done, some things are ultimately done differently because of his tirades. He impresses the mind of his age by setting people of all kinds thinking and wondering about culture and economics and social affairs. And the common people, whom he despises as democrats but not as men, are to benefit chiefly from his preachings. *Past and Present* is one of the most deeply read books among democratic leaders, who, like their followers, welcome his criticism of the commercial system and laugh at his strictures on democracy. Carlyle's influence is indirect and partial. His dialectic colours the thoughts of Ruskin and Morris and reaches even wider fields by its influences on the didactic novelists. Dickens, George Eliot, Mrs. Gaskell, and, nearer our own day, George Meredith and Mark Rutherford, owe much to him which they pass on to their myriad readers. But it is only his opposition to the evils of unrestrained commercialism which wins their support. They may approve occasionally his remedies, but then only in so far as he is abstract or idealist! Ruskin and Morris, on the other hand, have their own remedies which Carlyle in turn thinks frivolous or utopian. The didactic novelists and those they influence are sentimental reformers. They doubt not with Tennyson that

> *through the ages one increasing purpose runs,*
> *And the thoughts of men are widened with the process of the*
> *suns.*

Carlyle has no such illusion.

RUSKIN

The thing which no merely historical investigator can understand, or even believe . . . belongs exclusively to the creative or artistic group of men, and can only be interpreted by those of their race, who themselves in some measure also see visions and dream dreams.

JOHN RUSKIN

I

Carlyle is so overcome by contemplation of the folly of mankind that he can do little more than scold. Ruskin is just as convinced that our civilization has taken the wrong turning, but he explores the immediate causes more diligently and tries to show how to recover the right path. They condemn the same evils, but although Ruskin hails Carlyle as his Master, there are differences in their methods and remedies. Carlyle believes in moral salvation by work, hard work and plenty of it. Ruskin qualifies the prescription by associating work with aesthetics. Unlike Carlyle he does not believe that money is the root of the evil. He regards money as evil when we seek to make more of it rather than much of it. Nor is there hope alone from the Carlylean faith in supermen. We are more likely to find a remedy in the consistent pursuit of good living by lesser-men, each doing his best for the love of doing it and not for pecuniary reward.

Like Carlyle he opposes the prevading Liberalism of his day: 'I hate all liberalism as I do Beelzebub.' But though he calls himself a Tory of the old school, he refuses to be classed as a Conservative, or to recognize opposition between the two doctrines. The opposition is between 'Liberals and Illiberals'; that is between people who desire liberty, and those who dislike it. He proclaims himself 'a violent Illiberal'. But it is not safe to accept even his own labels, for he is capable of adding confusion to political terminology by saying that although he was 'bred a Tory' he has 'gradually developed into an indescribable thing—certainly *not* a Tory,' and again by proclaiming himself a Socialist,[1] and later, a

---

[1] 'Of course I am a Socialist—of the most stern sort—but I am also a Tory of the sternest sort.' *Friends of a Lifetime Letters to Sydney Carlyle Cockerell*, Ed., Viola Meynell (1940), 26.

Communist.[1] But all these arguments mean little more than a refusal to be tied down to arbitrary concepts. At the same time he is a decided and consistent opponent of the ideas of freedom and democracy. He is convinced that 'all freedom is error' and he tells working men, presumably democrats, that their opinions are 'not worth a rat's squeak'. He believes with Carlyle that 'the wisest system of voting that human brains could devise would be of no use as long as the majority of the voters were fools, which is manifestly as yet the fact'.

He sees the devastation wrought by *laissez-faire* as clearly as Lord Shaftesbury, Disraeli, and Carlyle did, and opposes to that doctrine proposals for a return to orderliness in affairs aided by good taste, neither of which can be obtained without discipline towards an approved end. With Carlyle he therefore challenges what he calls 'that treacherous phantom which men call Liberty', but demands something more incisive than the legal controls inaugurated by Shaftesbury, and something less political and more realistic than the Tory Democracy of Benjamin Disraeli. 'The first duty of every man in the world is to find his true master, and, for his own good, submit to him; and to find his true inferior, and, for that inferior's good, conquer him.'

2

The fundamental characteristic of Ruskin's teaching is the welding of aesthetics and ethics into a doctrine of social as distinct from financial values. In this teaching he is furthest removed from his master, yet in contact with the chosen enemy of both—the political economist. Where the economist estimates value in terms of goods or money, Ruskin estimates it in terms of life. Ruskin's economics pro-

[1] 'I myself am a Communist of the old school.' *Fors Clavigera*, 7.

vide for the soul of man as well as for his body. For support of these theories we are to turn from the economists to the *Bible*—which is ever at his hand for encouragement and citation. He speaks as God's agent, and is convinced that it is 'the intention of Providence' that art and affairs should be united and 'grow together into one mighty temple; the rough stones and the smooth all finding their place, and rising, day by day, in richer and higher pinnacles to heaven'.

His attacks upon railroads, mechanical noises, the smoke nuisance, the pollution of rivers, slums, poverty, and ignorance, whatever their cause, together with his dislike of the architecture of the Houses of Parliament, the National Gallery, the new parts of Edinburgh, the north suburb of Geneva, and the city of New York, all of which he would have rebuilt or destroyed without rebuilding, are welded into a general attack upon commercial civilization. In such matters he is an iconoclast. The obverse of the medal is a desire to keep what he considers worth keeping: 'I want', he says, 'to keep the fields of England green, and her cheeks red', but he wants also to keep the beauty and character of our English country towns and villages before they were besieged by railways and factories and the suburbs of speculative builders.

Art is not solely a matter of pictures and poems, no matter how admirable. It is equally a code of manners and tends to be bad or good according to the quality of the life lived by artists and the presumed appreciators of their works. Art at its best is 'the expression of man's joy in his work'. But Ruskin is not out (as too many Ruskinians have supposed, with tiresome results) to make artists, or, yet, craftsmen. His efforts 'are directed', he says, 'not to making a carpenter an artist, but to making him happier as a carpenter'. Even his Professorship of Art is made to serve that aim, and his efforts in that post 'would be accomplished if . . . only the English nation could be made to understand that the beauty which is indeed to be a joy for ever, must be a joy for all'. There can be 'neither sound art, policy, nor religion' until

G

we restore 'the rule of the spirits' who reward 'with constant and conscious felicity, all that is decent and orderly, beautiful and pure'.

3

He is the evangelist of taste in everyday affairs and ordinary behaviour, of obedience to the demands of quality in raw materials and the goods which are made from them. 'Taste is not only a part and index of morality—it is the only morality.' And, 'Bad taste', he says, 'is our cardinal modern sin, the staple to the hinge of our taste for money, and distaste for money's worth, and every other worthiness.' Money in this sense is anathema. 'As much care must be taken to forbid and prevent Riches as to prevent Pestilence.' Wealth, on the other hand is to be fostered, for 'wealth means that which conduces towards life', not money but the sum of all those things and experiences which contribute to health and joy: 'There is no Wealth but life. Life, including all its powers of love, of joy, and of admiration. That country is the richest which nourishes the greatest number of noble and happy human beings; that man is the richest, who, having perfected the functions of his own life to the utmost, has also the widest helpful influence, both personal, and by means of his possessions, over the lives of others.' And although he has no fundamental objection to luxury, he would postpone the satisfaction of luxurious tastes and habits until they could be shared by all. 'Luxury is indeed possible in the future—innocent and exquisite; luxury for all, and by the help of all; but luxury at present can only be enjoyed by the ignorant; the cruellest man living could not sit at his feast, unless he sat blindfolded.'

Ruskin is the first man of his time to realize the interdependence of art and affairs, and he seeks for a plan to correct the evils of that free competition for financial gain which in spite of changes in methods, still seem to be undermining civilization. He is a utopist but a practical, even a militant, utopist. At Hawarden once he met the Duke of Argyll who was so puzzled at the turn of Ruskin's talk that he said, 'You seem to want a very different world, Mr. Ruskin'. 'Yes, verily', was Ruskin's reply, 'a new heaven, and a new earth, and the former things passed away.' Ruskin's remedy is a planned society, 'founded on a perception of the connection of all branches of art with each other', and the whole with life.

4

It is curious to reflect (and significant as well) that the first decline in Ruskin's popularity was caused by resentment against his economics. The teacher was acceptable so long as he kept to art. This view, however, entirely ignores the important and indisputable fact of his theory of economics, to the explanation and advocacy of which he devoted half his life, and all his books from the first column of *Modern Painters* to the last part of *Fors Clavigera*. He returns resentment with contempt or replies to it with the most brilliant and logical of reasoning and the most passionate of invective. There is never the slightest inclination to hedge or compromise, or to placate relative, friend or foe.

John Ruskin, at first almost single-handed, carries on a war against the financial valuation of life with all the weapons he can command and with the utmost energy and courage. And it is not too wild to suppose that had he possessed organizing ability as well as the vision to see and the power to explain he would have brought about a revolution which might have given a different and a better complexion to the years since his death in 1900.

5

His gospel of economics, for it is more than a theory, is not confined to books or lectures, it enters into his talk and his correspondence and pervades all his being. In his books it is coldly logical or carefully eloquent. In his letters (including *Fors Clavigera*) he lets himself go, and invective seems to get the better of him. But whether it is stated in the almost Euclidian definitions of *Munera Pulveris*, the measured eloquence of *Unto this Last*, in the invective of *Fors*, or the private letters, it is the same theme, the same conviction differing only in expression, and one method of expression is as deliberate and as well considered as the other. When he is most furious he is not losing his temper, he is finding and applying it.

One of the most significant examples occurs in a letter of 1862 to Dr. John Brown, who warns him that a criticism of the sacrosanct commercial system might do him harm. Ruskin replies: 'Those expressions of mine may do me harm, or do me good: what is that to me? They are the only true, right or possible expressions. The Science of Political Economy is a lie—wholly and to the very root (as hitherto taught). It is also the damnedest—that is to say, the most utterly and to the lowest pit condemned of God and his Angels—that the Devil, or Betrayer of Men, has yet invented, except his (the Devil's) theory of Sanctification. To this "Science" and to this alone (the professed and organized pursuit of Money) is owing *All* the evil of modern days. I say All. The Monastic Theory is at an end. It is now the Money theory which corrupts the Church, corrupts the household life, destroys honour, beauty, and life throughout the universe. It is *the* Death incarnate of Modernism, and the so-called science of its pursuit is the most cretinous, speechless, paralysing plague that has yet touched the brains of mankind.' Then, feeling no doubt that his friend might think he is over-doing it, he explains that the expressions he has used indicate no mere 'state of mind'. He is not particularly wrought up. What he says is 'the cool, resolute result of ten years' thought and sight. I write it as coldly as I should a statement respecting the square of the hypotenuse. ... The matter of this letter is as deliberate as if I were stating an equation to you, or a chemical analysis.'

He reiterates this opinion in several places, notably in the Introduction to *Unto this Last*, and finally in a passage found among his papers and presumed to be an Epilogue for *Fors Clavigera*, where he expresses the belief that 'society is rapidly drawing to a crisis in which all that *Fors* proclaims false will be found fatally so, and in which, of pure necessity, some respectful experiment will be made on the lines it has pointed out'. The experiment should he thinks, take the form of the organization of labour as pleaded by him in *Unto this Last*, but he says with prophetic insight when we recall what has taken place in Germany—'it ought all to be concentrated into the order and discipline of totally governing power'.

6

Like Carlyle he suffers from a sensitive conscience; but from different causes. Carlyle was born poor, Ruskin was born rich. The one works hard for a living and allows a chronic shortage of cash to colour his critique of the commercial system. The other is influenced by the opposite condition, for although, in spite of an opulent inheritance, he is never tempted to fall into vulgar indulgence, he is never quite able to shake off a feeling of guilt in his great possessions. 'My chief trial', he writes, 'is in the cowardice and sensuality and luxury of my own character which keeps me down—ashamed to take any true leadership—unwilling to give up my own mean ways of rich life—but I shall be driven to something desperate soon—I believe.' It is in this mood that he becomes a reformer: 'as a byework to quiet my conscience, that I might be happy in what I supposed to be my own proper life of art-teaching.'

Some of his vituperation against the commercial system may be a reflection of this sense of guilt, as his Utopian dreams are consolations for having to live in a civilization which is uncongenial to him. Guilt and spiritual discomfort are interchangeable terms in the cosmography of Ruskin. He is a social misfit, a square peg in a round hole ever trying to soothe his outraged sensibilities by dreams of what might have been. Through all these permutations and enthusiasms we obtain evidence of the effects upon a sensitive genius of a remarkable home life. From one point of view John Ruskin is the victim of the possessive love of a prosperous father and a puritanical mother: 'the fondest, faithfullest, most devoted, most mistaken parents that ever child was blest with, or ruined by.' The mother is an evangelical martinet, and the father a masterful business man, and they love their only child literally to distraction. He and his father 'disagree about all the Universe. . . . If he loved me less, and believed in me more, we should get on; but his whole life is bound up in me and yet he thinks me a fool—that is to say, he is mightily pleased if I write anything that has big words and no sense in it, and would give half his fortune to make me a member of Parliament if he thought I would talk, provided only the talk hurt nobody and was all in the papers.' This form of affection galls him 'like hot iron', reduces him to a 'subdued fury' and dries 'all the marrow out of every bone' of him.

7

No incident in biography is more curious than the early days of the child who is to become the art dictator of England. The moral and religious cramming to which he is subjected with the object, presumably, of controlling or exterminating unruly desires, succeeds only in driving them inwards. The picture of the small child of genius being forced to read the *Bible* for hours every day and to learn long passages by heart arouses pity to-day, although in after life he attributes some of his literary taste to that experience. 'Walter Scott and Pope's Homer were reading of my own selection, but my mother forced me, by steady long toil, to learn long chapters of the Bible by heart; as well as to read it every syllable through, aloud, hard names and all, from *Genesis* to the *Apocalypse*, about once a year; and to that discipline—patient, accurate, and resolute—I owe, not only a knowledge of the book, which I find occasionally service-able, but much of my general power of taking pains, and the best part of my taste in literature.' Ruskin is obviously making the best of a bad job, with characteristic loyalty to the more trying of his parents. But granting such a harvest from such a sowing the credit is not wholly due to a dom-ineering mother who looks for a less worldly reward.

He is a sensitive and sociable boy of great promise, need-ing sympathy and a cheerful setting for the normal develop-ment of his character. These conditions are to some extent obtained, but he is subjected to more discipline and solitude than is necessary, with the result that his growth is warped and he remains abnormal throughout life. But his childhood is not unhappy nor his home-life without colour or move-ment. There is much in it to favour the growth of a child of genius. Quietness and regularity are invaluable if they are not too irksome, and those conditions of Ruskin's early life help to form the meditative and orderly habits without which his books would not have been composed precisely as they were, if written at all. His parents, though strict and some-times narrow, were kind and sympathetic, encouraging his studies and reading his books with enthusiasm and pride. In spite of all restrictions, confidence existed between parents and child. In *Præterita* he tells how he would read the previous day's work 'to papa and mamma at breakfast next morning as a girl shows her sampler'. His father's taste for pictures gives his outlook upon life an aesthetic bias. It might easily have led him away from writing to painting. For several years to come he looks upon himself as a painter, and although he becomes a writer, he never relinquishes his early love of drawing in which he shows a mastery, not even now sufficiently appreciated. But with the publication of the first volume of *Modern Painters* (1843) when he is only twenty-four, he establishes his reputation as a writer. Even then he is no tyro, for he began writing verse and prose twelve or more years earlier, his first poem being printed when he was eleven.

8

It is the sterner influence of his mother which introverts his mind. 'She reads good books and makes herself unhappy, and me', he says, 'profoundly sorrowful.' The *Bible* is her favourite weapon, but Mrs. Ruskin has no interest in the *Bible* as literature. She lives in the passionate hope that her gifted son will enter the Church and become a Bishop. To an analytical mind such as his the literal interpretation of the scriptures must ultimately have been unacceptable. But underground preparation must have preceded the collapse of this maternally imposed faith although it does not show itself until he is half-way through his life. It is believed that he never wholly recovered from the shock. That, however, is doubtful. The shock from which he never recovers is not solely the result of a religious crisis. A crisis in the affections coincides with the religious crisis and may have precipitated it. The emotional disturbance induces a sceptical condition which prompts him to question the well-meaning tyranny of his parents. These upheavals, whatever their cause, release energies which have long been dormant.

They constitute an important stage in his progress towards self-mastery. He feels that something within him has been suppressed, and as he becomes more conscious of a desire for self-expression, he realizes that the parental dominance which is warping his instincts promises to do the same for his mind. 'I've suffered so fearfully from *Reticences* all my life,' he says 'that I think sheer blurting out of all in one's head is better than silence. . . .'

It is not easy to estimate the ultimate effect of the peculiar rigidity of his early life. It is probable that his unduly prolonged adolescence is constitutional, but there is no doubt that the condition was aggravated by his parents, particularly his mother. She looks upon him from the first as a gift from heaven to be shaped to her own will. She begins early by dedicating him to God before he is born, and although her wish that he should become a bishop is not fulfilled, she maintains her moral and religious tyranny over him until her death. To the end this hard-boiled puritan treats her brilliant son as if he were an unmanageable child. In one sense it could be argued that he was born old but did not grow any older. He is aware of the peculiarity, for in his last work, *Præterita*, he finds himself unchanged from the days of his youth: 'Some of me is dead, more of me stronger. I have learned a few things, forgotten many; in the total of me, I am but the same youth, disappointed and rheumatic.' And when he is an old man he tells Sir Oliver Lodge that his life only began when he was over thirty. 'My old age is really youth,' he confesses—a statement which Sir E. T. Cook believes to be 'true in a wider sense' than Ruskin intends.

The repressions continue far beyond childhood, beyond even his youth, they pursue him into middle age. When he is past forty and 'at the height of his literary reputation . . . he was still a child in the house of his parents', and he complains of the 'unendurable solitude' of a house made painful to him 'by parental love . . . which was cruelly hurtful without knowing it'. He loves his parents, but does not hesitate to charge them with thwarting him. His father, he says, 'would have sacrificed his life for his son, and yet forced his son to sacrifice his life to him, and sacrifice it in vain'. He is not thinking retrospectively for the domestic tyranny continues throughout the lives of his parents. He is rarely free of an uncomfortable feeling that he has missed something. In a letter to his father in 1863 (Ruskin is then forty-four), he expresses his belief in discipline, but with a difference: 'Men ought to be severely disciplined and exercised in the sternest way in daily life—they should learn to lie on stone beds and eat black soup, but they should never have their hearts broken.' He believes that the peculiar discipline of his own upbringing broke his heart. 'The two terrific mistakes which Mama and you involuntarily fell into were the exact reverse *in both* ways—you fed me effeminately and luxuriously to that extent that I actually now could not travel in rough countries without taking a cook with me!—but you thwarted me in all the earnest fire and passion of life.' But he blames himself: all would have been well if he had only stood up to the parental tyranny: 'If I had had courage and knowledge to insist on having my own way resolutely, you would have had me in happier health, loving you twice as much . . . and full of energy for the future—and of power of self-denial.' As it is he is forced into all sorts of selfish ways at a time when 'a man ought to be knit for the duties of middle life by the good success of his youthful life'.

In an estimate of his life and advantages (April 1856) he says: 'I am untroubled by any sort of care or anxiety, unconnected with any particular interest or group of persons, unaffected by feelings of Party, of Race, of social partialities, or of early prejudices.' Yet his life is an effort to ease the unrest caused by thwarted self-expression rather than to gratify desires—or even whims. It is true that he is exposed to temptations without the power to yield to them and that his desires are always nipped in the bud, but that is only half the trouble. He wants to love and to be loved, but to love and be loved in the normal way is denied him. A boyish affair ends in failure: his marriage is annulled; and a late passion ends tragically. 'I wonder mightily', he says, at the end of his life, 'what sort of creature I should have turned out, if instead of distracting and useless pain, I had had the joy of approved love, and the untellable, incalculable motive of its sympathy and praise.' But he comes to believe that 'such things are not allowed in this world', or that 'men capable of highest imaginative passion are always tossed on the fiery waves of it'.

9

Ruskin's appearance has been described as 'quaint', an unfortunate word because it has no very exact meaning. We may suppose that those who have used it to illustrate his personal looks intend to convey something out of the ordinary without being grand or heroic: not the typical scholar, or the typical poet, or the typical gentleman. 'Quaint' would thus mean a digression from the typical. It would also mean a certain kind of digression. Carlyle, Thoreau, and Whitman all digress from the typical but no one ever calls them 'quaint'. Even Whitman's lace-trimmed shirts never earn him that epithet, whilst Carlyle's capacious hats were 'characteristic', and Thoreau's tramp-like aspect merely 'eccentric'. William Morris dresses in navy blue serge and likes to be mistaken for a sea-faring man, and Emerson looks the scholar and gentleman that he is. Wherein then lies Ruskin's quaintness?

There are numerous word-pictures of Ruskin and most of them emphasize his volatility and volubility. He is kinetic and talkative, and if dogmatic, always helpful and kindly, and if earnest, ever gracious and charming. He is of medium height, fair-haired, with full lower lip scarred from a dog-bite in childhood, and bright blue eyes. Joanna Horatia

Ewing calls them 'turquoise blue', and all records agree that it is no ordinary shade of blue. His clothing is odd, and he is known to have mingled homespuns with a frockcoat. He was comfortably rather than elegantly 'turned out' even in his early manhood, but later he sets his own fashion, allowing his clothes to become crumpled and wearing a pale blue cravat of an unusual shade.

So much for the details, and now for the *ensemble*. In his youth he is frail and of a consumptive appearance. In middle life, active and virile without being vigorous. And in old age, patriarchal in long white beard, at last looking the prophet he is. The best glimpse of him in his prime comes from his Oxford disciple, Canon Scott Holland. 'How quaint, the mingling of . . . wistfulness in the face with the spotted blue stock and the collars and the frockcoat, which made him look something between an old-fashioned nobleman of the Forties, and an angel that had lost its way. The small bird-like head and hands and figure, had nevertheless, a curious and old-world pomp in their gait and their motions. The bushy eyebrows gave a strength to the upper part of the face which was a little unexpected, and which found its proper balance in the white beard of his last years. He, somehow, moved one as with the delicate tenderness of a woman; and he looked frail, as if the roughness of the world would hurt and break him; and one longed to shelter him from all that was ugly and cruel.'

10

Both Scott Holland, and, later, Ruskin's biographer, Sir Edward Cook agree that the quaintness is due to a peculiar combination of mental and physical characteristics. Scott Holland associates wistfulness with odd clothes, and Cook a 'quaintness of costume' which 'accurately' reflects 'something of the quaintness of his mind and talk'. But these reasons are not entirely convincing. There is another characteristic, noted by them all, without which his blue eyes and blue cravat and odd costume would not have supported the term. Mary Russell Mitford, in 1848, calls it 'a sort of pretty waywardness that is quite charming'. Ruskin was then twenty-nine. In the following year Dr. Furnivall meets him and is also impressed by his charm of manner, and describes it as 'partly feminine'. At thirty-six Charles Eliot Norton finds in him 'an almost feminine sensitiveness and readiness for sympathy'. When Joanna Ewing meets him he has reached the age of sixty. He still has great charm and is 'so much gentler and more refined' than she expected to find him and, she tells her husband, 'he had been out to buy buns and grapes for *me* (!), carrying the buns himself very carefully so that they might not be crushed!'

It is not then so much his appearance as his manner which is called 'quaint', and his manner is quaint because it is gentle, sensitive, sympathetic, charming, feminine. Charles Eliot Norton calls his 'pleasure in pleasing others by lavish liberality . . . one of the sweet feminine traits of his nature'. There is something feminine even in his economics. He is fond of drawing deductions from domestic life and his reforming zeal has something of the feminine fervour of spring cleaning. He would like to spring clean the world, and given the opportunity he would have done it with all the thoroughness of a good housewife.

Ruskin forms delightful friendships with women who are the recipients of some of his most charmingly playful letters. Such volumes as *Hortus Inclusus* and the privately printed letters to the daughters of Mr. Gladstone, are evidence of this amiable trait. But his preference is nearly always for young girls, and whether these relationships are tutelary, avuncular, or romantic, they are always above reproach. The breath of scandal never touches John Ruskin. 'I don't like married women; I like sibyls and children and vestals,'

he tells Mary Glynne teasingly before her marriage with
Alfred Lyttelton. His friendship with girls is always playful
and often includes a 'make-believe' love-affair with the
exaggerated use of terms of affection. When his newly-wed
correspondent challenges the statement just cited, he
replies: 'I didn't mean, and never have thought, that girls
were higher or holier than wives. Heaven forbid. I merely
said I liked them better, which, surely, is extremely proper
of me.' In the society of girls he is able to express a phase of
his life which might otherwise have been starved. He loves
nothing better than to give them lessons in botany and
geology or to instruct them in his own brand of domestic
economy, or to teach them how to draw, and he once thought
of establishing a school of drawing for girls, with Kate Greenaway as headmistress. His idea of what a young girl should be
taught is crystallized in *Sesame and Lilies* and *The Ethics of
the Dust*, based upon a series of lectures given at a girls'
school. The ostensible purpose of these lectures is 'to awaken
in the minds of young girls . . . a vital interest in the subject
of their study'.

It is not without significance that he shows no such
interest in the welfare of boys. There is something in him
which responds to the very idea of girlhood. He associates it
with all those gracious and kindly things in life to which he
devotes so much of his genius. He tells an audience that all
pretty girls are angels. At the same time he enjoys their
playfulness and has no wish to put them on too high a
pedestal. He indulges in mock-flirtations and likes a romp
with the hoydens. He boasts that 'nice girls make quite as
much fuss about me as I do about them.' He goes 'crazy
about St. Ursula and other saints—chiefly young lady
saints'; Leighton wins his heart 'by painting some pretty
girls', and at another time his sole physical want is 'one of
those Graces out of Botticelli's picture of the Spring'. He
'can't make out how that fellow was able to see such pretty
things, or how he lived among them'.

I I

His diaries have only been published in extract, and his letters have been carefully edited by friends and disciples during a period which made a virtue of suppression and encouraged the maintenance of a virtuous reputation by the same methods. Thus it is not possible to do more than guess at the inner meaning of those emotional incidents which play so conspicuous a part in his middle years. But such details as we now have of a repressed and more than conventual childhood during which he was even dressed like a girl, together with our knowledge of his later feminine characteristics, indicate a deficiency of masculinity. He complains of his effeminate upbringing, and although he suffers from it, adaptation of these peculiar characteristics towards a balanced life are continually going on and with considerable success.

Like some other great men of his time he is sex-shy. He seeks something beyond, something pure and holy. If he had fallen in love with a temperate or a phlegmatic woman, or a woman, like his mother, who had transmuted her passion (if she ever had any) into moral fervour, with her only child as an experimental station, he might have imagined he had found what he wanted and so have been free to concentrate on his job without anxieties or misgivings. Instead of that he falls in love at different times with girls whom he idealizes and who leave him. Adèle Domecq plays with him for a while and then flies to the arms of a more normal lover. Rose la Touche excuses herself on the grounds of his heterodox religious opinions, and dies. Euphemia Gray marries him and then runs away with his friend John Everett Millais. Neither Adèle nor Euphemia is the sort of girl who can live on idealization, and they jilt the egoist who looks into their eyes only to see himself, much as Clara Midleton jilted Sir Willoughby Patterne for a similar reason.

The case of Rose is more complex. She is a delicate child

of nine when Ruskin, aged forty, begins to take an interest in her. His relation at first is avuncular. She is a pet and he pets her with education. Then comes love and an understanding which was to have led to marriage. But when, after seven years, he proposes marriage, Rose, who has become religious and tuberculous, hesitates, rejects him, and dies at the age of eighteen. The objections to Ruskin, which her mother shares, are his age as well as his religious views. But there can be little doubt that the same causes are at work as with Adèle and Euphemia. His insistant idealization frightens the girls, for he not only idealizes them but he seeks to educate them up to his own intellectual level. Adèle shows no interest in that sort of thing, but Euphemia and Rose do. His relation towards them is that of teacher as well as lover. He is ten years Euphemia's senior and 'took pleasure in cultivating her taste and improving her mind'.

Women like Ruskin. They feel, rightly, that they can trust him. But they do not want to marry him. They are attracted, unconsciously, by what is feminine, not what is masculine, in him. His patience with them, his thoughtfulness, his infinitude of kindliness, and his great courtesy are obvious and legitimate attractions. But much as they appreciate these high qualities, I think on the whole they are amused rather than moved by him, and he inclines to treat them as rather nice toys or brittle ornaments. He not only idealizes them, but he is capable of writing the most astonishing nonsense about them. 'I believe', he writes in *The Seven Lamps of Architecture*, 'that most women would, in the end, prefer the pleasure of having built a church, or contributed to the adornment of a cathedral, to the pride of bearing a certain quantity of adamant on their foreheads.' Obviously an opinion which will surprise many men, and most women. But much as he enjoys the company of women and much as he is dependent on them for comfort and sympathy, he is always a little suspicious of them. Remembering his mother, he fears petticoat rule. At Brantwood he considers his rest is 'greatly troubled and darkened and lowered by the horrible arrangement of there being women in the world as well as mountains and stars and lambs, and what else one might have been at peace with—but for those other creatures'.

12

Ruskin side-tracks his passions and is disturbed by the consequences. He is aware of some emotional defect but believes that at some time in the past his passions were normal. 'I believe I once had affections as warm as most people; but partly from evil chance, and partly from foolish misplacing of them, they have got tumbled down and broken to pieces.' He goes on, with an attempt at self-justification, to argue that he is equally cold in all his human contacts, with relatives as well as with friends, and to say that he has no friendships and no loves, which is an exaggeration. He is on good terms with his relatives, has many friends, is always, as we have seen, indulging in innocent little love affairs, and at least one of his masculine friendships, that with Charles Newton at Oxford, on his own admission, 'had possibilities of some heroic attachment . . . in the manner of Theseus and Pirithous'. Love has been unfortunate and painful, as he confesses in a letter to Rossetti at about the same time. 'I have had boundless love from many people during my life, and in more than one case that love has been my greatest calamity. I have boundlessly suffered from it.' He has only been able to get 'understanding from two women' (one was Burne-Jones's wife), which is significant. Normal lovers do not want or expect understanding. Ruskin does and his lovers run away from him and in the end he becomes 'nearly sick of being loved'.

Like Emerson and Thoreau he fears physical contacts and although he is made for friendship rather than for love he is

H

conscious of a distance between himself and his masculine friends. He is kind and generous to all his friends and his letters prove that some of those friendships must have been satisfying, yet none so satisfying as a mountain, a thirteenth-century building, or a picture. These mutely accept his idealization. 'Men are more evanescent than pictures, yet', he says, 'one sorrows for lost friends, and pictures *are* my friends. I have none others. I am never long enough with men to attach myself to them; and whatever feelings of attachment I have are to material things. If the great Tintoretto were to be destroyed, it would be precisely to me what the death of Hallam was to Tennyson. . . .' Perhaps Ruskin's apparent sublimation of sex is diffusion. He is a spiritual Don Juan with two *grand* passions—the pictures of Turner and Mont Blanc.

13

After the death of his mother, he is depressed by 'the sense of loss of that infinitude of love' she gave him 'and the bitter pity of its extinction'. Yet he is conscious of having been over-mothered, when he wants above all things to be himself and to express himself and his own ideas and experiences in his own way. Neither his mother nor his father will permit that much liberty. 'Never', he confesses to Norton, 'did good fond parents meaning to do right do worse by a child than mine did by me.' They will do anything for him but leave him alone or let him grow up, with the result that he has what looks like an attack of deferred wild oats at sixty-five and when he is eighty he is still adolescent.

He takes the united opposition of his parents lying down until he is nearly forty—then he gets up and kicks over the traces, not by having what is vulgarly known as a 'good time', but first by rejecting the literal interpretation of the scriptures imposed upon him by his mother, and next by resenting the objection raised by his father to the alternative —salvation by social reform. His father had opposed the publication of the essays which afterwards become *Munera Pulveris* and earlier he had prevented him from 'saving Turner's work'. Ruskin protests in a letter which is not only a revelation of an amazing relationship between a genius of forty-three years old and a stern father, but a clear indication that the son is making a bid for freedom. 'The *only* thing you can do for me', he says, 'is to let me follow out my work in my own way and in peace. All interference with me torments me and makes me quite as ill as any amount of work.' The depression from which he is suffering can only be reduced when he accomplishes what he intends and recovers 'in some degree the lost ground of life'. He has made up his own mind and 'My opinions', he asserts, 'will never more change—they are now one with Bacon's and Goethe's—and I shall not live long enough to be wiser than either of these men. (I trust I shall not change by becoming foolisher.)'

He may have said some foolish things during the next half of his life, but he sticks to his resolution. He becomes a political economist, remains one, and resents all the attempts of his parents and his friends, to turn him from the path which he convinces himself is the right one. 'The only vexation of my life', he tells Norton, 'which you have it really in your power to allay is the continual provocation I receive from the universal assumption that I know nothing of political economy, and am a fool—so far—for talking of it. . . .'

14

During this more than usually disturbed period of his life he flirts with the notion of abandonment as Emerson had done, and at all times he is frankly puzzled by the

puritan fear of the flesh and the knowledge that great men
have been neither puritans, nor saints. He notes that Homer,
Shakespeare, Tintoretto, Veronese, Titian, Michael Angelo,
Sir Joshua Reynolds, Velazquez, Correggio, and Turner,
'are all of them boldly Animal' and that 'Francia and
Angelico, and all the purists, however beautiful, are poor
weak creatures in comparison'. He confesses that he does
not understand it. 'One would have thought purity gives
strength, but it doesn't.' And he concludes that 'A good,
stout, self-commanding, magnificent animality is the make
for poets and artists'. . . . He will not believe that Paul
Veronese, for instance, 'whose finger is as fine, and whose
eye is like the morning' is 'a servant of the devil' and 'the
poor little wretch in a tidy black tie' to whom he had been
'listening this Sunday morning expounding Nothing with a
twang—is a servant of God'. It is all very well 'for people to
fast, who can't eat; and to preach, who cannot talk or sing;
and to walk barefoot, who cannot ride, and then think themselves good. Let them learn to master the world before they
abuse it.'

In his thirty-eighth year he is at Turin studying Paul
Veronese in the mornings and enjoying the opera in the evenings, 'and', he writes, 'I've found out a good deal—more than
I can put in a letter—in that six weeks, the main thing in the
way of discovery being that, positively, to be a first-rate
painter—you mustn't be pious; but rather a little wicked, and
entirely a man of the world. I have been inclining to this
opinion for some years; but I clinched it at Turin.' This
desire to break away from the old moorings persists. Two
years later he is still 'seriously and despairingly, thinking of
going to Paris or Venice and breaking away from all modern
society and opinion, and doing I know not what'. And a year
later he says he is 'tired of benevolence and eloquence and
everything that's proper' and is going to 'cultivate himself
and nobody else, and see what will come of that'.

15

When past fifty he confesses that he is 'woefully dependent on affection and praise', and his writings are a continuous advocacy of a society which might be supposed to soothe the hypersensitive nerves of a Ruskin. But it is unsafe to take any of his statements too literally, for he is paradoxical by nature and ready to round on one with an equally emphatic pronouncement to the contrary. It is necessary to consider what he means at the moment and what are the circumstances which govern that meaning. For instance, a few years before the above statement is made, he says: 'No one can do me any good by loving me: I have more love, a thousand-fold, than I need, or can do any good with; but people do me good by making *me* love *them* —which isn't easy.' He inclines like most men to outbursts of grumbling, but his sharp mind realizes that it is not entirely external influences that are wrong. Although his father checks expenditure on Turner's pictures and opposes his political opinions, and his mother makes him 'effeminate and vain', nevertheless he confesses 'it will be justest . . . to blame either Fate or me myself, for all that I suffer, and no other person'.

As he grows older he confesses to Norton, 'the evil about us takes more definite and overwhelming form in my eyes, and I have no one near me to help me or soothe me, so that I am obliged often to give up thinking and take to walking and drawing in a desperate way, as mechanical opiates'. . . . At the time he is on a continental holiday with his parents. During these years he is burdened with 'the sense of the terrific call of human crime for resistance and of human misery for help—though it seems to me as the voice of a river of blood which can but sweep me down in the midst of its black clots, helpless'.

These however are the wayward intimations of inverted

feelings. Ruskin is a competent and sensitive draughtsman, but even if he had been impious or 'a little wicked' he could never have become a painter, which was never a serious intention. His drawing, with a minor exception or so, is documentary. Its purpose has only been to collect data—never for its own sake. In the wider sense, however, he was an authentic artist, especially as a writer of prose, and the purport of his ethics was the creation of an artistry in life. His gospel might be summed up as living as a fine art.

The hesitations and frustrations which arrest his art ultimately find expression in a passionate moral code which might have ended in mere eccentricity had Ruskin possessed an ordinary mind. This moralism is another stumbling-block to any pure artistry, even of words, and if the divergent conditions result in a contradiction in artistic terms justifying somewhat Whistler's malicious gibe that 'Ruskin is an artist among political economists and a political economist among artists', they unite in producing a fearless criticism of society and an inspired moral synthesis which may yet benefit humanity.

16

An acute sensibility makes him restless and tends always to overwork his faculties in the interest of his own pet interests: justice and beauty, prompted, as he rightly diagnoses, by good nature and vanity which are the media of his overwhelming desire for self-expression. Of this desire he was always more or less conscious, and in a letter to his father (1852), he puts it into frank and precise words. His idea of genius is a thing that consists mainly in a man's doing 'intellectual' things because 'he can't help it'. 'There is a strong instinct in me', he says, 'which I cannot analyse, to draw and describe the things I love—not for reputation, nor for the good of others, nor for my own advantage, but a sort

of instinct like that for eating and drinking. I should like
to draw all St. Mark's, and all this Verona stone by stone,
to eat it all up into my mind, touch by touch.'

17

Like Thoreau he is a naturalist and an observer, but with
a more romantic bias for the picturesque. He discourages the use of the microscope among his pupils for *two*
characteristic reasons: one romantic, because it spoils taste
'by diminishing interest in distant effects of things'; and the
other Ruskinian, because there is more to be seen with the
naked eye than a hundred eyes could see. Seeing with him is
believing. His genius is fired through his eyes and he seems
to see more of everything than anyone else ever saw. Compared with him, Flaubert, another master of observation,
only saw surfaces. Ruskin sees all the world and all the
heavens in a stone, a shell, or a snowflake. 'What a lovely
thing a bit of fine, sharp, crystallized snow is, held up
against the blue sky, catching the sun! Talk of diamonds!'
If he turns everything into a theory and sees in everything
a symbol of something else, he first observes accurately—as
accurately as a Flaubert, and more profoundly. He possesses
both the insight and the observation of genius. *Modern
Painters* is a piece of observation as well as a sermon and
it is as much about mountains as pictures. He sets out 'to
see the Alps in a simple, thoughtless, and untheorizing
manner', and becomes their supreme watcher and recorder.
No other writer has painted such word-pictures of Alpine
scenery. Literature has no greater purpose for him than to
see accurately and to report faithfully. Poets are physical
as well as visionary seers.[1] He believes that part of his

[1] He believes that the description of the Alps in Tennyson's 'Come down,
O Maid, from yonder mountain height', is 'perhaps the most wonderful piece
of sight in all poetry'. 'Letters', *Works*, xxxvi, 326.

mission is to give eyes to a hurrying, careless world. 'There can be no question . . . of the mischievous tendency of the hurry of the present day, in the way people undertake this very looking.' But he is not content with Thoreau to observe infinity in a grain of sand or a snowflake, he stares himself into ecstasy over Venice or Mont Blanc. He gives 'three years' close and incessant labour to the examination of the chronology of the architecture of Venice; two long winters being wholly spent in the drawing of details on the spot.' He devotes a long life endeavouring to make people see things in his way, and it is still with the eyes of Ruskin that many people see the Alps and the show-towns of Italy. Seeing with him is as important as doing and more important than thinking. If we would only 'look at a thing instead of thinking what it must be like or do a thing instead of thinking it cannot be done, we should all get on much better'.

18

His evangelical upbringing convinces him that the pursuit of pleasure is wrong and that all things founded on pleasure pass away and that even where 'Art has been followed *only* for the sake of luxury or delight, it has contributed, and largely contributed, to bring about the destruction of the nation practising it'. Doing what you like is not 'the way to heaven', and when he tells you that he takes a pleasure in doing good even he does so with a sort of defiance: 'My pleasures are in seeing, thinking, reading, and making people happy (if I can, consistently with my own comfort). And I *take* these pleasures. And I suppose, if my pleasures were in smoking, betting, dicing, and giving pain, I should take *those* pleasures.' In his early twenties, he feels that it is no time 'to be spelling letters, or touching of strings, counting stars or crystallizing dewdrops, while the

earth is falling under our feet, and our fellows are departing
every instant into eternal pain'. And ten years later he looks
back upon his past life with discomfort, for, he tells his
father, he has always been working for himself in one way or
another: 'Either for myself, in doing things that I enjoyed,
i.e. climbing mountains, looking at pictures, etc.: or for my
own aggrandisement and satisfaction of ambition, or else to
gratify my affections in pleasing you and my mother . . . I
had never really done anything for God's service.' It was
this feeling which turns the evangelist into a Socialist, for
however loudly he calls himself a Tory his teaching is fundamentally socialistic. He seeks to do God's work not so much
by saving souls as by saving bodies, or rather by saving
souls through the redemption of the body politic. And he
comes to despise gratification of whim even in an artist.
He is primarily a teacher and a preacher and he teaches that
life must have purpose and that the purpose must be the
improvement of life. It is this didactic attitude which ultimately breaks his friendship with Rossetti. He cannot
bear to see Rossetti doing just whatever he likes 'as puppies
and tomtits do'. Doing what you like is the way neither to
Heaven nor Utopia.

19

In spite of these outbursts of penitence, and after the first
real break with parental authority, Ruskin becomes not
only more and more Ruskinian, but more and more a social
reformer. His last struggle with his father is over the
development of the unorthodox views on politics and
economics which take the place of his belief in the literal
interpretation of the scriptures and continue to absorb him
for the rest of his life. The tendency is always present. It
begins in *Modern Painters* and ends in *Præterita* and in all

the oceans of prose in between it is easy to discover this search for that religion of humanity which declares itself frankly for the first time in the *Political Economy of Art* (1857), and he sums it up, as far as it can be briefly summed up, in *Fors Clavigera* (Letter 76) where he declares 'that in resolving to do our work well is the only sound foundation of any religion whatsoever'.

Ruskin looks upon the change as a conversion which is not complete until a year after the publication of the *Political Economy of Art*. He calls the abandonment of his old evangelical faith 'unconversion', and dates it from the sudden realization of the contrast between a service in the Waldensian Chapel in Turin where 'a little squeaking idiot was preaching to an audience of seventeen old women and three louts that they were the only children of God in Turin', and the *Queen of Sheba* of Paul Veronese which glowed in the afternoon light, whilst from outside came the strains of a military band that seems to him more devotional 'in their perfect art, tune, and discipline than anything' he remembers of 'evangelical hymns'. And as the perfect colour and sound assert their power over him they seem finally to 'fasten' him in the 'old article of Jewish faith, that things done delightfully and rightly were always done by the help and in the spirit of God'.

20

It is permissible and easy to make personal deductions from the works of Ruskin, for they are almost entirely autobiographical. 'As for the things that have influenced me,' he says, 'I believe hard work, love of justice and beauty, good nature and great vanity, have done all of me that was worth doing.' Whether he preaches, describes, argues or denounces; whether he writes *Modern Painters* or *Fors*

Clavigera, Unto this Last or *Præterita*; whether his subject be pictures or minerals, mountains or buildings, education or currency or economics, it is always a microcosm of John Ruskin. From one point of view he is like an archaeologist digging into the past, but in his case the past is himself or some object of research apropos of himself. He gives everything he studies new significance and nothing is insignificant for him. Consciously or unconsciously he projects himself into all his themes and activities.

Nowhere is this habit so characteristic or so curious as in the titles of his books, which are more peculiar to himself than those perhaps of any other writer. They have rarely any meaning for his readers until he has explained them—which he does at length and with a relish. And some of his biographers and commentators have felt it necessary to explain his explanations. Ruskin himself devotes two and a half pages of the second of the *Fors Clavigera* letters to an explanation of that bewildering title, and Sir E. T. Cook finds it necessary to devote no less than five pages to the task of disentangling and setting out in logical order 'the intrinsic play of thought in Ruskin's mind around *Fors* as Force, Fortitude, and Fortune, and *Clavigera* as bearing the Club, the Key, and the Nail'.

His books are exhibitions of his whims and fancies as well as of his considered ideas; his letters and diaries are confessionals. This accounts for marked inconsistencies of opinion which should never be attributed to caprice. They are natural changes of mind such as most experience and indulge. Most writers, however, keep these wayward and temporary opinions to themselves. Ruskin has no such caution. He is always thinking aloud, and if his innate exhibitionism will not permit him to keep anything to himself, his natural honesty and intellectual courage prevent him from disguising the variations and eccentricities of his opinions. But apart from that he is as usual perfectly honest about these inconsistencies, as he is in all things. They are not always involuntary and he is prepared to defend them:

'I am often accused of inconsistency; but believe myself defensible against the charge with respect to what I have said on nearly every subject except that of war.' On that subject he finds it impossible to write consistently, for he has come to 'two precisely opposite conclusions'. And here he is not alone.

He is also fond of taking his readers off the main route of his theme into by-paths where he may find an excuse to talk to them about his own personal affairs. You never know the moment he will digress from a discussion upon pictures or minerals, on clouds or social reform, into details about his parents, his schooldays, his travels, or even his fantastic and frustrated love affairs, but each digression will be linked to the main theme with consummate ingenuity. He is disarmingly frank about this habit. 'I rather enjoy talking about myself,' he says in *Fors*, 'even in my follies' (Letter 75). And it is obvious that he enjoys self-revelation, even when he is sorry for himself, although he deprecates a similar habit in others. He is ashamed of Carlyle in the letters to Emerson. 'My own diaries are indeed full of mewing and moaning, all to myself,' he says, 'but I think my letters to friends have more a tendency to crowing, or at least, on the whole, try to be pleasant.' That is true, but they mew and groan also, and if he does not yield to self-pity with Carlylean gusto, he likes to contemplate his own troubles and he revels in diatribes against a naughty world.

All literary phenomena, however disguised, are a reflection of self, and nowhere is this more obvious than in the works of Ruskin. There is little, if any, attempt at disguise. His interest in his own desires prevents him from realizing that they nearly always father his thoughts. If, however, he is not conscious of all the implications, he is aware of this self-absorption, which so often amounts to conceit, and defends it on the grounds that 'there are two kinds of self-estimation—a fool's, and that which every man who knows his business has of himself'. Self-absorption is responsible for many outbreaks of candour which disturb even his friendships, as well as the Press, and sometimes precipitate him into more complicated difficulties. But criticism aggravates rather than allays his egotism. On being trounced by the *Athenæum* for 'vaingloriousness' in his pamphlet on *Pre-Raphaelitism* he vows that in speaking of art he will never be modest any more. He keeps to his vow, and not only about art.

2 I

His sociology reflects his own outraged feelings before the wastefulness and unseemliness of an acquisitive society. He spends both life and fortune trying to clear up the mess of a machine-age which has not yet learnt how to behave itself. His theory of joyful work is a projection of his own enthusiasm and friendliness, for if he writes of life apropos of himself, he lives also for others apropos of himself, seeking no other reward than the joy of doing so. His life is a continuous public spiritedness. He wants to be good and he wants to do good. 'People, be good', were the first words of a sermon he preached to his family when he was almost a baby. 'I must tell you, Professor,' a would-be disciple said, 'how much I admire your books.' 'I don't care whether you have admired them or not,' Ruskin snapped, 'have they done you any good?' Pictures and poems are means of doing good. He tells Mrs. Browning that poetry must not only be made as good as possible, it must be made to do as much good as possible. Doing good is in the nature of a spiritual purge. 'I write these letters,' he says in *Time and Tide*, 'not in any hope of their being at present listened to, but to disburthen my heart of the witness I have to bear, that I may be free to go back to my garden lawns, and paint birds and flowers there.'

This attitude towards life and affairs is put concisely at

the beginning of his last phase in the opening of *Fors Clavigera* where he announces that he 'will put up with this state of things, not an hour longer'. 'I am not an unselfish person, nor an Evangelical one,' he says, 'I have no particular pleasure in doing good . . . but I simply cannot paint, nor read, nor look at minerals, nor do anything else that I like, and the very light of the morning sky, when there is any—which is seldom, now-a-days, near London—has become hateful to me, because of the misery that I know of, and see signs of, where I know it not, which no imagination can interpret too bitterly.'

22

You may find examples in any of his works, but nowhere is it more amusingly or emphatically revealed than in this passage from a letter expounding the Guild of St. George (1869):

'Do not think it is a nonsensical fastening on my own particular fancies when I tell you that my first object in all law will be grace and beauty in all external things. There shall be no riches on the one side, no noisomeness nor vulgarity on the other. I have been planning this finally ever since I passed the Alps this year, and yesterday it got hammered down into me by a curious chance. I had been all the morning in the Venetian Gallery looking down at Victor Carpaccio's history of St. Ursula, in which every figure, and there are hundreds, is refined in feature and beautiful in dress, with a purity as perfect, though as various, as wild flowers. There are old and young—hinds and poor labourers, saints and rough soldiers, but they are all different only as violets and ivy, or roses and meadow grass, all lovely and human and pure.

'Well I had been an hour or so among these people, and

then came here[1] in a glorious afternoon, with the mountains of Titian all purple in the North, but with four Americans in the carriage with me (1st class) one man and three women, who, of all the wretches I ever endured the presence of, were the noisomest and most abominable, in the ingrained essential desperateness of degradation of mind. I can't enter into details about them, but I won't endure for my part the state of things which produces such vermin. If I fence myself only into a few fields I will have about me at least nothing but what shall tend to true laws of pleasantness and peace—not loathsomeness and wrath.'

The personal attitude becomes more emphatic and aggressive as he grows older. He dogmatizes and resents interference or opposition. Candid friendships are not encouraged. A certain amount of acceptance is demanded. At times, if he is taken literally, he demands even more; 'I will associate with no man', he tells Rossetti, 'who does not more or less accept my own estimate of myself.' It was no uncommon thing for his friends to attempt to save him from himself, especially when he offends intellectual or religious susceptibilities. Even the faithful but timid Norton had to be rebuked for such kindnesses. 'You were to me', Ruskin tells him, 'what many of my other friends and lovers have been,—a seeker of my good in your own way, not in mine.'

23

Ruskin strives towards accurate statement, desiring always the truth without exaggeration, not alone as 'an accomplishment of language', but as 'a principle of honour'. Yet, although you can feel him striving after accuracy in all his works, he sometimes writes in haste and withdraws at leisure, not, however, because of mis-statement

[1] Ruskin had travelled from Venice to Verona.

but rather to tone down some harshness, truth in itself, but likely to cause undeserved pain. He exaggerates in spite of himself especially in his talk and in those of his works which take the epistolary form and thus approximate to talk. His pursuit and statement of truth become exaggerations from sheer love of the thing: 'Nothing that I say is my saying or thinking, but simple truth by all men ascertainable as the law of gravity.' Exaggeration with him is constitutional. It is the over-statement of conviction, not an attempt to deceive.

He often seeks effect in the manner of *épater les bourgeois*, or 'writing piquantly' as he calls it, and like most intellectuals he enjoys opposition, is often deliberately contentious, and in the absence of anyone else he contradicts himself: 'I am never satisfied that I have handled a subject properly till I have contradicted myself at least three times.' On one occasion at breakfast in Downing Street he puzzles Mr. Gladstone by suggesting that the community not the criminal should be responsible for crime. When, for instance, a murder is committed, the residents in the vicinity of the outrage should draw lots to decide who should be hanged for it. 'How excellent the moral effect,' beamed Ruskin, 'if the man on whom the lot fell were of a peculiarly high character.' His wife ventures to tell him that he is 'a great conservative in France, because there everybody is radical, and a great radical in Austria, where everybody is conservative'. He accepts the rebuke, supposing that: 'One reason why I am so fond of fish (as creatures, I mean, not as eating) is that they always swim with their heads against the stream. I find it for me the healthiest position.'

But his manner is as varied as his interests. Sometimes he is arch, at other times even silly, and versatile as he is, he is given to obsessions which are not always normal. At times he suspects even a predominating enthusiasm and goes so far as to confess that he has been insane about Turner and Rose la Touche. But his weakness is versatility rather than obsession. He has ever 'a thousand things' in his head 'pushing each other like shoals of minnows', and again, the thousand things flitter in his mind 'like sea-birds for which there are no sands to settle upon' (*Fors*, Letter 60). He cannot resist the temptation of doing several things at once until in the end he loses power of concentration, and before the final exhaustion of his apparently endless mental reserve, those who care for him see him scattering the force of a tottering brain, 'upon new schemes almost daily which could never be completed.' Another eye-witness reports that Ruskin's mental collapse of 1878 was due to the 'utterly spendthrift way in which (with imagination less and less controlled by judgment) he has for these last years been at work with a dozen different irons in the fire—each enough to engage one average man's mind . . . his emotions all the while as hard-worked as his intellect—they always blowing the bellows of its furnace'.

24

Ruskin's versatility was not that of a Leonardo da Vinci or a William Morris. It was not the capacity of practising with genius several different crafts, but rather a desire to do a number of the same things at once, like an amateur of many hobbies. He remains an amateur throughout life and an amateur very much at the mercy of enthusiasm and whim. There is something incredible about his activities, and he takes a delight in bragging about them. During his first Professorship of Art at Oxford (1870–8) he publishes works on Botany, Geology, and Drawing; founds an Art museum, a library of standard literature, the Companionship of St. George, engages in such social experiments as sweeping the streets of St. Giles, opening a shop for the purpose of selling tea at a fair price, as well as lecturing, writing to the newspapers on many subjects, and publishing as well as writing the monthly parts of *Fors Clavigera*.

In several instances these operations are carried on simultaneously. In October 1875 he tells Norton that he has 'now on hand altogether seven big books going on at once'. Ten years later he informs him that he is arranging a case at the British Museum 'to show the whole history of silica'; lecturing at Oxford; 'writing the life of Sta. Zita de Lucca' and 'an essay on clouds', which has 'pulled' him into a lot of work on 'diffraction and fluorescence', the preface for Collingwood's *Alps of Savoy*, and he is 'doing a *Fors* now and then.' In addition he is teaching Kate Greenaway 'the principles of Carpaccio', beginning to reform the drama 'with the help of Miss Anderson', producing *The Tempest* with George Richmond's grandchildren; and finally he is 'making the children learn chimes' on the 'three sets of bells (octaves)' which he has presented to Coniston School.

His unwritten works of all kinds are extensive, and in the preface to *Deucalion* he refers to a list of seventy-three projected volumes, including ten volumes on Northern Thirteenth-Century Art, six volumes on Florentine Art and three on Attic Art. In addition, he is collecting materials for a life of Walter Scott, with an analysis of Epic Art, in seven volumes, a life of Xenophon, with an analysis of the principles of Education, in ten volumes, a commentary on Hesiod, a 'final analysis' of the principles of Political Economy, in nine volumes, and a work on the geology and botany of the Alps, in twenty-four volumes.

He also works hard at his private charities, keeps up a continuous correspondence with relatives, friends, colleagues and strangers; and is one of the most active and pungent of letter-writers to the public press. A collection of these last letters was published in 1880 with the title *Arrows of the Chace*, and the variety of the subjects discussed, and discussed brilliantly, is in keeping with a versatility which is equalled only by his powers of absorption and concentration. He also enjoys everything he does and is convinced that his latest hobby is the best. 'I never get any credit for my geology', he tells Mary Gladstone, 'and it is the best of me by far.' That was in 1878, but his high opinion of his work as an economist, on the publication of *Unto this Last* (1862), is nearer the truth as we understand Ruskin to-day.

25

There is little doubt that much of this energy is the result of an unfulfilled physical life, which also encourages those anxieties and fears which dominate him. His work is an instance of what psychologists call sublimation, but it is involuntary sublimation. He works to forget and to let off steam. Rest means discomfort. He is always as busy as an ant, and is known to have worked at different subjects on twelve successive days. If he is not travelling or talking, or drawing, he is writing or reading or pottering about with his minerals and pictures, or etching into his mind 'touch by touch' the stones of Venice or Abbeville or Verona or the rocks of Switzerland or Savoy, and when these fail he stares at clouds and birds and flowers and twists their beauties into dreams and theories; not merely sitting and staring for the fun of it. Everything he sees is observed and memorised, and, as like as not, stored in a note-book for future or present use.

It is inevitable that in such a life, admirable and useful as it is, there should have been periods of doubt and depression. And it is not surprising that something should have snapped in the end. Nothing is so pathetic as the sight of this unworldly genius in one such moment toying with the idea of the value of the ordinary prosaic life where 'nothing prevails finally but a steady, worldly-wise labour—comfortable—resolute—full of animal life—affectionate—compassionate'. And it is to fight down or side-track such normal wishes that he arms himself with a variety of activities. The chief of them is writing. He is always writing, 'he wrote anywhere, anyhow, with anything, and on everything'. Work with him for long periods is an aid to forgetting. 'My work is an opiate,' he confesses. It is also a sedative bringing calm if not always sleep: 'I can only breathe freely when I am at work.' Work thus does for him what a full animal life—affectionate and compassionate—does for those who possess blunter sensibilities.

26

His periods of depression are not always produced by obvious causes. They are often vague and what is popularly called constitutional. His ingrown emotions make him peculiarly sensitive to the flight of time. This condition is reflected in his work, much of which is concerned with the idea of permanence. From one point of view the *Stones of Venice* is a passionate appeal for the protection of the noble architecture of that city and an equally passionate plea for the revival of social conditions under which architecture as noble and as durable might come into the world again. His politics no less than his political economy seek to conserve. There he is 'by nature and instinct Conservative, loving old things because they are old, and hating new ones merely because they are new'. The words are his own. Liberty means mutability and destruction; democracy leads to confusion and ugliness. Uncontrolled commerce is ravaging the countryside of England, destroying her agriculture, and building smoke-grimed factory towns. Restoration is playing havoc with the past as represented in ancient buildings. 'Every thirteenth-century cathedral in France, and every beautiful street in my favourite cities, has been destroyed. Chamouni is destroyed—Geneva—Lucerne—Zurich—Schaffhausen—Berne—might just as well have been swallowed up by earthquake as they are now. There are no inns, no human beings any more anywhere; nothing but endless galleries of rooms, and automata in millions. I can't travel, I have taken to stones and plants.' The 'withering and disgusting pain' which afflicts him when faced with the results of modern progress is tempered by memories of 'unchanged beauties', but not sufficiently to obliterate his indignation when he continues to find beloved places 'changed into railroad stations and dustheaps'.

But if in the main he is trying to save himself under the impression that he is saving beauty, he throws a clear light upon the fundamental weaknesses of a system which seeks material prosperity at all costs, and he strives disinterestedly for a progress nearer, not only to his heart's desire, but nearer (in theory at least) to that of many sensible people. Further, and it is a tribute to his honesty of purpose as well as to the integrity of his social conscience and the growth of his mind from romantic enthusiasm to sense of fact, his attack on predatory commerce becomes more realistic as the years pass. And if some of his aesthetics are questionable, and if his utterance at times is too emphatic, his social doctrines, stripped of their rhetoric and pruned of their egotism, are not only as he believes them to be—the most useful of his writings—but more useful to the present age than any other teaching that has survived the century he helped to make illustrious.

WILLIAM MORRIS

My work is the embodiment of dreams in one form or another.

WILLIAM MORRIS

Ever since William Morris became a Socialist attempts have been made to separate his art from his politics. The attempts fail because there is never a time when Morris does not associate art with the problem of living. With Carlyle and Ruskin he feels a personal responsibility in social affairs, and his conversion to Socialism is the inevitable consummation of his attitude towards the arts. 'The tremendous import of his teaching', said his daughter, colleague and editor, 'depended upon his experience as poet and artist.'[1] Like his master, John Ruskin, he repudiates art for art's sake as emphatically as he repudiates political economy for commercial profit. He tells the students of the Birmingham School of Art, in 1879, that 'it is not possible to dissociate art from morality, politics, and religion'. But he is fully aware of his responsibilities as an artist, and although he devotes an increasing amount of time to preaching, his art escapes didacticism, except towards the end of his life, when he writes a handful of propagandist songs and two equally propagandist romances. The songs are not much better than the average efforts of the kind, but the romances, *News from Nowhere* and *A Dream of John Ball*, are generally acknowledged to be among his masterpieces, and in recent years they have achieved something like classical status.

Those who would separate the poet and designer from the politician and Socialist overlook the fact that in spite of appearances to the contrary, the poetry, even the earliest poetry of Morris, as well as his designs and manufactured articles, are intensely subjective. He is seeking all the time to objectivize an emotional condition, largely subconscious, which makes some conception of a perfect state inevitable if

[1] May Morris. Intro., *William Morris and the Early Days of the Socialist Movement*, J. Bruce Glasier (1921).

he is to find peace. He lives always in a state of conflict with his internal and external environment, and being a man of energy he seeks to allay the inward stress by action. The writing of poetry and fiction, painting and designing, manufacturing and shop-keeping, lecturing and Socialist agitation, are all attempts to resolve this inward conflict by the processes known to psychologists as objectivization and sublimation.

2

When still a young man, he feels that all is not well with the world, and dreams of retreat into the Church, or alternatively, a Brotherhood of poets and artists. The Church as a refuge is abandoned early, and the idea of a Brotherhood loses its original monastic character by becoming the Morris Workshop and the germ of the Arts and Crafts Movement which ultimately restores the lost sense of design to the decorative arts. The ideas of design and craftsmanship which inspire the enterprise and give it importance are ultimately projected into an ideal commonwealth which Morris thinks can be brought into being by means of Socialism.

The social character of his attitude towards the arts is fundamental at all stages of his life. He does not immediately find his right direction, but when he does there is no break with earlier impulses. He does not change, he evolves. Under the influence of his parents, particularly his mother, he considers the idea of entering the Church, but decides finally upon architecture as a career. Both the Church and architecture appeal to that communal purpose which governs his life, and at an early age he looks upon architecture as the mother-art embracing all the rest and finding full expression in an ideal city, or even state. No better starting-point could have been chosen for the budding utopist, whose superabundant energy is already demanding expression.

Morris is not at his ease in Street's architectural office, but the experience is useful if only because he meets there Philip Webb, who becomes a life-long friend and comrade in craftsmanship. In this unsettled mood he listens to Satan in the person of another early friend, Dante Gabriel Rossetti, who advises him to abandon architecture for painting. Morris is tempted and with characteristic energy decides, as a preparation, to devote six hours a day to drawing 'besides office work'. He feels, doubtless, that neither architecture nor painting is his destiny, otherwise he would not have objected to the drudgery of an architect's office or succeeded in completing no more than one picture. Drudgery is a relative term depending upon whether you like what you are doing. The monotony of office routine interpreting other people's ideas is the essence of drudgery to Morris. 'One won't get much enjoyment out of life at this rate,' he complains, and here he postulates one of his chief demands: happiness.

Morris demands happiness for himself and for others, and it was natural that he should become a supporter of the Ruskinian doctrine of joy in work. Even at the age of twenty-three Morris has approached this doctrine, for in the same letter he associates 'love and work'. Two further passages are even more significant. The first represents his early retreatist (not 'escapist') attitude towards affairs. 'I can't enter into politico-social subjects with any interest, for on the whole I see that things are in a muddle, and I have no power or vocation to set them right in ever so small a degree. My work is the embodiment of dreams in one form or another. . . .' This attitude finds its final expression in the familiar introductory verses of *The Earthly Paradise* (1868), which it must be noted he calls an 'Apology':

Of Heaven or Hell I have no power to sing,
I cannot ease the burden of your fears,
Or make quick-coming death a little thing,

> *Or bring again the pleasure of past years,*
> *Nor for my words shall ye forget your tears,*
> *Or hope again for aught that I can say,*
> *The idle singer of an empty day.*

Instead he turns again, for a little while, to the dominion of dreams, conscious none the less of the languors and boredoms of such a realm:

> *But rather, when aweary of your mirth,*
> *From full hearts still unsatisfied ye sigh,*
> *And, feeling kindly unto all the earth,*
> *Grudge every minute as it passes by,*
> *Made the more mindful that the sweet days die—*
> *—Remember me a little then I pray,*
> *The idle singer of an empty day.*

The image of an Earthly Paradise is none the less the background of all his dreams and recurs throughout his poetry and his prose. It sometimes takes the form of a Palace of Art remote from the toil and trouble of common affairs and it ultimately becomes the Utopia of *News from Nowhere* and the Socialist Republic of his propagandist lectures. His prose romances are all set in dreamland, their lovely titles alone suggesting the dominant utopian image, *The Waters of the Wondrous Isles*, *The Well at the World's End*, *The Roots of the Mountains*. But although the dreamland is nowhere it always follows the pattern of past times and particularly of the middle age. William Morris spends his spare time in an idealized medieval England.

3

Morris is ready to 'feel kindly unto all the earth' but his eyes are set neither in the ends of the earth nor in some romantic future. If he looks to the past for an example, it is because he finds the present survivals of the craftsman-ship of a past age so admirable that they might become guides into a future which he would inaugurate here and now. In the best sense of two much-abused words, William Morris is both realist and nationalist. He flirts with the ancient cultures of Northern France and Scandinavia but loves England. He is a revolutionary because he realizes that the separation of art from work, and production for profit rather than use, are together destroying the England that he loves so much more passionately than those who oppose him. His noblest and most inspiring words in poetry and prose are steeped in this passion for England. His life-work as a craftsman and a politician is devoted to the pre-servation of England before she becomes the chattel of those who think of nothing but buying and selling.

Here again his politics are derived from his aesthetics. He repudiates the idea that the English lack the art-sense. 'Let us dispose of the dictum', he says, 'which used to be popular in dilettante circles, that the English are essen-tially a non-artistic people. I must call that a good deal less than a half-truth, and you have only got to go to the first (unrestored) medieval building you can get at to test that view of the subject. As a matter of fact, until art failed throughout civilization, the English had a very different style of Art of their own, which clearly expressed their thoughts and their lives, and of which beauty, almost it seems to us unsought for, was an essential part; while as far as our own days go, it is, as I have said before, to non-artistic England that some glimmer of insight into the possible future of Art has come. In short, it is no use going further afield than this country to find the artists and craftsmen that we need: when you find them you will undoubtedly find that they have shortcomings which those of other countries have not; but also they will have their own special excellencies, which we had better make the most of.'

This art of England is born of the spirit of the English people blending with and re-creating the English countryside. It expresses itself in houses and barns and churches and the common objects and utensils of ordinary life: 'I say, without fear of contradiction, that no dwelling of men has ever been sweeter or pleasanter than an English house.'

One of the outstanding joys of his life is the discovery and acquisition of such a house in the remote Oxfordshire village of Kelmscott. He cannot speak of that 'mass of grey walls and pearly grey roofs which makes the House, called by courtesy the Manor House', without tenderness. For a quarter of a century that old place mingles with his life and thoughts. 'It is a house that I love,' he says, 'with a reasonable love I think; for though my words may give you no idea of any special charm about it, yet I assure you that the charm is there; so much has the old house grown up out of the soil and the lives of those that lived on it; needing no grand office-architect, with no great longing for anything than correctness, and to be like Julius Caesar; but some thin thread of tradition, a half-anxious sense of the delight of meadow and acre and wood and river; a certain amount (not too much let us hope) of common sense, a liking for making materials serve one's turn, and perhaps at bottom some little grain of sentiment. This I think was what went to the making of the old house. . . .' When he takes that other old house of a later period on the Upper Mall at Hammersmith, he names it after his beloved Oxfordshire home, and his last, and, for him, happiest work, is called the Kelmscott Press.

4

He rejoices in our great Cathedrals and fights valiantly to save them from vandalism and 'restoration', but he has a special tenderness for our country churches: 'Take note of them, I say, to see how art ran through everything: for you must not let the name of "church" mislead you: in

times of real art people built their churches in just the same
style as their houses; "ecclesiastical art" is an invention of
the last thirty years . . . I myself am just fresh from an out-
of-the-way part of the country near the end of the navigable
Thames, where, within a radius of five miles, are some half-
dozen tiny village churches, every one of which is a beautiful
work of art, with its own individuality. These are the works
of the Thames-side country bumpkins, as you would call
us, nothing grander than that.' It is significant that he
associates himself with those old English country bumpkins. A large part of his effort is devoted to an attempt to
revive the kind of work they did and the conditions under
which they worked.

Houses and churches, no matter how beautiful they are,
are not for him things in themselves any more than art is a
thing in itself. They are details in a beautifully ordered
country-side. Nature and art are to be blended if they are to
be of real value to men. He has little of Ruskin's love of
wild nature. For Morris 'the crown of nature' is 'the life
of man upon the earth'. 'In all old civilized countries, even
when we are in the country, out of sight of a single house,
the aspect of the place is largely influenced by the work of
man: the hedgerows, the road, the lanes leading out of it, the
trees which have all been planted with man's hands, the
growing crops, the tame beasts and sheep, the banked and
locked river, all these go to making up the loveliness which
lies before us . . . in these landscapes we have before us
history in its most delightful, I will say its most instructive,
shape. And, furthermore, in such landscapes England (in
all country-sides which have not been ruined by our artificial
poverty) is fruitful.' He sees in the middle ages in England
circumstances of life which led the 'genius of our fore-
fathers' to what he calls 'the embroidery of the general face
of the country' giving it 'individuality and character', and
'their generously built manor houses and homesteads . . .
once made an English country-side a special treasure not to
be seen anywhere else'.

5

He is no sentimental antiquarian praising things merely because they are old. The houses and churches are beautiful because they are well-made, of good materials under happy conditions, by the people who are going to use them: 'and though the new house would have looked young and trim beside the older houses and the ancient church ... yet it would have a piece of history for the time to come and its dear and dainty cream-white walls would have been a genuine link among the numberless links of that long chain, whose beginning we know not of, but on whose mighty length even the many-pillared garth of Pallas, and the stately dome of the Eternal Wisdom, are but single links.'

Nor is he thinking of 'ideal houses' or 'rare marvels of art of which few can be vouchsafed to the best times and countries'. He is thinking of 'a yeoman's steading at grandest, or even his shepherd's cottage'. 'There they stand at this day,' he says, 'dozens of them yet in some parts of England: such an one, and of the smallest, is before my eyes as I speak to you, standing by the roadside on one of the western slopes of the Cotswolds . . . there stands the little house that was new once, a labourer's cottage built of the Cotswold limestone, and grown now, walls and roof, a lovely grey, though it was creamy white in its earliest days; no line of it could ever have marred the Cotswold beauty . . . 'tis in fact beautiful, a work of art and a piece of nature.' Such buildings in Oxfordshire or Berkshire, in the Thames or Severn Valleys, or sometimes among the orchards of Kent or the gentle hills of his native Essex, are the raw materials of the recurring utopia of his poems and romances, which are written out of fear that all this English loveliness is about to be destroyed by a predatory and insensate commerce.

6

The favourite projection of his phantasy, in point of time, is into Chaucer's England, where he always imagines himself most at home. This is evident in *The Earthly Paradise*, but two or three years earlier he exhibits the same preference in an apostrophe to Geoffrey Chaucer, which he drags into the text of the otherwise objective poem, *The Life and Death of Jason*:

> *Would that I*
> *Had but some portion of that mastery*
> *That from the rose-hung lanes of woody Kent*
> *Through these five hundred years such songs have sent*
> *To us, who, meshed within this smoky net*
> *Of unrejoicing labour, love them yet.*
> *And thou, O Master!—Yea, my Master still,*
> *Whatever foot have scaled Parnassus' hill,*
> *Since like thy measures, clear and sweet and strong,*
> *Thames' stream scarce fettered drave the dace along*
> *Unto the bastioned bridge, his only chain.—*
> *O Master, pardon me, if yet in vain*
> *Thou art my Master, and I fail to bring*
> *Before men's eyes the image of the thing*
> *My heart is filled with: thou whose dreamy eyes*
> *Beheld the flush to Cressid's cheeks arise,*
> *When Troilus rode up the praising street,*
> *As clearly as they saw thy townsmen meet*
> *Those who in vineyards of Poictou withstood*
> *The glittering horror of the steel-topped wood.*

We have another glimpse of the vision which fills his heart in the opening lines of the Prologue to the *Earthly Paradise*:

> *Forget six counties overhung with smoke,*
> *Forget the snorting steam and piston stroke,*
> *Forget the spreading of the hideous town;*

Think rather of the pack-horse on the down,
And dream of London, small, and white, and clean,
A clear Thames bordered by its gardens green;
Think that below the bridge green lapping waves
Smite some few keels that bear Levantine staves,
Cut from the yew wood on the burnt-up hill,
And pointed jars that Greek hands toiled to fill,
And treasured scanty spice from some far sea.
Florence gold cloth, and Ypres napery,
And cloth of Bruges, and hogsheads of Guienne,
While nigh the thronged wharf Geoffrey Chaucer's pen
Moves over bills of lading—mid such times
Shall dwell the hollow puppets of my rhymes.

In *A Dream of John Ball* (1888) the Earthly Paradise again takes the form of an unspoiled English country-side of the middle ages:

'It was, as to the lie of the land, an ordinary English low-country, swelling into rising ground here and there. The road was narrow, and I was convinced that it was a piece of Roman road from its straightness. Copses were scattered over the country, and there were signs of two or three villages and hamlets in sight besides the one near me, between which and me there was some orchard land, where the early apples were beginning to redden on the trees. Also, just on the other side of the road and the ditch which ran along it, was a small close of about a quarter of an acre, neatly hedged with quick, which was nearly full of white poppies, and, as far as I could see for the hedge, had also a good few rose-bushes of the bright red, nearly single kind, which I had heard are the ones from which rose-water used to be distilled. Otherwise the land was quite unhedged, but all under tillage of various kinds, mostly in small strips. From the other side of a copse not far off rose a tall spire white and brand-new, but at once bold in outline and unaffectedly graceful, and also distinctly English in character. This, together with the unhedged tillage and a certain unwonted

146

trimness and handiness about the enclosures of the garden and orchard, puzzled me for a minute or two, as I did not understand, new as the spire was, how it could have been designed by a modern architect; and I was of course used to the hedged tillage and tumble-down bankrupt-looking surroundings of our modern agriculture. So that gardenlike neatness and trimness of everything surprised me.'

When he enters the dream-village, his heart is 'quite ravished' with the 'extreme beauty, elegance, and fitness' of the church to the general scene, and the reader who is un-aware that the masterpiece was composed as a Socialist tract, is soon made to realize that the countryside, so lovingly por-trayed, is such a countryside as William Morris wishes to restore to life.

7

The vision changes in detail from work to work, but it never loses its integrity, and finally in *News from Nowhere* (1891), he extends it into a complete social system fit for a William Morris to live in. He is no longer four hundred years backward but a hundred forward, and the setting is much the same. He dreams he is near his own house at Hammersmith a hundred years hence and with 'bewildered eyes' looking eastward towards the bridge, as-tonished at the changes that have taken place on the banks of the London River:

'For though there was a bridge across the stream and houses on its banks, how all was changed from last night! The soapworks with their smoke-vomiting chimneys were gone; the engineer's works gone; the lead-works gone; and no sound of rivetting and hammering came down the west wind from Thornycrofts. Then the bridge! I had perhaps dreamed of such a bridge, but never seen such a one out of an illuminated manuscript; for not even the Ponte Vecchio at Florence came anywhere near it. It was of stone arches, splendidly solid, and as graceful as they were strong; high enough also to let ordinary river traffic through easily. Over the parapet showed quaint and fanciful little buildings, which I supposed to be booths or shops, beset with gilded vanes and spirelets. The stone was a little weathered but showed no marks of the grimy sootiness which I was used to on every London building more than a year old. In short, to me a wonder of a bridge. . . .

'Both shores had a line of very pretty houses, low and not large, standing back a little way from the river; they were mostly built of red brick and roofed with tiles, and look, above all, comfortable, and as if they were, so to say, alive, and sympathetic with the life of the dwellers in them. There was a continuous garden in front of them, going down to the water's edge, in which the flowers were now blooming luxuriantly, and sending delicate waves of summer scent over the eddying stream. Behind the houses, I could see great trees rising, mostly planes, and looking down the water there were the reaches towards Putney, almost as if they were a lake with a forest shore, so thick were the big trees. . . .'

8

The desire to embody this dream is the impelling motive of his life. The persistent desire for the restoration of the beauty of England dominates his activities. William Morris is clearly a patriot who wishes to give more to his country than he takes out of it. He not only desires to do so, he strives to do so. There can be no peace for him so long as our English country-side is being disfigured by speculative builders, our rivers polluted by the excreta of factories, our towns begrimed by smoke and our public places by litter. When he speaks of beauty and happiness, as he so often does, he is not pinning his faith to abstract terms. These words represent concrete and practical alternatives to the ugliness and misery produced by uncontrolled business activity. He has no use for beauty which does not lead to happiness, or to happiness which does not lead to beauty.

In this spirit he founds the Society for the Protection of Ancient Buildings and the workshops at Merton Abbey, and later, joins the Socialist League and writes *News from Nowhere*. His life is devoted to the preservation and creation of beautiful things. But with all his idealization of the past he is far more a protector of the present and a builder of the future. He will preserve an old church or an old cottage or an old barn, not so much because they are old but because they are the beautiful records and expressions of a time when, as he believes, men worked more joyfully than they do now. His poems and romances, furnishing fabrics and stained glass, illuminated manuscripts and printed books are his practical contributions to the realization of this dream of an Earthly Paradise. He looks upon himself as a workman and his creations as useful goods, and he does not shrink from sharing with his fellow-workmen the drudgery of public-speaking, and hawking Socialist periodicals and pamphlets at street corners in London or in the industrial towns of the North.

9

William Morris is a revolutionary but no mere agitator, He does not live on exhortation but on action, and he is prepared at all times to practise what he preaches, for no other reward than the joy of doing so. Nor is he content to confine his activities to the more spectacular work of his various enterprises. He is ever on the alert to take advantage of the nearest and humblest action towards the realization of his dreams. Wherever he is, and whatever he does England is better for his presence and his activity. Where he settles beauty is restored. His environment becomes the logical embodiment of his dreams. All his habitations partake of this power of dream-realization—the workshops in Red Lion Square, and at Merton Abbey, the shop in Oxford Street, and above all in his homes: the Red House at Upton which he built from the designs of his friend Philip Webb, the Georgian town house overlooking the Thames at Hammersmith, and the Elizabethan manor house of Kelmscott on a tributary of Matthew Arnold's 'stripling Thames' in the heart of the English countryside.

One of his permanent anxieties is for the constant and increasing encroachment of ugliness and vulgarity upon what remains of the Earthly Paradise of the England he loves. Ruskin wishes to visit the workshops at Merton Abbey where Morris is making some stained glass for the Master. 'I need not say that I should be very glad to see you at our place at Merton Abbey: though', he adds, 'I fear it would be a grief to you to see the banks of the pretty Wandle so beset with the horrors of the Jerry-builders; there is still some beauty left about the place however, and the stream itself is not much befouled: I am doing my best to keep the place decent, and can do so in the seven acres our works command; but as to the rest can do but little.' Wherever he goes he notes the desecration of the countryside, and where he can, protests against such vandalism, particularly where it has victimized our old English churches. His letters as well as his lectures contain frequent references to such misfortunes, for much of the evil is due to that too-common kind of 'neglect and stupidity' which has 'so marred the lovely little' church at Inglesham which he visited on a beautiful afternoon in August 1888. Nor is he interested only in English architecture. He has an equal affection for the ancient towns of Northern France. On his last visit, in

1891, he observes all sorts of changes for the worse. Beauvais, for instance, he tells Emery Walker, is 'very pleasant' after Amiens, 'which is dull, bourgeois, and, in a word, gritty', and 'much improved for the worse . . . by the addition of some beastly building of the 3rd Napoleonic style inconceivable almost outside Zola's books'.

I O

The theory behind this attitude and these dreams comes from Ruskin, but he gives it a professional and practical application which the Master could not attain. Ruskin is a professional teacher, Morris is a professional worker. Ruskin practises one art with genius: the art of prose, and the art of drawing with talent, superb talent, but not more than that. Morris expresses his practical genius in poetry and prose, as well as in many of the decorative arts from the designing of wall-papers to the printing of books. Ruskin's attempts to put his theories into practice (roadmaking at Oxford and a tea shop at Paddington) were amateurish failures. Morris is a successful manufacturer, printer, and shop-keeper, who revives those Decorative Arts which Ruskin knows only how to expound. Morris, in short, practises what Ruskin teaches. But for Ruskin Morris might have remained in the hothouse of the fine arts with his friends Rossetti and Burne-Jones, or his contemporaries Tennyson and Browning. All of whom are ready to applaud him when he makes beautiful poems and decorations so long as they are unrelated to common affairs. But when he comes into the open to fight for better conditions, they are horror-stricken. Those who are content to barricade themselves against an ugly and ruthless world in a Palace of Art look upon him as one of the lapsed and lost. 'He must be crazy!' Tennyson exclaims.

I I

Since Morris moves along the path of the Decorative Arts to his idea of an Ideal State, an understanding of his attitude towards art is necessary to a clear understanding of his attitude towards his own life and that of the community. His theory comes from Ruskin from whom he differs only in motive and procedure. Ruskin is Christian and Moral, Morris, Pagan and Hedonist. They reach agreement on the superiority of qualitative over quantitative production, and of commerce for use not profit, but by different roads, although there are many convergences on the way. An implication of Ruskin's teaching is that if you are good you will be happy. Morris is more willing to believe that if you are happy you will be good. In outward action both Ruskin and Morris desire to build the House Beautiful and agree upon the terms of reference, namely, the nature of Gothic. But where Ruskin would set members of the comfortable classes road-making for the good of their souls, and encourage workmen to seek inspiration in museums and art galleries, Morris teaches the middle classes to revolt against Victorian taste and the working class to revolt against industrial conditions.

The subjective character of Morris's teaching is revealed in his lectures on art and particularly in 'The Aims of Art' which was delivered in the early days of his conversion to Socialism and printed by him in *Signs of Change* (1888). The Pagan and hedonistic note is struck in the opening passage:

'In considering the Aims of Art, that is, why men toilsomely cherish and practise Art, I find myself compelled to generalize from the only specimen of humanity of which I know anything; to wit, myself. Now, when I think of what it is that I desire, I find that I can give it no other name than happiness. I want to be happy while I live; for as for death, I find that, never having experienced it, I have no conception of what it means, and so cannot even bring my mind to bear upon it. I know what it is to live; I cannot even guess what it is to be dead. Well, then, I want to be happy, and even sometimes, say generally, to be merry; and I find it difficult to believe that that is not the universal desire; so that, whatever tends towards that end I cherish with all my best endeavour. Now, when I consider my life further, I find out or seem to, it is under the influence of two dominating moods, which for lack of better words I must call the mood of energy and the mood of idleness: these two moods are now one, now the other, always crying out in me to be satisfied.'

The result is that he 'must either be making something', he says, 'or making believe to make it'. But whether making or making-believe, working or playing, what he does is art, in the sense (his and Ruskin's) that art is joyful work, and he is convinced that 'all men's lives are compounded of these two moods in various proportions, and that this explains why they have always, with more or less toil, cherished or practised art'. It is for this personal reason, so clearly and frankly stated, that Morris sets out to build Utopia

In England's green and pleasant land.

I 2

He believes that 'the manner in which our buildings, and especially our houses, are built is really the foundation of the whole question of art', and that the separation of architecture and the fine arts from the common or useful arts is not only the cause of the degeneration of taste, but the underlying condition of the degradation of labour and of social decay. Under such a system both the greater and the lesser arts suffer. The greater lose 'their dignity of popular arts, and become nothing but dull adjuncts to unmeaning pomp, or ingenious toys for a few rich and idle men'. The lesser arts 'become trivial, mechanical, unintelligent, incapable of resisting the changes pressed upon them by fashion or dishonesty'. He believes, with Ruskin, that luxury under such conditions is unfair, that labour under such conditions is dull and uninteresting, and that art under such conditions is unhealthy, 'it even scarcely lives; it is on the wrong road, and if it follow that road will speedily meet its death on it.' There can be no healthy or happy social system until art is once again 'made by the people for the people as a joy for the maker and the user'. He goes even further for he doubts that art can exist 'unless it is shared by all the people; and', he adds, 'for my part I don't wish that it should'. And he does not hesitate to push this idea to a logical conclusion by demanding a nation of artists. 'If we attempt to keep art alive on other terms, we are bolstering up a sham, and that it would be far better for us to accept the other alternative, the frank rejection of art, as many people do and they not the worst of us, have already done.'

It is with 'grief and pain' that he comes to realize how 'many men notice but little' the 'contrast between times past and the present day'. He believes that a 'revulsion to pessimism' is 'natural to a man busily engaged in the arts' and for that reason is compelled in his earlier days to 'hope that the ugly disgraces of civilization might be got rid of by the conscious will of intelligent persons'. But he finds as he strives to 'stir up people to this reform', that the causes lie deeper than he had thought, and gradually he is driven to the conclusion that 'all these uglinesses are the outward expression of the innate moral baseness into which we are forced by our present form of society, and that it is futile to attempt to deal with them from the outside'. Whatever he has written or spoken on these 'social subjects', he declares is the result of Socialism meeting his 'early impulse, and giving it a definite and much more precious aim'.

13

Throughout all his teaching there is evidence that one of the predominating causes of his attack upon social conditions of his day is an innate fear of boredom. His own restless energy is a symptom of that fear, and it is natural for him to feel that others must suffer in the same way; yet he is not wholly convinced, for he desires and fears rest simultaneously. The one anxiety of the people in *News from Nowhere* is that work will die out, but the sub-title of this Utopian romance is 'An Epoch of Rest'. In the introductory verses of *The Earthly Paradise*, he poses as

> *The idle singer of an empty day,*

whilst being in actual life one of the most energetic workmen of all time. In fact he is incapable of idleness, and his friends believe that he worked himself to death.

When Morris speaks of restlessness he means boredom— a word he rarely if ever uses. 'Restlessness', he says, 'makes hapless men and bad citizens', and 'the restraining of rest-lessness is clearly one of the essential aims of art'. Fear of being bored underlies his love of decoration. We must decorate the things we make so that we shall not be bored whilst at work, and articles must be decorated in order that they shall not bore us in use. He uses the significant phrase 'eventfulness of form' to express the quality which he sees in natural forms and would re-create in craft forms. The very word 'eventful' is a bulwark against the boredom he fears.

Morris is incapable of repose. In moments of enforced idleness, as Bruce Glasier records, there is a 'constant rest-lessness of his hands, and indeed of his whole body, as if overcharged with energy'. He has a rolling sailor-like manner of gait, and he gesticulates as he talks. On the lecture platforms he is rarely still, waving his arms to emphasize a point and walking about if there is room. When a young man he was called 'Topsy' by his friends because of his untidy shock of curly hair. But he is not only shaggy of hair and beard, both hair and beard bristle with energy, especially during moments of impatience or irritability. Bruce Glasier, in the early days of their association, arouses this quaint fury by a derogatory reference to the work of Burne-Jones. 'Hardly had I completed my sentence', he records, 'than Morris was on his feet, storming words upon me that shook the room. His eyes flamed with actual fire, his shaggy mane rose like a burning crest, his whiskers and moustache bristled out like pine needles.'

14

Bruce Glasier is obviously writing at the top of his voice, but all records of Morris contribute something to the legend of his vehemence. The above romantic account may therefore be usefully compared with the evidence of such a master of understatement as William Hale White ('Mark Rutherford'): 'Morris, Earthly Paradise Morris, came to dinner with us. He is unlike any fancy picture which the imagination might draw of him. He is broad-shouldered, ruddy, wears a blue shirt with no neck-tie, and talks with great vehemence; oftentimes with a kind of put-on roughness, I think—as if he meant to say "If you think that I am an Earthly Paradisiacal creature with wings you are egregiously mistaken".' These outbursts, though free of rancour and never far removed from good humour, were too frequent and spontaneous to have been put-on. They may have been fantastic but they were none the less real.

Explosions of the kind invariably follow any frustration of his taste or will. He dislikes, for instance, the way a piece of tapestry is going on one of the Merton Abbey looms and lunges his stick through it, swearing with great fury. Expletives were a constant accompaniment to these expressions of overwrought feelings. Sometimes he prances up and down the studio to an accompaniment of curses which on calming down, he explains away as 'talking to nobody in particular'. Vandalism in connection with the restoration of ancient buildings is a constant cause of these explosions. On a visit to Glasgow Cathedral with Bruce Glasier he stops abruptly, 'as if struck by a rifle-ball, his eyes fixed furiously on some object in front of him. As he glared he seemed to crouch like a lion for a leap on its prey, his whiskers bristling out. "What the hell is that? Who the hell has done that?" he shouted to the amaze, alarm, and indignation of the people near by.' The offending object is a white marble sarcophagus of recent date, placed inappropriately against the old grey stone of the cathedral! Morris ultimately directs this wrath against modern civilization.

15

However, Morris is no impossibilist and when he attacks the commercial system which he loathes, he is calm and reasonable. He is also very practical, knowing little and caring less about economic theories. This dislike of theories has a characteristic sequel when at a Socialist meeting he is asked to clarify his attitude towards Karl Marx and his 'theory of value': 'To speak quite frankly,' he replies, 'I do not know what Marx's theory of value is, and I'm damned if I want to know.' The effect of the explosion is immediately liquidated by a good-humoured explanation, which illustrates the other side of the man, for he is no curmudgeon: 'Truth to say, my friends, I have tried to understand Marx's theory, but political economy is not in my line, and much of it appears to me to be dreary rubbish. But, I hope, I am a Socialist none the less. It is enough political economy for me to know that the idle class is rich and the working class is poor, and that the rich are rich because they rob the poor. That I know because I see it with my eyes. I need read no books to convince me of it. And it does not matter a rap, it seems to me, whether the robbery is accomplished by what is termed surplus value, or by means of serfage or open brigandage. The whole system is monstrous and intolerable, and what we Socialists have got to do is to work together for its complete overthrow, and for the establishment in its stead of a system of co-operation where there shall be no masters or slaves, but where everyone will live and work jollily together as neighbours and comrades for the equal good of all. That, in a nutshell, is my political economy and my social democracy.'

There is little of the pedant about William Morris, and his written lectures suggest the spontaneity of conference rather than studious deliberation. He knows he is primarily an artist and a poet, but he also wants to be a man among men. He believes passionately in neighbourliness. Men could and should live happily together. If they don't it is because circumstances and environment prevent them. With him Socialism is subjective: he feels a personal responsibility for modern conditions. In his early days he contemplates escape into a religious or an artistic sanctuary. Later he toys with the idea of reform. But he finally realizes that there lies no hope in either of these retreats. The idea of a community of social equality within the present system is also considered and abandoned. He has no desire to be either an anchorite or a member of an exclusive group. Then in a confession which reveals the bigness as well as the pathos of the man, he says: 'I don't want to get out from among my fellow men, for with all their faults—which are not theirs but only our own—I like them and want to live and work among them. My Utopia must be pitched square in the midst of them or nowhere. But, as I say, I often feel conscience-stricken about enjoying myself, and enjoy myself much I confess I do in my art and literary work, while the mass of my fellows are doomed to such a sordid and miserable life of servitude around me. Were it not for my work and the hope of Socialism, I believe life would be positively unendurable to me—as in truth it should to any man possessed of any aesthetic or moral feeling at all.'

When time has winnowed the grain from the chaff of William Morris's works it will be found that he has put the best of himself as a thinker as well as a writer of prose into *A Dream of John Ball.* He puts into the mouth of the leader of the Peasant Rising in Kent his ripest thoughts, and one phrase alone: 'Fellowship is life, lack of fellowship is death,' contains the essense of his religion. All his æsthetics and his politics, his craftsmanship and his hedonism, are directed towards the realization of that dream of fellowship—when, in the words of John Ball, 'man shall help man, and the saints in heaven shall be glad, because men no more fear each other; and the churl shall be ashamed, and shall hide his churlishness till it be gone, and he be no more a churl; and fellowship shall be established in heaven and on earth.'

16

In the early days of his Socialist activity he believes that the revolution which would inaugurate the Utopia of his dreams is close at hand. But he underrates the obstacles, particularly that of human nature, and is ultimately forced to admit that it will take much longer than he imagined even to prepare the way for the desired event. His aim is to instil converts with 'Intelligence enough to conceive, courage enough to will, power enough to compel'. Neither the intelligence, the courage, nor the power is effective in his own immediate circle because the comrades could not agree among themselves. Almost the last words addressed by him to his Socialist friends refer to the bickerings and jealousies which ultimately drive him out of the fighting line: 'I appeal to all Socialists, while they express their thoughts and feelings about them honestly and fearlessly, not to make a quarrel of it with those whose aim is one with theirs, because there is a difference of opinion between them about the usefulness of the details or the means . . . let us forgive the mistakes that others make, even if we make none ourselves, and be at peace among ourselves, that we may the better make war upon the monopolist.' But already differences of opinion about methods as well as persons have arisen in his own mind. He not only doubts the value of the means, but he feels also that there is a difference between himself and his comrades about ends.

His attempts to inspire the British Socialists with the splendour of his own dream and the unselfish honesty of his mind and heart recall Max Beerbohm's cartoon of Walt Whitman inducing the American Eagle to soar! There were, of course, those who could appreciate the value of such a gift of genius to the cause, but the majority could not and did not; and, more ironic, some who worked in closest touch with him were the least understanding. He gave himself, his material and his spiritual wealth, freely and generously, subsidizing and editing and contributing to the Socialist journal *Justice*; lecturing in frowsy club-rooms, or speaking at street corners, or on slag-heaps outside iron foundries; advising, cheering, and helping in any way no matter how small, and he is finally defeated not by the Capitalists but by the Socialists, and in the end falls back upon his own Utopia at Merton Abbey and his great experiment in printing at Hammersmith. The Kelmscott Press affords him the last glimpse of an Earthly Paradise, and he maintains his effort to spread his dream to all by means of his own Socialist Society which he conducts from a small hall translated out of the stable at Kelmscott House on the Upper Mall at Hammersmith. Morris presides at weekly meetings composed of all that was imaginative and thoughtful in the Movement, and here he is happy, sowing the seed not of revolt, but of hope.

17

His work for the revival of craftsmanship and design in the decorative arts has happier results, although even in so obviously useful a field those results are sometimes ironical. Morris, for instance, is a democrat, and hopes that his works will be popularly accepted, but he never succeeds in winning the patronage of more than a comparatively few cultured people, many of whom buy his fabrics and his furniture merely on fashionable grounds, and when the designs and colourings, which are protests against commercial exploitation, eventually become popular, it is by means of the commercial vulgarization which he opposes.

Forty years ago the ideas of Morris were cheapened under the title of the *New Art*. The handicrafts became a hobby like fretwork or pokerwork. Copper was teased into quaint shapes, picture frames and overmantels were cluttered with coloured fabrics; women were draped in trailing robes of autumnal tints, even men let their hair grow and put on butcher-blue shirts and red ties. Enterprising manufacturers took advantage of the craze by making pottery and hardware with all the crudities and flaws of handicraft mechanically produced. Morris was almost completely side-tracked, and to this day self-respecting people shudder at the word 'artistic' because it brings back painful memories of 'art' muslin and 'art' colours, 'arty' people and 'artistic' temperaments.

Morris did not live to see the full cheapening of his great idea, and he recognized long before his death that the world cannot be saved by Art alone. 'Yet as I strove to stir up people to this reform,' he wrote, I found that the cause of the vulgarities of civilization lay deeper than I had thought, and little by little I was driven to the conclusion that all these uglinesses are but the outward expression of the innate moral baseness into which we are forced by our present form of society, and that it is futile to deal with it from the outside.' He thus came to add revolutionary Socialism to his activities.

18

Since his death the mechanized Society he dreaded has been established; yet he might have found more inspiration in the passionate life of to-day, with all its banalities and blunders, than he found in the shallow pomposities and poses of the closing decades of the last century. For, if he attempts to restore the lost tradition of quality in goods and sanity in design by throwing back to the middle ages, he is only a tentative medievalist. Morris has all the audacity, energy, and versatility of an artist of the Renaissance, which rang down the curtain on the long drama of the middle ages and inaugurated a new era of which our civilization is the culmination—and perhaps the end. However much he may like to imagine himself as the reincarnation of a guildsman of the twelfth century, his spiritual prototypes are Michael Angelo and Leonardo da Vinci.

His plaint that he is 'born out of his due time' must not be taken too literally. It is a piece of self-pity which hardly does justice to the circumstances. William Morris was a product of his time, and its irritations made him. We have no means of knowing how he would have behaved in a more perfect state, but his abounding energies might have found a range of new irritations in the 'epoch of rest' which he imagined in *News from Nowhere*. In an individual era obsessed by the profit-motive he is obviously a misfit, but being practical as well as forceful he manages to make the best of a bad job, discovering for himself and his friends an oasis in the desert of Victorian commercialism from which he and they can work somewhat as they like, and attack the system they dislike at the same time. But it is not sufficiently recognized even yet that Morris was a successful man of affairs. He was that rarity, a doer as well as a talker, and in addition to being a poet, a craftsman and a teacher, he set up in business as a decorative artist and provided himself with profitable occupation for over twenty years. The firm of Morris & Co. commemorated its fiftieth anniversary by the publication of a booklet on the 'Morris Movement' in 1911.

19

The 'firm' as it is called in the Morris circle, is no ordinary business. It pays its way but profit is not the object. Morris & Co. is a demonstration and a protest; a demonstration of design and handicraft, and a protest against mechanized production for profit. Following Ruskin's lead, Morris condemns mechanical production without considering the chances of teaching machines how to behave themselves. Had he lived to-day he would have had more machines to fight, but he could at least have seen that a machine can be a good servant—if a bad master. It is the mastery of machines and not machines that he opposes. He uses Ruskin's methods of attack on factories and railways, but he has not Ruskin's complete hatred of all mechanical devices. Common sense and William Morris are rarely separated for long and he is quite willing to admit that machines have a place in an organized social system. 'I have boundless faith in their capacity,' he says, and he adds that he believes machines 'can do everything, except make works of art'. But, as he looks forward to a time when all workmen will be artists, it is clear that machines will not be allowed to do as they like in his Utopia. There is no mechanization in *News from Nowhere* or in his favourite historical periods. *News from Nowhere* is to some considerable extent a reply to the mechanized Utopia of Bellamy's *Looking Backward*, described by Morris as a 'cockney Paradise'.

It may be that, infected with his own enthusiasm, we have expected too much of him. Most sociologists would now admit that his attack upon the commercial conditions of his day was justified. The mistake he made was to think it easier to arrest industrialization than to adjust it to reasonable standards. If he had lived to-day he might have allied himself with the trend of convenience and order in design which is a happy characteristic of our time.

20

In spite of his passion for the past, Morris also allies himself with the future, and comes near to anticipating the idea of design which underlies the modern decorative arts. How far he has influenced the newer movement it is difficult to estimate. But it would be a mistake to assume that because his work as such has been by-passed his ideas have been ignored. From the point of view of aesthetic procedure Morris's ideas are much more important than his works. Those beautiful articles possess an integrity of their own, but could hardly be integrated with life as it is now lived. William Morris produces beautiful but ineffectual masterpieces. His tapestries, books, tiles, carpets, illuminated manuscripts, and stained glass windows are museum-pieces from birth. He is born out of his due time in this respect to a far greater extent than even he imagined, because he can never shake himself free of his medieval idiosyncrasies.

There is also a tendency to forget that Morris is a Victorian with a Victorian's faith in reform, education, and the innate goodness of human beings if things are properly explained to them. There is only a difference of expression between his moral, as distinct from his hedonistic ideas, and those of Carlyle, and Ruskin, Tennyson and Browning. Further, he is anchored, in some degree, to the Gothic Revival and the Tractarian Movement through early associations even when in opposition, and his personal attitude to life and art exposes him to friendly dominance. Thus he is kept a medievalist by Burne-Jones, but those stained-glass windows which Jones designs and Morris executes but which are as incongruous in a modern city as the mock-Gothic churches which they generally adorn, and he condemns, come into existence because the Church provides one of the few openings for the decorative arts.

21

William Morris has an exact understanding of the relationship between design and decoration, but, because of his personal preference for decoration, and a belief that it is a remedy for boredom, the two functions are often confused. He knows better than most craftsmen of his time that design should be determined by function, and he goes back for inspiration to the Middle Ages because he finds there what he believes to be the practical application of his own idea of design. But apart from that, and for purely personal reasons, he looks upon any plain surface, no matter how beautiful in form, as an invitation to indulge his passion for decoration. Thus everything he makes, beautiful as it is, tends to be over-ornamented. It is here that he is most at variance with modern needs and contemporary taste. Yet he believes in an Art which might express a recaptured simplicity in the technique of living. Even then, however, he is not interested in simplicity for its own sake, but rather as a means of checkmating the influence of machines. He believes that if we learn 'to do without' we shall 'choke both demand and supply of mechanical toil', and by so doing keep machines in their place. 'And then', he concludes, 'from simplicity of life would rise up the longing for beauty, which cannot yet be dead in men's souls, and we know that nothing can satisfy that demand but Intelligent work, rising gradually into Imaginative work: which will turn all "operatives" into workmen, into artists, into men.' So far as we can see, this dream of Morris is farther away than ever, and although the 'operative' may be having a better time of it, he certainly is not any more of an artist than he was, nor is there any evidence that he wants to be.

Yet the significance of William Morris increases in spite of the inevitable revaluation of his work and of his attitude towards the life and industry of his times. The craftsmanship he inspired may have died of commercial vulgarization, as the Communism for which he drudged died of inertia and human fallibility. And both may have been born again in such questionable shapes that Morris, even at the moment of his greatest disenchantment, would not have recognized them. Yet he did not work in vain. He dreams of a Utopia where work is so joyfully performed that people fear lest there may not be enough of it to go round. That happy state may seem farther off than ever, for the thing which he dreads has come to pass and the way is blocked by machines, which make monotony so inevitable that, instead of finding recreation in their jobs, workers have to be entertained by other machines in order to rescue them from the evils of boredom which he fought and hoped to conquer by useful work. The ornamentation which he hopes to revive for the expression of man's joy in his work has been side-tracked by the austerities of functionalism; and the genial Communism which he preaches, with its democracy, fellowship, handicraft, and freedom, has become autocracy, with enforced mechanization and standardization of men and materials as its ideals. He lived and worked for the common people, but his poetry and romances have never been popular, and the works of his hands are the treasures of the rich.

2 2

William Morris is remembered to-day as the most splendid failure of the nineteenth century. Many fail because they are wrong. Morris fails because he is right. He has the courage to make no compromise with the social system he condemns. He believes that men must live in fellowship and have joy in their work or they will perish, and until we have found a working substitute for that doctrine, the failure of Morris can only be relative, and, perhaps, temporary. He lives in these days of violence and transition as an example rather than an influence. He is often rude, but never condescends or patronizes; he is often rough, but never cruel. He swears without cursing, and insists on himself and his own way of doing things without causing injury to others. The social consciousness is none the worse for the doctrine that 'fellowship is life, lack of fellowship is death'. The arts are all the better for his reassertion of the principles underlying the association of form and utility in the creation of common things, and the personal example of his disinterested and varied activities must for ever remain an inspiration for those who are not merely predatory or meretricious.

EMERSON

No more will I dismiss, with haste, the visions which flash and sparkle across my sky; but observe them, approach them, domesticate them, brood on them, and draw out of the past, genuine life for the present.

RALPH WALDO EMERSON

I

Emerson is by nature a student and a quietist. Ideas rather than actions inspire him, although he is persuaded that ideas should end in actions. His vocation is talking, and for the greater part of a long life he talks with voice and pen as few men have talked before or since. Like Walt Whitman he is the advocate of a national culture for America, but in several respects he is the opposite of Whitman. He calls himself an 'incorrigible spouting Yankee', but he is American only in his readiness to challenge orthodox thought and conventional behaviour. This challenge, however, is always rhetorical, and is not allowed to interfere with his blameless life. The only risks he ever takes are intellectual. Where Whitman will spend Emerson will save. Whitman lives his own life with almost impudent egoism, but Emerson, the evangelist of self-reliance and the inspirer of Whitman, has to argue himself into being himself, and even then he is doubtful of the results.

Virile as his utterance of faith can be, his journals reveal a vacillating character, and a sufferer from morbid diffidence. He is aware of this disposition and is disturbed by the feeling that lesser intelligences can dominate him. In his own words: 'The least people do most entirely demolish me. I always find some quarter, some sorts of respect from the mediocre. But a snipper-snapper eats me whole.' He believes himself to be deficient in vital force, a 'puny, limitary creature', unable to stand 'the dissipation of a flowing and friendly life'. No wasting of substance in riotous comradeship for him. As a young man he strives to keep his soul 'in a polite equilibrium' and in middle age he husbands his strength and contemplates apotheosis as 'a well-preserved old gentleman'. But as a young man he is elderly, remote, empedestalled— an American Goethe without Goethe's sexual inquisitiveness. He runs to intellect. Nathaniel Hawthorne thinks it 'impossible to dwell in his vicinity without inhaling, more or less, the mountain atmosphere of his lofty thought'. His prevailing moods are lofty. He was not, as we say now, a good mixer, but a superior person incapable of ease and friendly contacts with ordinary people or the homely virtues. The thought of having received a gift makes him squirm. Somebody remarks that he 'always seems to be on stilts', and the cap fits. 'It is even so,' he admits, 'most of the persons whom I see in my own house I see across a gulf. I cannot go to them nor they come to me.' He feels that his speech is frigid and laborious with such people and although he recognizes the 'ludicrousness of the plight', he can find no remedy.

2

The editors of his *Journals* note this characteristic and attribute it to a desire to stand on his own feet. That is true, but it does not solve the problem. Emerson's attitude towards his friends and surroundings is remote and tinged with hauteur, because of a suspicion of inferiority which pesters him throughout his life. At the age of thirty-one he attributes his diffidences and hesitations to an excess of reverence which makes it impossible for him to realize that he is a man. 'He never', he says, 'assumed equality with strangers, but still esteemed them older than himself, though they were of his own age or younger. He went through life postponing his maturity and died in his error.' Yet he desires superiority and upholds himself with kindness and simplicity. But superiority at any price does not satisfy him. He is as fastidious in mind as in manners, but although he has little hesitation in selecting fine passages or ideas from literature or philosophy, he looks over memories of saints and heroes without finding the man he would be.

This superior pose is evident throughout his writings.

He is a professed Olympian, demanding 'only the eminent experiences'. Once he regrets that he has 'made a bargain' instead of throwing himself wholly on his protagonist's 'sense of justice', because 'the Olympian must be Olympian in carriage and deeds wherever he can be symmetrically, not rudely—and he must dare a little and try Olympian experiments'. His Olympian pose is, perhaps, his only consistency. He is Olympian even to himself and never bends or descends in the ten volumes of the private journals which form a full record of his intellectual and spiritual life from youth to age.

His humility thus swings into place as the mask of pride. He rarely rebukes his opponents or argues with them. After a lecture in his early theological period a brother minister who dissented from him prayed aloud, 'We beseech Thee, O Lord, to deliver us from ever hearing any more such transcendental nonsense as we have just listened to from this sacred desk.' When discussing this outburst later, all Emerson has to say is that his detractor 'seemed a very conscientious plain-spoken man'. This was neither humility nor candour.

3

It is not surprising to learn that he will be content with any sort of government in which 'the rulers are gentlemen', as in England, where power appears to be 'confided to persons of superior sentiment'. He is obviously no democrat, but neither is he an advocate of hereditary aristocracy. He believes in a nobility of moral superiority. 'Virtue', he says, 'is the only gentility.' He is offended by the 'gruff, Jacobin manners of the village politician', and prefers an aristocracy or even a benevolent despotism to majority rule. Majorities are 'the arguments of fools, the strength of the weak'. But he is also sufficiently near to European liberalism to believe that government is best when it is least. One of the good signs of the times is the importance given to the single person. 'Everything that tends to insulate the individual— to surround him with barriers of natural respect, so that each man shall feel the world is his, and man shall treat with man as a sovereign state with a sovereign state;—tends to true union as well as greatness.' ('The American Scholar.')

Emerson, as well as Thoreau and Whitman, seem to push their innate liberalism to its logical conclusion in anarchism. But their anarchism is philosophical and personal, almost a private affair, and, in the last resort, like their British counter-parts, Carlyle, Ruskin, and Morris, they would seem to pre-fer some form of benevolent dictatorship. The problem of the individual existence, that of a Shakespeare or a Milton, is clear enough, 'but why the million should exist, drunk with the opium of Time and Custom, does not appear'. Emerson's objection to the commonplace extends to affairs as well as to ideas and things. Whitman likes to picture him-self as the average man, and acclaims what is easiest and commonest as his allies: Emerson, the superior man, in the most famous of all his phrases, hitches his waggon to a star. He is not content with men as men but wishes he could treat them all as gods. At the same time he is not always certain of his faith even in great men: 'By courtesy we call saints and heroes such, but they are very defective.' Unless the hero is wise he is useless. 'The wise man is the State.' But wisdom, according to Emerson and the Transcenden-talists, is not to be acquired, for it is innate and waiting to be brought forth. 'A nation of men will for the first time exist' when 'each believes himself inspired by the Divine Soul which also inspires all men.'

Thus he is neither an unqualified lover of the people, nor does he suffer fools gladly. He laments that most men are 'dupes of the nearest object', and given to talking with inferiors without knowing it. It is a pity 'that we do not know how to say fiddle faddle to people who take our time and do not exercise our wit'. In the Emersonian formula you must not talk down to the herd. The people may be right but it is 'a low sort of right'. In his works he is never less than a patrician and scholar, and he handles the vernacular primly as though wishing to improve its social status. His feeling is for genteel rather than powerful expressions. On one occasion he uses 'fib' for lie. Yet, with what we shall soon recognize as a characteristic somersault, he regrets that 'we cannot curse and swear in good society'! and would like to domesticate the 'stinging dialect of sailors'.

He approves American exuberance, believing not only that intellectual man must have 'faith in the possible improvement of man' but that the tendency of all thought is towards Optimism. For him, as for Ruskin and Morris, the Golden Age is yet to be. There is hope in the present even for America. 'The worst times that ever fell were good times for somebody. There is always someone in the gap.' But in spite of these cheerful remarks and although he has the 'culture of the Old World with none of its intellectual despair', you feel that his cheerfulness is superficial. An innate melancholy is revealed throughout his journals.[1] Thoreau courts solitude, Emerson shuns it. 'Solitude is fearsome and heavy-hearted,' he says. 'I have never known a man who had so much good accumulated upon him as I have. Reason, health, wife, child, friends, competence, reputation, the power to inspire and the power to please; yet, leave me alone a few days, and I creep about as if in expectation of a calamity.' He goes so far as to admit that 'after thirty, a man wakes up sad every morning, except perhaps five or six, until the day of his death.'

There are two sides also to his advocacy of self-assertion. He hates with a 'perfect hatred' the man who persistently thinks of himself, yet he upholds a faith in egoism which was so novel in those days as to seem over bold. He is in the anomalous position of one who fears to stand alone yet resents the support of others. In spite, however, of this

---

[1] 'His optimism becomes a bigotry, and, though of a nobler type than the common American conceit . . . he has hardly less of the quality of fatalism.' C. E. Norton, *Letters* (1913), i, 503.

hesitancy, he succeeds in differentiating himself from the crowd, and living his own life without upsetting middle-class conventions. He overcomes even his repugnance for material progress, on the assumption that it heralds the dawn of a new civilization rather than, as many now believe, a civilization in twilight.

4

At the age of twenty-one he turns from the world to his studies and will 'have nothing to do with society'. He contemplates the passing of his 'unpleasant boyhood' and the waning of youth into manhood without regret. For what 'are the unsuppressed glee, the cheering games, the golden hair and shining eyes of youth to me?' He withdraws himself from their spell. But if a 'solemn voice' bids him retire and his 'tongue has stammered where fashion and gaiety were voluble' and if he has 'no grace amid the influences of Beauty and the festivities of Grandeur', he will not hastily conclude that his 'soul is ignobly born'. Yet at thirty he is so chagrined with his 'weakness' and his 'quiet', that he would like to hide himself 'in the dens of the hills'. He is pained by the discovery that we can only give to each other a rare and partial sympathy, and he complains that he lacks the 'skill to live with . . . such men as the world is made of', and those he delights in he seldom finds. 'It seems to me,' he concludes, 'no boy makes so many blunders or says such awkward, contrary, disagreeable speeches as I do. In the attempt to oblige a person I wound and disgust him. I pity the hapless folk that have to do with me.' And when he is thirty-five he looks sadly back at thirty, after which year a man becomes 'sensible of the strait limitations which his physical constitution sets to his activity'. In his fortieth year he complains that the 'capital effect' of his 'nature for society' is 'want of animal spirits . . . the power of the present'.

He hears of the energetic performances of others with fear. He wants to become a rousing orator and is never more than an impressive lecturer. 'When I address a large assembly . . . I am always apprised what an opportunity is there: not only for reading to them, as I do, lively miscellanies, but for painting in fire my thought, and being agitated to agitate.' But the fiery cross is not for him. He lacks the necessary fervour. 'I was born cold,' he writes, 'my bodily habit is cold, I shiver in and out; don't heat to the good purpose called enthusiasm a quarter as quick and kindly as neighbours.' Though he is 'full of tenderness, and born with as large a hunger to love and to be loved as any man can be, yet its demonstrations are not active and bold, but passive and tenacious'. In spite of that his love 'has no flood and no ebb, but is always there under silence, under displeasure, under cold, arid and weak behaviour'. He contents himself with moderate, languid actions, and never transgresses the staidness of village manners. 'Herein', he says, 'I consult the poorness of my powers. More culture would come out of great virtues and vices perhaps, but I am not up to that. Should I obey an irregular impulse, and establish every new relation that my fancy prompted with the men and women I see, I should not be followed by my faculties; they would play me false in making good their very suggestions.'

There is no time in his life when he is not conscious of a desire to husband his resources, to be prudent in the expenditure of time, thrifty of the emotions, and economical in all human relationships, guiding his 'moods as anxiously as a miser his money'. He is easily upset: parties, packing, proof-reading, put him out of tune for writing or even reading, and he has been known to go to bed to escape an argument. His feelings react like exposed nerves to what with most people would be normal contacts. 'Pleasant these jets of affection that relume a young world for me again. Delicious is a just and firm encounter of two in a thought, in a feeling.' To healthy people that would be a sufficient reward, not so with Emerson, for 'we must be tormented presently by baffled blows, by sudden unseasonable apathies, by epilepsies of wit and of animal spirits in the heyday of friendship and thought. Our faculties do not play us true.' The curious thing is that although he is tortured with such thoughts, he knows that his prudence is a weakness and a hindrance to complete self-expression, but he can do no more than aggravate his condition with self-pity.

5

Everything he does has its attendant doubt. He is best known through many years of his life for his lectures, but even those lectures, which were so brilliant and successful a contribution to the culture of his time, arouse in him painful reflections. Emerson is descended from seven generations of preachers, and like so many distinguished and undistinguished Americans, both before and since, he lives by and for preaching, but there are several indications in his letters and diaries that he dislikes the profession. It is not only that he doubts his oratorical gifts, he suspects that he lacks constitutional vigour to live up to his topics. 'I ought', he writes, 'to seek to lay myself out utterly,—large, enormous, prodigal . . . but a hateful experience has taught me that I can only spend twenty-one hours on each lecture, if I would also be ready and able for the next.' Up to this point he might be indulging no more than a normal lament over natural exhaustion, but he knows he is holding himself back, saving when he should be spending. 'Of course,' he continues, 'I spend myself prudently; I economize; I cheapen, whereof nothing grand ever grew. Could I spend sixty hours on each, or, what is better, had I such energy that I could rally the lights and mights of sixty hours into twenty, I should hate myself less.'

6

It is indeed a source of surprise that in such a society at such a time there should have been audiences of regular listeners to so complex a thinker as Emerson. This was noted in 1841 by John Sterling, who doubted whether anywhere in Britain, except in London, a hundred people could be found capable of appreciating the mental fare which found so ready an acceptance in America. Whatever the cause of this lecture-habit, the machinery for gratifying it was already there and surprisingly complete. Almost every town in New England had its 'lyceum' and Emerson could have found an audience every night in the year. Perhaps thirst for knowledge and interest in ideas are not the only causes of this enthusiasm. Emerson is an entertaining lecturer and social distractions are few, so it is more than likely that a proportion of his audience is composed of people seeking respite from themselves and from the monotony of colonial society. Emerson is not only entertaining, he offers these people, who have few newspapers or theatres or dance-halls, a self-contained philosophy which is a substitute for entertainment, and perhaps, for thought. Interest would have been impossible if his lectures had been dull. Their wide appreciation was partly due to his gift for sparkling paradox and earnest contradictoriness. 'The secret of his popularity,' someone was heard to say, 'is that he has a *damn* for everybody.' That is only half true. Emerson may spice his praises with faint damns, but he rarely damns with faint praise.

But however witty and sparkling he may have been, the dramatization of himself on the platform does not enable him to escape from that intellect, which he suspects with reason, for it trips him up whenever he approaches the idea of a life of action. 'People who know how to act', he admits, 'are never preachers.' The quietist in him never learns to be quiet. He can't even read with a clear conscience but fears what he calls the 'cardinal vice—intellectual dissipation', or the 'sinful strolling from book to book and from care to idleness'.

7

Lacking the will to action and suspecting intellectual sub-stitutes, such as reading and talking, he places the doer higher than the thinker. He is ever conscience-stricken at his own inaction. Thinking is talent, doing is genius. 'When a zealot comes to me and represents the importance of this Temperance Reform,' he says, 'my hands drop—I have no excuse, I honour him with shame at my own in-action. Then a friend of the slave shows me the horrors of Southern Slavery—I cry Guilty! Guilty! Then a philan-thropist tells me of the shameful neglect of the schools by the citizens: I feel guilty again. Then I hear of Byron or Milton, who drank soda-water and ate a crust whilst others fed fat, and I take the confessional anew. Then I hear that my friend has finished Aristophanes, Plato, Cicero, and Grotius; and I take shame to myself. Then I hear of the generous Morton, who offers a thousand dollars to the cause of Socialism, and I applaud and envy. Then of a brave man who resists a wrong to the death, and I sacrifice anew.'

Because his brain always challenges his heart he is moody and diffident. 'Sadness is always the comparison of the Idea with the Act.' He is an intellectual who denies the intellect: 'Intellectual tasting of life will not supersede muscular ac-tivity;' a bookman to whom books are only tools, a man of letters to whom the end of writing is 'the dead limbo we call literature'. He will and he won't and on the whole doesn't, for no philosopher ever sits on the fence so delicately, or, it must be admitted, so instructively. If he had lived more re-cently he might have written an essay against prohibition and voted for it on the grounds that you can get drunk on water as well as alcohol. 'I have very good grounds for being a Unitarian and a Trinitarian too,' he says, 'I need not nibble for ever at one loaf, but eat it and thank God for it, and earn another.' He is ancient and modern, nominalist and realist, classic and romantic, egoist and altruist, alternatively and even simultaneously—if he is to be judged by his words. But judged by the standard of his behaviour he is a scholar and a gentleman of puritan caste trying in vain to adjust himself to a colonial society in decadence.

8

This duality is worth following further because Emerson ultimately recognizes it and makes it, if not the basis of his philosophy, at least one of its modes, and it must not be forgotten that his philosophy is for practice, and not an end in itself. At one time he thinks that because he is 'confounded by interrogatories' and 'put on his wits for a definition', he is unable to reply without injuring his own truth. Later he believes the condition 'proper to man' is to 'live his own definitions' rather than waste time in trying to formulate them in words, so when a problem appears which he cannot solve with all his wits, he leaves it until 'faithful truth live at last its uttermost darkness into light'. Which would be very well if it were as easy as that, but what is truth? 'I am nominally a believer,' he says, 'yet I hold on to property: I eat my bread with unbelief. I approve every wild action of the experimenters. I say what they say concerning celibacy, or money, or community of goods, and my apology for not doing their work is preoccupation of mind. I have a work of my own which I know I can do with some success. It would leave that undone if I should undertake with them, and I do not see in myself any vigour equal to such an enterprise. My genius loudly calls me to stay where

I am, even with the degradation of owning bank-stock and seeing poor men suffer, whilst the Universal Genius apprises me of this disgrace and beckons me to the martyr's and redeemer's office.' Even on so simple an issue as his professed desire for a true American expression we have the familiar wobble. In his 'weak hours', he confesses to looking fondly to Europe and thinking how gladly he would live in Florence and Rome. But in his 'manly hours' he manages to resist these temptations and to allow duty to prescribe his place. It is clear, however, that consciousness of dilemma solves nothing.

His life, like that of many gifted men, is an intermittent dilemma. He desires to obey his genius, but reason is always getting in the way. When he visits England this peculiarity does not go unobserved. George Gilfillan records that Emerson's 'lectures were chiefly *double entendres*' and that he saw him 'scanning an audience ere he resolved which of two lectures he should give'. This high-minded but discreet Mr. Facing-Both-Ways, knows that he cannot have his cake and eat it any more than he can serve God and Mammon, and that knowledge puzzles, even vexes him. He longs to have both rural strength and religion for his children, and 'city facility and polish', for himself. But he naïvely confesses that he cannot have both. His essays are an elaborate defence of the inevitable anomalies of his position; and finally he falls back upon the idea that there is an intellect of a special quality which existed prior to intellect. It is, he says, a god, whose other name is inspiration.

9

He cannot abandon himself, even to his own ideal. He fears abandonment above all things. Yet he preaches, 'trust the instinct to the end, though you can render no

reason'.[1] He is subdued and puritan; but the fabric of his
quietism is shot with pagan colour and unrest. He allows
his sedate but seething brain to brood upon the notion of
abandonment. 'Life is ecstasy', he announces, and like
William Blake he toys with the idea of excess and would
have made a good 'best man' at the poet's marriage of
Heaven and Hell, although he might have tried to dodge
his responsibility at the altar. His ingrowing genius finds
continual consolation in the idea of intoxication. The idea is
constant, almost pivotal, but always hedged about with protective reservations. 'Tea and coffee are my wine', he begins
one reference, but soon lets his fancy roam from such lady-
like tipples, bragging that he has 'finer and lighter wines
than these'. An intellectual man will naturally use some sort
of nectar, 'for he will soon learn the secret that beside the
energy of his conscious intellect, his intellect is capable of
new energy by abandonment to the nature of things'. But
not only intellectuals, 'all persons avail themselves of such
means as they can to add this extraordinary energy to their
normal powers. One finds it in music, one in war, one in
great pictures and sculptures; one in travelling, one in conversation; in politics, in mobs, in fires, in theatres, in love,
in science; in animal intoxication.' He then catalogues
'finer and lighter wines' than his habitual tea and coffee.
He takes many stimulants of the kind and often makes an
art of inebriation. Brave words fill him with hilarity and at
the sight of them his heart dances, his sight is quickened, he
beholds shining relations between all beings and 'is impelled
to write and almost to sing'. Such experiences are not uncommon, but they are normally taken in our stride, not deliberately as stimulants. The emphasis Emerson gives them
is symptomatic of his congenital low-spirits. There is a profound difference between the welcome given to an induced
experience and the enjoyment of one that happens.

Here also we find the difference between Emerson and

[1] 'The road of excess leads to the palace of wisdom.' William Blake, *The
Marriage of Heaven and Hell* (1790).

life. He is an idealist because he cannot live up to his instincts. His well-known lines:

> *Cast the bantling on the rocks,*
> *Suckle him with the she-wolf's teat;*
> *Wintered with the hawk and fox,*
> *Power and speed be hands and feet,*

are little more than a sentimental chirrup in comparison with Whitman's 'barbaric yawp'. He is only burbling. Any reality of the kind would have pained or shocked him. He prefers life glossed with comfortable sentiment. Wildness is admirable as the raw material of tameness. He always gilds the realistic pill. His admiration for vitality and wildness are a romantic reaction from his own softness and nonresistance. When this gracious writer and mild-mannered man praises hard expressions and hard manners, he is playing the part of a mollusc. He wants to be thought hard and is disturbed when his innate kindliness is approved. 'Why should they call me good-natured? I too, like puss, have a retractive claw.' If he has he never uses it. But he is too honest to succeed wholly in deceiving himself, and there are moments when he realizes that brave words are no more than a protective covering for an ineradicable timidity. 'We love to paint those qualities which we do not possess . . . I who suffer from excess of sympathy, proclaim always the merits of self-reliance.' But if he had followed his more vigorous sentiments he would not have been the urbane apostle of culture, and might have anticipated Theodore Roosevelt. The strenuous life, however, is not for him, nor does he welcome a too literal interpretation of his more daring ideas. He is willing to consider life as an experiment about which we are not to be too 'squeamish', but he is never quite easy about the experimental lives of his great disciples Thoreau and Whitman.

I O

With Thoreau he despises money, yet this scruple might be overcome and 'filthy lucre' made 'beautiful by its just expenditure'.[1] You must never indulge in anything for itself but for some extrinsic reward. Nature for instance, which fires the genius of a Jefferies or a Hudson and suffices Gilbert White, must offer something more than delight to justify the attention of an Emerson in his austerer moods. It is permissible to 'marry Nature' but not to 'use her for pleasure'. We must domesticate her in order to win her favours. More even than that, she must be intellectualized for 'Nature is a discipline of the understanding in intellectual truths', and 'the world exists to satisfy the desire for beauty'. His moral ideas are a protest or a protection against nature: 'every natural fact is trivial until it becomes symbolical or moral.' At the same time nature is apparently a reliable guide to conduct: 'a virtuous man is in unison with her words' and 'willingly does she follow his step with the rose and the violet, and bend her lines of grandeur and grace to the decoration of her darling child.' Yet again, we are not out of the wood for 'nature lives by making fools of us all' although she 'adds a drop of nectar to every man's cup'. There is the same duality in his attitude towards the arts. Art has moral as well as aesthetic purpose, and style in writing is not, as some suppose, the expression of a man, but 'the best thoughts run into the best words'.

[1] Emerson's compromise in this and other places will recall William Penn's 'Never marry but for love; but see that thou lovest what is lovely.' *Reflections and Maxims*, 79.

I I

Love is acceptable as a moralizing force. Women are angels unawares 'made, not to serve, but to be served', and to be appreciated by good men, although only woman can 'tell the heights of feminine nature, and the only way in which man can help her, is by observing her reverently, and whenever she speaks from herself, and catches him in inspired moments up to a heaven of honour and religion, to hold her to the point by reverential recognition of the divinity that speaks through her'. Women of to-day might resent such idealization and shrink from its responsibilities, if they could be convinced that it was not ironical. But Emerson is not merely talking this time. He means it, and proceeds to bring up his own experience in support.

He can 'never think of woman without gratitude for the bright revelations of her best nature which has been made to me, unworthy'. The use of the qualification 'best' is significant. It governs much of his thought. Fine living is a rhythm from best to best, from intrinsic to extrinsic best, the best within us being the sure guide to the best without us. Even 'Nature is loved by what is best in us'. It is a moral concept and is particularly emphasized in his attitude towards love. The admirable thing about woman it would seem, is to be a conductor of divine intimations, to be venerated for her 'oracular nature': the help-meet, obviously, of a low-vitality male. 'The angel', he continues 'who walked with me in younger days shamed my ambition and prudence by her generous love in our first interview. I described my prospects. She said, I do not wish to hear of your prospects.' The woman was, of course, right; but her rightness was natural, not angelic. Any woman who is a true female (which does not always follow) will have the man, or men, of her choice unconditionally. Emerson is also true to type, not that of the true male, but that of the philosopher who praises life in the raw but prefers it cooked.

He is a temperate lover seeking rather the solace of friendship than the raptures of passion. He believes that 'all affections to persons are partial and superficial'.[1] There are reasons for believing that this opinion is the expression of something more than low vitality. When he is a young widower of no more than one and thirty and about to marry again, he says that 'there is no greater lie than a voluptuous book like Boccaccio', the reason being that it misrepresents the duration of 'pleasures of appetite, which only at rare intervals, a few times in a life-time, are intense, and to whose acme continence is essential, as frequent, habitual, and belonging to the incontinent . . .'[2] In marriage he notes 'how fast the frivolous external fancying fades out of the mind', and for that reason husband and wife should be taught not to mourn 'the rapid ebb of inclination'. Once gone, 'no luck, nor witchcraft, nor destiny, nor divinity in marriage . . . can produce affection, but only those qualities that by their nature extort it', for 'all love is mathematical', or, as we should now say, rhythmical.

Doubtless there is truth and even wisdom in the attitude, but it seems here to be confessed for consolation. This becomes increasingly evident when similar passages in the *Journals* are related and compared. There is one which strikes deeper than the rest and was later turned into a poem: 'You must love me as I am. Do not tell me how much I should love you. I am content. I find my satisfactions in a calm, considerate reverence, measured by the virtues which provoke it. So love me as I am. When I am virtuous, love me: when I am vicious, hate me; when I am luke-warm, neither good nor bad, care not for me. But do not by your sorrow or your affection solicit me to be somewhat else than I by nature am.'[3]

---

[1] When he undertook the editing of Thoreau's *Familiar Letters* he aimed at producing 'a most perfect piece of stoicism', and he thought Thoreau's sister had 'marred his classic statue' by inserting some tokens of her brother's 'natural affection'. F. B. Sanborn, *Thoreau* (1882), 306.

[2] *Journals*, iii, 456. The sentence is unfinished in the book.

[3] *Journals*, v, 394. He was then thirty-four years of age.

1 2

It is only by inference that we can form a cognate idea of the man. Emerson is not prone to candid confession and when he confesses to himself, as he finds it necessary to do in his journals, his candour is accidental. In most of the intimate notes he is obviously playing hide and seek with himself. His favourite subterfuge is evasion, aided and abetted by sublimation—in itself but another form of evasion. He is, for instance, conscious of coldness and persuades himself that it is only superficial; and when he fears mental impotence, which he frequently does, he attributes it to indolence. Each of these characteristics he attributes, in his more realistic moments, to lack of vital force. There can be little doubt now that his diagnosis is correct. His case is one of morbid diffidence rather than incapacity, and the opposite treatment to that which he administers to himself, namely, more diffidence, might have brought relief, if relief were desirable, for in the end a man is what he is and the portrait of him is what he does. Emerson's repressions are the result of a wrong mixture of honesty and timidity expressing itself in undue caution which at times resembles cowardice.

He is not impotent, but afraid of sex. Here doubtless his puritan ancestry has him by the heel. The condition is common in New England, whose early settlers, unlike those of the South, were not seeking adventure so much as escaping from it. Moral repressions gave them an unwholesome delight. Emerson is a sceptical branch of this tree. He can't grow straight for staring at himself and the longer he stares the more crooked he grows. He stares his heart out of countenance, as congenital spinsters do. He is, in fact, a male spinster, over-nice, dreading coarseness, desiring anything but desire. Such men break women by emotional attrition. Emerson tries to dodge the flesh and its contacts, and is consequently in a chronic state of unrest alternating between repressive excitement and post-coital melancholia. He exposes himself unawares, and in no place so much as in the passage cited above where he desires to be loved for what he is, if he is virtuous. He will excuse even hate if he is vicious and indifference if he is lukewarm.[1]

Yet he believes inwardly, at least, that all is not well. On a June morning in his thirty-seventh year he finishes the transcription of the essay on 'Love', an obvious effort towards self-justification, and realizes its inadequacy. He confesses privately that he has disguised or omitted his own experience, and he is obviously under the impression that this confession absolves him from complicity in what amounts to public misrepresentation. Emerson can resist everything but the temptation to cook his intellectual books, and yet he is ever defeated by the laws of expression which give him away in the very lineaments of his disguise.

His dissertation upon love, in spite of that silence in which 'we must wrap much of our life, because it is too fine for speech, because also we cannot explain it to others, and because somewhat we cannot yet understand', is as much a testimony as the confession just cited. The essay is inadequate, he says, because, in his own words, 'I, cold because I am hot, cold at the surface only as a sort of guard and compensation for the fluid tenderness of the core'. He has had more experience than he admits, more, he says, 'than I will or can write'. This is probably an inverted brag,[2] because if he has repressed his affections so seriously as the previous sentence implies, his experiences must have been other than such as he suggests, though not less real to a man of Emerson's introspective habit.

[1] 'I do *wish* one knew something about Emerson's *first* wife! . . . And *did* the second one like always being called "*Dear* Lidian"! Did *either* wife ever kiss him on the tip of his nose, I wonder!—I fear Lidian never!' Anne Douglas Sedgwick, 6, ii, 1931. *Letters* (1936), 256.

[2] His coldness was life-long. In 1825, when he is only twenty-one, he feels the defect so deeply that he records it in verse:

> *My pulse is slow, my blood is cold,*
> *My stammering tongue is rudely turned.*

I 3

Emerson has also the puritan's fear of luxury. His faith in Goethe, who is one of his heroes, is shaken when he realizes not only that the German Olympian revels in grandeur, but that he is incapable of self-surrender to the moral sentiment. Michael Angelo's 'struggles and mortifications' are 'a more beautiful wreath than the milliners made for Goethe'. Anything likely to arouse passion arouses his suspicion. On his first visit to Florence, he condescends to witness a ballet, and enjoys it. But his conscience gets the better of him, for he cannot help feeling that it were better for mankind if there were no such dances. He is consoled however with the discovery that God is on his side, because 'all the *ballerine* are nearly idiotic'. He fears the betrayal of something false within, for he is never quite sure of himself in the presence of a pretty woman. Instead of being grateful for such normal delights he turns the other way. After the same ballet he reflects that one ought not to be 'too easily satisfied with the accomplishments of vulgar pretty women'. Vulgarity is the badge of his distaste.

Naples was one of the first European cities he ever saw, and the contrast of Neapolitan life with that of Concord, or even Boston, must have been startling. His feelings, when his morals are exposed to the advances of this strangely passionate life, compared with which life in New England is in its infancy, can be no more than guessed. It may be that, like his contemporary idealist, Wordsworth, he is tempted. Whether he 'fell' or not is unknown. He is certainly disturbed, and reflects that 'our virtue' needs all the 'advantages . . . all the crutches', even 'fear' and 'want of appetite and press of affairs' as well as 'strength' and 'the just and sublime considerations of the love of God and self-respect. Not', he is careful to add, 'that any others will bear comparison with these, but because the temptations are so manifold and so subtle and assail archangels as well as coarser clay, that it will not do to spare any strength.' These admonitions are general or evangelical. They are not even rhetorically addressed to the Neapolitans to whom such temptations are no novelty. Emerson is fortifying himself. This is more clearly indicated by reference to his last line of defence, 'the remembrance of the affectionate, anxious expectations with which others 'regard' your contest with temptation is a wonderful provocative of virtue'. It cannot be doubted that Emerson, if in real danger, would have exercised all these precautions, but he is doubtless saved in advance by 'want of appetite', a prophylactic not without honour in his own country, and ours.

The reason he gives for one of his literary repressions is that 'we do not live as angels, eager to introduce each other to new perfections in our brothers and sisters, and frankly avowing our delight in each new trait of character, in the magic of each new eyebeam, but that which passes for love in the world gets official, and instead of embracing, hates all the divine traits that dare to appear in other persons'. The implication here would seem to be that he cannot for reasons of expediency penetrate further into the Holy of Holies of transcendental love. If that is what he means, it might be suggested that he could not very well have gone further than the essay on 'Love', which frankly advocates the distillation of sex-passion into an immaterial essence and the use of that essence in the pursuit of an abstract idea of beauty. This is evident because in the journal he refers to 'a better and holier society' where greater frankness will be possible because 'we shall have brave ties of affection, not petrified by law, not dated or ordained by law to last for one year, for five years, or for life; but drawing their date, like all friendship, from itself only'. All of which reads like advocacy of free love as understood by the moderns, but it is no more than a piece of special pleading for love as understood by the Platonists.[1]

[1] The essay on 'Love' is supported everywhere in Emerson's *Journal* which abounds in such admonitions as 'Reduce the body to the soul' (ii, 478), 'Put away your flesh, put on your faculties' (ii, 494).

14

These 'brave ties' are no anticipation of the ties in Mr. Aldous Huxley's *Brave New World*. They are 'brave ... because innocent, and religiously abstinent from the connubial endearments'. Such love can never be human nature's daily food, for nobody who is not 'good' can believe it possible. Those who are not good are no better than 'cows and bulls and peacocks' who 'think it nonsense'. With these words he consoles himself against the 'imputations of unnecessary hardness and stoicism' which he thinks he has incurred 'from those who compose the Court and Parliament of Love'.

The essay on 'Love' is Emerson's considered attitude, and it is one of the most emphatic pronouncements against the physical expression of affection outside the works of professional saints. 'Hitch your waggon to a star', comes into full operation when he faces love.[1] Affection must be dredged of all fleshly taint and become a relation of 'transcendent delicacy and sweetness' such as 'roses and violets hint and foreshow'. The lover must protect himself against any coarsening of the soul by contemplation of that beauty which lies beyond mere passion; and if, 'accepting the hint of these visions and suggestions which beauty makes to his mind, the soul passes through the body, and falls to admire strokes of character, and the lovers contemplate one another in their discourses and their actions, then they pass to the true palace of beauty, more and more inflame their love of it, and by this love extinguish the base affection, as the sun puts out the fire by shining on the hearth, they become pure and hallowed'.

The path of even ideal love is not always smooth. There is a stage during which 'the soul which is in the soul of each,

[1] 'I saw a maiden so pure that she exchanged glances only with the stars.' Ib., v, 35.

craving a perfect beatitude, detects incongruities, defects, and disproportion in the behaviour of the other. Hence arise surprise, expostulation, and pain.' Yet this state is only temporary for by 'the purification of the intellect and the heart, from year to year, is the real marriage, foreseen and prepared from the first, and wholly above their consciousness. . . . That which is so beautiful and attractive as these relations must be succeeded and supplanted only by what is more beautiful, and so on for ever.'

15

Emerson is a self-torturer haunted by the desire to strike a balance between good and evil. He has a bad conscience, inherited from a long line of puritans, and his philosophy is devoted to excusing or pacifying it. His journals are confessions of this conflict, and his essays studies in expiation. Yet, in a famous passage, he announces that our lives are for living not expiation, but he is not certain what sort of life is the true life, and he never even succeeds in convincing himself that he is doing right by the faith of his fathers or the inward light which should guide his steps. He is pained by the thought that his actions do not always conform with his principles. He believes in the 'wholesomeness of Calvinism for thousands and thousands' but he is disturbed because he cannot foster what he does not practise and is thus guilty of a 'hollow obeisance to things' he does not himself value. His most familiar solatium is the Pantheistic notion of self-projection into nature, and he is encouraged by a desire to be associated with all men, although, at the same time, he believes that 'the true and finished man is ever alone'.

His work suggests an endless argument with himself as well as a brilliant piece of special pleading for exalted ideas, but it is his object to convert or inspire himself as much as

his readers. He cannot escape from his tyrannical conscience
even here, and is ever trying to evade responsibility for his
beliefs and disbeliefs, by attributing them to something outside himself or beyond his own desires. Thus he justifies his
idealism by associating it with nature: 'Nature is the true
idealist'; a tendency to exaggerate is excused on the grounds
that 'Exaggeration is a law of Nature'. He worships God not
because of any wish to do so but because 'God in us worships
God'. He tries to escape responsibility for his idiosyncrasies
and his moods by communalizing them: 'Every man beholds
his human condition with a degree of melancholy.' He is
teased by ideas of sloth and unprofitable living and consoles
himself with the thought that 'it is the highest power of
divine moments that they abolish our contritions'. And when
he disapproves of an idea or a movement, he blames the interpretation of it, not the thing itself. When he says that 'there
is nothing of the true democratic element in what is called
Democracy', he is associating with the obscurantists who excuse the deficiencies of professing Christians by saying that
Christianity has not failed because it has not been tried. All
of which are familiar tricks of unconscious self-justification.

Knowing as he does that his own blood is tepid, that his
enthusiasms are so checked by prudence that abandonment
of any kind for him is impossible, he notes that 'the one thing
which we seek with insatiable desire is to forget ourselves, to
be surprised out of our propriety, to lose our sempiternal
memory, and to do something without knowing how or why',
for 'nothing great was ever achieved without enthusiasm',
and 'the way of life is wonderful; it is by abandonment.' He
never kicks over the traces, so 'genius is always ascetic'; car-
nal tastes are taboo for him, so 'appetite shows to the finer
souls as a disease'. And in his popular dissertation on 'Self-
reliance', at once one of the bravest and most inspiring essays
and a startling piece of self-revelation, he confesses: 'I do not
wish to expiate, but to live.' Life is for itself and not for a
spectacle; and this high-minded and fastidiously proper man
tries to persuade himself that he would prefer life 'of a lower

strain, so it be genuine and equal, than that it should be glittering and unsteady'.

A typical piece of advice to himself is, 'Adhere, sit fast, lie low', yet on almost every page of his sparkling essays he exhorts his readers to be themselves and to live boldly in the present, to take risks, ignore conventions, opinion, even prudence, for there is a time when philosophy and imagination are absurd, when 'one must act, count, measure, plunge, strike, and die'. But he wonders whether he is a hypocrite, because he is not only disgusted with vanity everywhere but preaches self-trust every day, and is not above reproaching himself for allowing 'every little pitiful instance of awkwardness and misfortune' to keep his 'nervous system on the rack' and thus convict him of succumbing to the 'disease' of being unduly 'respectful to the opinion of others'.

16

Emerson is one of the first of the moderns to venture a good word for wilfulness, and it is interesting to note that a self-willed girl inspires one of his most heroic aphorisms. He so approves of her lofty will that he wishes to say to her: 'Never strike sail to any. Come into port greatly, or sail with Gods the seas.' It would be even more interesting to know if he ever carried out his wish, but the words thus inspired later find a key-position in his essay on 'Heroism', where his insistence upon heroic doing as the consummation of heroic being exalts like wine, and under its spell quite ordinary readers are apt, temporarily, to feel like gods. But reading this essay in a more sober mood, one cannot escape the feeling that when he is exhorting his reader he is reproaching himself. When he says that there are 'immense resources and possibilities proper to us, on which we have never drawn', he is reminding himself of something he thinks he has missed. When he writes 'Do not belive the past. I give you the universe now and unhanselled every hour,' he is exhorting himself, for he loves the past and has to batter himself into respect for the present; when he repudiates a taste for 'the great, the remote, the romantic' and announces that he embraces the 'common' and sits 'at the feet of the familiar, the low', he is dodging the consequences of his own priggishness. He is a dialectician who knows that 'life is not dialectics', and although he is always arguing with himself, if not with others, he rebukes himself with the thought that 'the children of the gods never argue'. When in his journal he says 'Use society: do not serve it', he is persuading himself and consoling himself simultaneously. He enjoys society especially 'where there is real affinity' and he can indulge his taste for ideas and poetry among his peers, but he complains, 'as soon as the tea-tray comes in, we feel the yoke of foreigners, and wish we were at home with our stupid familiars'. He is far from mean, but hospitality for him consists of 'a little fire, a little food, but enough', and as we might expect, 'immense quiet'.

His poems as well as his journals record a constant struggle with himself, a confessional and a controversy. At one moment he is all for dashing about; taking risks, at another for retirement and prudence. In the following lines, written in his twenty-ninth year, he anticipates the frenzied egoism of Nietzsche:

> *I will not live out of me.*
> *I will not see with others' eyes;*
> *My good is good, my evil ill.*
> *I would be free; I cannot be*
> *While I take things as others please to rate them.*
>
> *I dare attempt to lay out my own road.*
> *That which myself delights in shall be Good,*
> *That which I do not want, indifferent;*
> *That which I hate is Bad. That's flat.*
> *Henceforth, please Good, forever I forego*
> *The yoke of men's opinions. I will be*
> *Lighthearted as a bird and live with God.*

In the end prudence wins and daring and light-heartedness
are relegated to the realm of good intent. Yet prudence and
content are not always on good terms. Regret dogs the
footsteps of abstinence, remorse and indulgence. He sees
clearly enough but lacking the courage of his perceptions,
he argues himself into a perpetual indecision, for to the
dialectician there is a good reason for everything. So he
accepts and rejects, affirms and denies and in the end he is
discovered in retreat without ceasing to be on the side of
the angels.

17

Emerson's praise of genius and heroism is misleading because it is purely intellectual. His intellect is sentimental. He can persuade himself that boldness, courage,
even bravado, are good, but he never believes it in his heart.
'I think I have not the common degree of sympathy with
dark, turbid, mournful, passionate natures; but in com-
punction, in a keen resentment of violation, in shame for
idleness, in shame at standing still, in remorse for meanness,
in remorse for wounded affection, in rolling in the dust and
crying, Unclean! Unclean! when we have debased ourselves
to appetite, or undone ourself with injustice—I believe, I believe. I honour the retirements of men. I love the flush of
hope.' He places his inmost convictions under suspicion and
brings them to the bar of his own judgment. 'Why was not I
made like all these beatified mates of mine, *superficially* generous and noble, as well as *internally* so?' His kindness and help-
fulness, so obvious in his actions, are also under suspicion.
'I was born a seeing eye, not a helping hand. I can only comfort my friends by thought, and not by love or aid. But they
naturally look for this other also, and thereby vitiate our relation throughout.'

He is a high-brow, a bookman, an intellectual, by inclination and conviction, yet he craves the tonic of common, simple, and comfortable domestic life. Preaching and the study of books are sickly employments: 'The garden and the family, wife, mother, son, and brother are a balsam. There is health in table-talk and nursery play. We must wear old shoes and have aunts and cousins,' yet 'shall our conversation when we meet, O wife, or sister Elizabeth, still return, like the chime of seven bells, to six or seven names, nor we freemen of nature be able long to travel out of this narrowed orbit?'

18

He believes, as Whitman and Thoreau do, that life is here and now, and that no dashing about the earth to see the sights can add to its intensity, yet again he has to nudge himself to conviction. One night following an afternoon in the country with Thoreau, he goes out into the dark, and still, presumably, under the influence of his friend, sees a 'glimmering star' and hears a frog. Nature seems to say to him, as Thoreau must have done many times: 'Well do not these suffice? Here is a new scene, a new experience. Ponder it, Emerson, and not like the foolish world hanker after thunders and multitudes and vast landscapes, the sea or Niagara.' He knows the value of sincerity, 'yet how easily will any fop, any coat and boots, draw me to an appearance of sympathy with him and to an air of patronizing the sentiments; the commonest person of condition and fashion affects me more than is right, and I am mute, passive, and let their world wag, let them make the world, I being but a block of the same, I ought to go upright and vital and say the truth in all ways.' He is drawn to others because he longs for sympathy, but he believes an excessive desire for sympathy is a vice from which he prays God to defend him. The social round is always a difficulty with one who is socially-minded but whose spiritual prudency is so sensitive that he shrinks from all who would trespass upon the privacy of his soul.

He is prudent, conservative, moderate, on principle and by inclination, yet 'sad is this continual postponement of life'. He refuses sympathy and intimacy with people, as if he knew of some better sympathy and intimacy to come. 'But whence and when?' he asks, 'I am already thirty-four years old. Scarcely can I say that I see any new men or women approaching me; I am too old to regard fashion; too old to expect patronage of any greater or more powerful.' He will therefore 'suck the sweetness of those affections and consuetudes that grow near him'.

He confesses that he was born a hermit and must be content with his lot, and, characteristically swings round in favour of keeping aloof after all, and plucking 'the fruit from rare meetings with wise men', for thus 'the fruit of his own tree shall have a better flavour'. There is a curious link with his innate Platonism here. Persons as well as facts are disagreeable to him unless he can relate them with the 'universal consciousness'. When he can do so he can enlarge his 'charity one circle more and let them in'. He shuns his own personality for the same reason: 'break off your association with your own personality and identify yourself with the Universe.' It was in some such spirit that he left the Church, consoling himself with the characteristic paradox that 'in order to be a good minister, it was necessary to leave the ministry'.

19

Here, then, very clearly, is the phenomenon of a man at cross-purposes with himself and life, seeking and finding and repudiating alternately, in a perverse rhythm which, surprisingly is a kind of vitality. Nor does his life lack the quality of coherence, for his personal integrity is immeasurably superior to that of many men of genius. He is probably aware of this inward rectitude, which prompted him in early manhood, after one of his spiritual conflicts, to confess that his charge was to act faithfully upon his own faith, to live by it himself, and to see what a hearty obedience would do. And when he reflects upon what he has he desires no change. 'My direction of thought is so strong', he writes, 'that I should do the same things—should contrive to spend the best part of my time in the same way as now, rich or poor.' At that time he had scarcely lived half his long life, but thirty-five years later he would have made a like admission.

Such contradictions with lesser men might indicate absence of integrity; but with him they are the expression of an acute fastidiousness, morbid in some respects no doubt, but always scrupulous. His very timidity is a form of scrupulousness. Ever conscious of the criss-crossing of reason and understanding, instinct, and conscience, he feels that an idea, pure at birth, loses caste when it is written down. He seems to have a grudge against writing. 'The child', he says, 'is sincere, and the man when he is alone, if he be not a writer,' all of which is but another phase of his worship of the absolute. There is for him an abstract well of truth from which you can draw wisdom and guidance if your contacts are direct and spontaneous, 'your ear close to the soul'. When he was thirty and again when he is nearly sixty, he renounces all intention 'to refer, prefer, defer, or confer and differ', and determines to 'embrace the absolute life'. His ideas and impressions are carefully and frankly recorded in his journals, although in their passage from notebook to print they sometimes lose frankness. But whilst his disguises and contradictions reveal rather than hide his vital conflicts, they also reflect his honesty and his intelligence, and at the same time provide him with abundant opportunity for moral reflection in a prose which can be as simple and direct as *Pilgrim's Progress* and as delicately patterned as the *Hydriotaphia* of Sir Thomas Browne.

Life is as varied as he is and capable of still more variation.

Ordinary people believe that there are two sides to every question and one of them right. Emerson knows no such limitations. There are, for him, as many sides to a question as there are facets to a crystal and each of them right and wrong. It is all a matter of attitude. If you see things from a height you see more of them. Distance lends tolerance as well as enchantment to the view. Emerson, the Olympian, is looking on from afar. He is scrupulous as well as fastidious because he is intellectually generous as well as honest, and because he desires to reach truth by way of tolerance. Yet he longs to 'conceive the Universe without a contradiction'. Thus longing to be relieved from 'this perpetual perplexity of choosing', he strives to rationalize his perplexity: 'Why drag about this corpse of your memory lest you contradict somewhat you have stated in this or that public place? Suppose you should contradict yourself, what then?'

So this modern Hamlet, this, as Nathaniel Hawthorne puts it, 'everlasting rejecter of all that is, and seeker for he knows not what', sifts the gold from the dross and throws the nuggets away as quickly as he finds them, for 'there is nothing either good or bad, but thinking makes it so'. Yet he seems to be welding the parts of himself into a working cosmos, and opening doors and windows for others. He blows them open, for this suave and sedate teacher, this walking library, has, by his eagerness to awaken those who are habitually half-dead, become as invigorating as a summer's gale. His ideas have swept together the oddments of many a bewildered reader. His thoughts are darts that glance and prick. He pelts you with aphorisms which stick like burrs. And this breeziness is benevolent because it seeks to throw you not off your feet, but on to them. He is a master of verbal explosions and prefers to

> Mount to paradise
> By the stairway of surprise.

20

Emerson hides his self-concern behind a disinterested façade. He has no personal axe to grind, other than his own inward content, his aim being to startle you not out of yourself but into yourself apropos of himself and all he has thought or felt. You also must introvert your eye and so make your consciousness 'a taper in the desert of Eternity', for the Kingdom of God is within and can only be spread abroad by awakening latent and generally dormant genius. He is the romantic evangelist of spiritual escapades. He believes that the 'true emotion is wonder', and that the transformation of genius into practical power is 'the true romance which the world exists to realize'.

What that practical power may be is never wholly clear. Emerson's expressions are more concrete than his ideas, which are nearly always too abstract for his purpose. 'I hug the absolute,' he says. He does more, he takes refuge in it from the puzzles of action. 'The moment a man discovers that he has aims which his faculties cannot answer, the world becomes a riddle.' The instructions are further complicated by qualification. You must not only be yourself, but your better self. 'We wish to escape from subjection, and a sense of inferiority,—and we make self-denying ordinances, we drink water, we eat grass, we refuse the laws, we go to jail: it is all in vain, only by his obedience to his genius; only by the freest activity in the way constitutional to him, does an angel seem to arise before a man, and lead him by the hand out of all the wards of the prison.'

Emerson's motive is not, consciously, the expression of his own personality, although he does so express himself in every line he writes, for, in the last resort he is an artist, an artist in ethics. He is enamoured of moral perfection. It is a form of excitement. He is an idealist and looks upon idealism as 'the preparation for a strictly moral life'. The idea of moral excellence fills him with passion. 'It has separated me from man,' he says, 'it has watered my pillow, it has driven sleep from my bed. It cannot be defeated by my defeats. It cannot be questioned, though all the martyrs apostalize. . . . It is the soul of religion.' By it he understands 'all heroism, the history of loyalty and of martyrdom and of bigotry, the heat of the Methodist, the nonconformity of the Dissenter, the patience of the Quaker'. 'If the splendid function of seeing should lose its interest', he is consoled by the thought that he can still flee to the sanctuary of his moral nature, and 'trust, renounce, suffer, bleed'. The line of least resistance has no attraction for him. He is not sorry that it is very hard to be simple enough to be good.

2 I

In a particular sense, Emerson, despite his heterodoxy, is a product of the puritanism which did so much to mould New England character, and the history of whose influence he once dreamt of writing. Moral law is, for him, the highest standard of value, 'it lies at the centre of nature and radiates to the circumference'. Natural Science 'seems merely auxiliary to Moral' and he would 'learn the law of the defraction of a ray' hoping that it will 'suggest a new truth in ethics'. Beauty is 'the mark God sets upon virtue'. Pleasure only is suspect. The old puritan rises out of the mere thought of any action that is not purposeful. Pleasure is a form of nourishment, but you must be pleased 'without any misgiving' before you can be properly nourished. Even gardening if it gives pleasure comes under his ban, and labour enjoyed has little merit: 'nothing is easier or more epicurean.'

It is not always so easy to pin Emerson down, for you can never be certain under which thimble his latest idea rests, or whether indeed, it has not melted into thin air. He is as changeful as the sky, and his meaning is darkest when his firmament is fullest of stars. In one thing, however, he does not change, for he is always conscious of a purpose and he is always in earnest about it. Life without purpose is as ambiguous for him as a man without a purpose. 'You must exercise your genius in some form that has essential life now; do something which is proper to the hour', and 'leave to God the care of the world'. 'I cannot help counting it a fault,' he says, that Thoreau 'had not ambition.'

Emerson is serious and solemn. Life is no joking matter. 'God never jests', nor do great men. 'Bacon and Plato have something too solid to say than that they can afford to be humourists.' He himself rarely laughs and thinks laughter in others disagreeable. 'The frivolous make me lonely.' He rebukes Carlyle for his 'playfulness' in the tremendous pages of the *French Revolution*. 'Why', he asks, 'should an imagination such as never rejoiced before the face of God, since Shakespeare, be content to play? Why should he trifle and joke?'

22

Emerson never cuts capers. His prose may dance, but he never does. Yet he is neither heavy nor morose even in his most earnest admonitions and exhortations. Roaring and moaning are not among his weapons; nor does he threaten. This unwearying evangelist of a better humanity is ever urbane, and he is convinced that the best is well within grasp were we but reasonable about it. Yet he is always preaching or teaching. In his most carefree moment he is didactic. Thoreau runs him close, but his didacticism does not prevent him from being interested in things for themselves, especially if he is not expected to own them; thus Thoreau's essays and journals open more often into joyous glimpses of birds and flowers, the glint of sun on leaves, the behaviour of a chipmunk or the moods of a muskrat.

Yet when it comes to behaviour the two sages meet on a common platform. Emerson appeals to the authority of abstract ideas but his teaching does not end in abstraction. Men must be good for something but even philanthropy must be associated with rectitude, and sacrifices must have conditions and safeguards. He has none of Whitman's passion for humanity in the raw. Men only begin to interest him when they show capacity for improvement. It is not, indeed, necessary that a man should live, unless he live and act rightly. Carlyle thunders the same idea through nineteenth-century England with even more magnificence, and as little effect.

Emerson is the most sedate of philosophers and, emphatic though he can be, there is nothing of the hot-gospeller about him. It is impossible to say with any certainty even whether he practises what he preaches, not so much because his advocacy has many facets, as because his philosophy is *laissez-faire*. You can prove anything from his writings, anything, of course, that is not wicked. He conforms, but conformity is far from being necessary to salvation. On the contrary, 'whoso would be a man must be a nonconformist'. That is clear enough, but it is equally clear that nonconformity is neither the aim nor yet the sole method. He means readiness to break with forms when they have served their purpose, and no break is advised unless dictated by that inner force which he calls genius. 'I shun father and mother and wife and brother, when my genius calls me.'

He would write on the lintels of his doorpost the word *Whim*, but he suspects spontaneity, and instantly qualifies the idea of abandonment by hoping that 'it is somewhat better than whim at last, but', he concludes, 'we cannot spend the day in explanation', forgetting that he has never done anything else. The difficulty is evidently very real, for, long before he condemned the whimsical with the bizarre as among those qualities which will not endure, we find him preparing the way for an exposition of the genius of Shakespeare by showing that the poet, to whom the average man might permit a margin of whimsical licence, is not thus advantaged. 'There is nothing whimsical and fantastic in his production, but sweet and sad earnest, freighted with the

weightiest convictions, and pointed with the most determined aim', which is a better definition of Emerson than of
Shakespeare.

23

Such inconsistencies do not however reduce his philosophy to absurdity. They are a further revelation of
the man rather than a devaluation of his ideas, and a tribute
to his ineradicable honesty. Emerson, as we have seen, like
Whitman, is not afraid of inconsistency. 'Damn Consistency!' is probably his strongest expression. It is characteristic of his habit of blowing hot and cold, of letting his mind
wobble like one who thinks aloud, revising as he goes. Indeed, there is nothing strange in that, for those whose terms
of reference are abstractions are no less consistent than those
who are buttressed by dogmas. The man who discovers the
elixir of life might easily be scared by his achievement, and a
nature-lover might lose faith in his mistress during an earthquake. So with Emerson, who realizes the force, variously
called whim, intuition, genius, and fears it because it can't
be controlled. His own genius is invariably right; it helps
him to perceive genius in others and, where ever it exists, in
his own time and place. He was Darwinian before Darwin,
Nietzschean before Nietzsche, Bergsonian before Bergson,
and Humanist before Irving Babbitt. All of which would not
have surprised him, or added to his conceit, for he believes,
with Thoreau, Carlyle and Whitman, that genius is all, and
that the great man is the summation of the genius of humanity. The great man, however, is not the strong man, but the
strong good man. Nature seems to exist for the excellent.
The world is upheld by the veracity of good men: they make
the earth wholesome.

He sees life as noble behaviour, and he sees himself in
great men; they are his mirror. Thus his main use of books
is to discover himself and this constant accumulation of bits

of himself from the works of others gives his essays the quality of mosaic, or of a well-chosen nosegay which, in his opinion, 'has its own charm, and affects the eye, as fields of the same flower cannot'. Sometimes you feel that he is not a man but a synthesis of many men, and he will be the first to agree with you. 'I go to Shakespeare, Goethe, Swift, even to Tennyson, submit myself to them, become merely an organ of hearing, and yield to the law of their being. I am paid for thus being nothing by an entire new mind, and thus, a Proteus, I enjoy the universe through the powers and organs of a hundred different men.'

24

His Olympianism comes out again in his numerous references to books. 'I think I will never read any but the commonest of books: The Bible, Shakespeare, Milton, Dante, Homer.' *Noblesse oblige!* And he makes a virtue of predilection, for readers of such noble books are almost as rare as their authors: 'Homer requires Homer to read him.' To understand Swedenborg requires a genius almost equal to Swedenborg's. So also a library is made perfect by weeding from the mass all books but the best. He is pursuing his old purpose all the time, and at his old tricks. Books are tonics for world-savers, 'magazines of beneficent dynamite'. The aim is to use and transcend them. 'The costliest benefit of books is to set us free from themselves.' And yet comes, ever and anon, the still small voice of the bibliophile within, telling him that he is after all a natural born reader and that in a 'true time' he would never have written.

The end of his system, as it is also of those of Whitman and Thoreau, is the production of great men, not so much a race of great men as sufficient of them to generate the elements of greatness in others. He anticipates Whitman's formula: 'produce great men, the rest follows', with the idea that one great man can become a kind of generating station for the revitalization of a society or a nation. 'We love to associate with heroic persons, since our receptivity is unlimited; and, with the great, our thoughts and manners easily become great. We are all wise in capacity, though so few in energy. There needs but one wise man in a company, and all are wise, so rapid is the contagion.' The problem of energy is again in evidence, the necessity of re-charging the human dynamo emphasized, and, later, in the same book he reasserts his faith in self-contained, mentally active, rather than dependent, physically active men.

Wholly admiring Plato he says, 'as a good chimney burns its smoke, so a philosopher converts the value of all his fortunes into his intellectual performances'. Partially admiring Napoleon, he sweeps aside the vitality which disturbed the dust of Europe, and notes that in his earlier years Napoleon was 'a model of prudence'. He prefers the prudent, conservative type, but above everything he admires men who have the courage and energy to live their own lives by conquering the frustrations of fear and convention. He joins Goethe and Napoleon 'as being both representatives of the impatience and reaction of nature against the *morgue* of conventions'. Swedenborg's philosophy, though suggestive, misses front-rank status because it is 'not vital, and lacks the power to generate life'. Swedenborg's idea of God lacks 'lustre' and fails to 'vivify the immense dependency of being'. The personal need for more vitality is again evident plus a hint at that despondency which Emerson with all his serenity can never wholly escape.

25

Throughout his admirable but frankly subjective studies of great men, you feel once more that he is searching for himself, explaining himself to himself. It is not so much

Plato, Swedenborg, Montaigne, Shakespeare, Napoleon, or Goethe, who leap out of these essays, as Emerson. He himself being eclectic rather than original, records with approval that 'great men are more distinguished by range and extent than by originality'. He is, however, convinced that talent alone is not enough, 'there must be a man behind the book', as strong, well-balanced, virile, as he would like to be.

The familiar duality is most clearly revealed in the essays on Plato and Montaigne. Emerson admires Plato, but loves Montaigne. Plato is what Emerson is, Montaigne, what Emerson would like to be. When he looks into Montaigne's mirror he thinks he sees himself, but he sees only what he might have been. He reads the 'prince of egotists' in Cotton's translation shortly after he leaves college and lives with him in delight and wonder. It seems that he himself has written the book, in some former life, so sincerely does it speak to his thought and experience. But it is only necessary to read on to find him describing his hero in terms not far removed from a self-portrait. Montaigne is frank and honest, his admirer is honest but far from frank; Montaigne 'runs into grossness'—but anticipates 'censure by the bounty of his own confession. . . . He pretends to most of the vices; and, if there be any virtue in him, he says, it got in by stealth. There is no man, in his opinion, who has not deserved hanging five or six times; and he pretends no exceptions in his own behalf.' Emerson is incapable of grossness and never, even in his most depressed moments, thinks of his weaknesses as other than negative. He only complains of his sins of omission, and is ever safe from cross or hemlock cup.

In the study of Plato he very nearly draws his own portrait: 'He is a great average man; one who, to the best thinking, adds a proportion and equality in his faculties, so that men see in him their own dreams and glimpses made available, and made to pass for what they are. A great commonsense is his warrant and qualification to be the world's interpreter. He has reason, as all the philosophic and poetic class have: but, he has, also, what they have not,—the strong solving sense to reconcile his poetry with the appearances of the world, and build a bridge from the streets of the cities to Atlantis. He omits never this graduation, but slopes his thought, however picturesque the precipice on one side, to an access from the plain. He never writes in ecstasy, or catches us up into poetic raptures.'

26

With such qualities Emerson sets out to slay the dragons of sloth and greed, and their litter of squalor of mind or heart or place. He is often sick at heart because his efforts have so little effect or receive such tardy appreciation; but he rarely reveals his melancholy—except to himself in the privacy of his journal. To the world he is full of good hope, Utopia is always round the next corner. He remains kind when he becomes famous, yet he is aloof from friends and disciples. He walks and talks with the leaders of American thought, and communes across the sea with Thomas Carlyle and John Ruskin, and, less intimately, with other admirers in England, where his works are as widely appreciated as in his own land. And if he feels rebuffed or disheartened, he never ceases to announce that the world is young or to believe in the efficacy of great men, and, significantly, it is the concluding words of *Representative Men* which sum up his own ambition and ethics most simply and clearly: 'We too must write Bibles, to unite again the heavens and the earthly world. The secret of genius is to suffer no fiction to exist for us; to realize all that we know; in the high refinement of modern life, in arts, in sciences, in books, in men, to exact good faith, reality, and a purpose; and first, last, midst, and without end, to honour every truth by use.' It is a dream which is far from being fulfilled either in America or England.

THOREAU

We should see that our dreams are the solidest facts that we know.

HENRY DAVID THOREAU

I

Thoreau, like Emerson, desires to expound a philosophy that will be a stimulus to men, but, unlike Emerson, he prefers to prove his ideas by personal experiment. It is impossible to avoid comparing him with Diogenes. He renounces the encumbrances of his age, has the same laconic wit, and though he does not live in a tub, he woos simplicity by living in a hut. The grand experiment of social renunciation is made on the outskirts of Concord where, undisturbed by sophisticated tasks and duties, he gives himself a reliability test, and at the same time hopes to make such discoveries as Emerson made in the library and on the lecture platform, and Whitman in the common ways of men among 'powerful uneducated persons'.

In appearance Thoreau is peculiar. Emerson describes him as short, long-armed, hairy, 'as ugly as sin, long-nosed, queer-mouthed, and with uncouth and somewhat rustic, although courteous manners'. Little wonder that he is sometimes mistaken for a pedlar or a tramp. Incidents of this kind flatter him for he congratulates himself upon 'enjoying the advantage to an unusual extent' of being 'the humblest, cheapest, least dignified man in the village'. He is not, he says, 'above being used, aye abused, sometimes'. He walks with long strides, fists clenched, and eyes apparently set on the ground but missing nothing that lives or grows in earth, air, or water. He dresses plainly and is not afraid of an old suit which has been worn long enough to become part of him. Anything dandiacal fills him with contempt. 'What I am must make you forget what I wear,' he says, 'the fashionable world is content to be eclipsed by its dress, and never will bear the contrast.'

2

Like Whitman, he can work at several trades; but unlike him, he believes in renunciation rather than acceptance, in solitude rather than concourse. 'He was bred to no profession; he never married; he lived alone, he never went to church; he never voted; he refused to pay a tax to the State; he ate no flesh, he drank no wine, he never knew the use of tobacco; and, though a naturalist, he used neither trap nor gun.' But these renunciations were not immediately inspired by any fear of living. On the contrary, their origin was a desire for more rather than less life, and although he compares himself with Zeno, the Stoic, who stood, he thought, in precisely the same relation to the world, his approach to life, in spite of all his austerities, is sensuous and epicurean. His renunciations resemble a cleansing of the palate in anticipation of a more delicate repast.

This is revealed throughout his writings, but nowhere so eloquently as where he strives to express his relations with nature. 'Can it be called a morning if our senses are not clarified so that we perceive more clearly?' In order to taste fully the exquisite flavour of life a superlative cleanliness is necessary. 'I should be as clean as ye, O woods, I shall not rest till I am as innocent as you.' This is renunciation with a difference. Thoreau's return to Nature is not in response to any 'call of the wild', it is medicinal and hygienic. He does not expect Americans to 'go native' but the native Indians to become civilized. When he is shown a primitive Indian pestle which has been found near Concord, he is interested in the archaic carving of the knob, and sets design above convenience. 'It is a great step to find a pestle whose handle is ornamented with a bird's-head knob,' because 'it brings the maker still nearer to the races which so ornament their umbrellas and cane-handles'. It implies thoughts and fancies such as he has, and is therefore a step towards redemption from 'the savage state' and 'enough of it might have saved' the Indians from extermination. That passage throws light on Thoreau's experimental philosophy, suggesting that his aim is more civilization, not less.

He rarely wanders far from the coteries of Concord, and he begins to imbibe humane ideas when a boy in his own home. His father is a pencil-maker of liberal views; his mother, an Abolitionist, and the Thoreau household a sanctuary for fugitive slaves. Such an environment might have done no more than turn the future philosopher and conscientious objector into a professional agitator. As it is he is not to be intimidated by threat of imprisonment. Such a man needs no persuasion to support the movement for slave emancipation, in which he exercises pluck as well as eloquence. This is proved when he becomes the sole public defender of John Brown the hero of Harper's Ferry. But such generous adventures are no more than prentice work, for if Thoreau stands for anything it is for the notion that revolutions should begin at home. He is not one to believe only in 'Freedom's cause as fur away as Paris is'.

3

There are other influences at work, in these early days the most irresistible of them is Emerson. He reads Emerson, meets Emerson, becomes Emerson's protégé, friend and domestic familiar. When little more than a youth he is admitted into the austere circle of plain livers and high thinkers who have made the small town of Concord the Athens of New England with Emerson as chief sage. He is classed with the Transcendentalists, and becomes acquainted with the leading figures of that group: Nathaniel Hawthorne, Margaret Fuller, Ellery Channing, and the Alcotts, but is intimate only with Emerson, Channing, and Bronson Alcott.

To the people of Concord he is a freak, and the intellectuals, except Emerson, are not certain whether he is a genius or a poseur. Ellery Channing is 'inclined to quiz him for his eccentricities: You are the same old sixpence you used to be, rather rusty, but a genuine piece?'

It must not be imagined that Thoreau is a mere imitator of Emerson, still less an uncritical disciple, although he is twenty years younger and might have sat at Emerson's feet without loss of poise. If he is a disciple at all it is more by affinity than conviction. Without Emerson he might have been no more than a local character, but it is Emerson who pulls the trigger which fires Thoreau's genius. 'I am very familiar with all his thoughts,—they are my own quite originally drest', says Emerson, in the early days of the friendship; but later the older sage goes as near as so proud an intellectual can towards admitting that there has been an interaction of influence, a natural give and take, and although they never lose respect for one another's ideas, they do not deny themselves the right of occasional disapproval. Many of Thoreau's sayings, such as 'we want great peasants more than great heroes', suggest that he is not docile before the master, and Emerson, who is not always a sound literary critic, shows jealousy when he classes Thoreau with Ellery Channing and Hawthorne as being superior to their writings.

The relation is never entirely literary or intellectual, and on one occasion Thoreau is able to serve Emerson by helping to restore his faith in himself when shaken by bereavements and depressed by public misunderstanding and neglect. He comes into Emerson's life at a period of crisis. Intermittent mental distress has been aggravated by the death of a favourite brother. The place of that brother Thoreau helps to fill at a moment when such a service is most needed. Emerson needs at all times the support of intimate friendships to shield him when life seems too hard, and to give eyes to those blind spots of which he is reluctantly conscious. Thus in his journal he records how his brother Charles saw nature for him and helped him to see, a service Thoreau ultimately performs for him or rather tries to teach him to perform for himself. The relationship recalls that of Dorothy to William Wordsworth. Emerson recognizes this influence and is disturbed by it. But, as in the case of Dorothy Wordsworth and her brother, Thoreau's influence is beneficent, for he helps the transcendentalist to earth without reducing his powers of flight. 'Thoreau', Emerson confesses, 'gives me, in flesh and blood and pertinacious Saxon belief, my own ethics. He is far more real, and daily practically obeying them, than I, and fortifies my memory at all times with an affirmative experience which refuses to be set aside.' One difference between them is that of practitioner and theorist. 'My brave Henry', Emerson remarks, perhaps wistfully, 'is content to live now and feels no shame in not studying any profession, for he does not postpone his life but lives already.'

4

Originality is largely expression and this faculty Thoreau possesses. He browses on the notions of the Concord circle, and rummages, like the rest of them, among the ideas and ideals of Europe and the then little-known East, turning what he finds, either directly or indirectly, into a style of his own. Emerson would not have accepted such an achievement as the final criterion of originality. He demands novelty of idea, but is ready to admit that his own ideas as well as those of his friend are part of the intellectual currency of the time.

Thoreau has not thrown any new ideas into circulation; on the contrary the Concord idea which Emerson thinks most original, the law of reciprocity and compensation, is, he admits, common to himself, Alcott, and Thoreau; and he thinks it odd that 'these three Gothamites' should be neighbours. It is safe to say, however, that Thoreau, the sensitive observer of nature, gives Emerson eyes where hitherto there has been little but mind. He even sets him, together with Ellery Channing, observing and recording the common objects of the countryside in the Thoreau manner. He may indeed, as he whimsically suggests, have started a fashion of outward observation, but such observations of nature as have come down to us from Emerson and Channing have none of the sharpness which Thoreau brings to his mission as inspector of natural affairs.

5

No writer lived more for the moment. His words even at their most poetic are rarely the result of the process described by Wordsworth as 'emotion recollected in tranquillity'. The impressions and observations of nature were written down on the spot and posted up in his journals from day to day. And when he came to turn his notes into books, which was always his intention, he did little more than organize them. There is no evidence of re-adjustment of impression or opinion in the perspective of memory. His idealizations also were so instantaneous, that he probably thought emotion or imagination played no part in them. Yet he believes that 'nothing remarkable was ever accomplished in a prosaic mood', and there is a passage in his *Journal* which suggests that he felt that this direct method was contrary to accepted theory, as, indeed, it was. He wonders why what is 'actually present is commonly perceived by the common sense and understanding only', and is therefore 'bare and bald, without halo, or the blue enamel of the intervening air'. What is past or to come is idealized. 'The imagination', he concludes, 'needs a long range. It is the faculty of the poet to see present things as if in this sense past and future, as if distant or universally significant. . . . We believe in spirits, we believe in beauty, but not now and here. They have their abode in the remote past, or in the future.' This purely romantic conception of poetry was never logically practised by Thoreau. He is the least romantic of the writers examined in this book, and for that reason is less remote from modern thought.

At the same time he has no intention of making scientific or literal records of what he observes. 'I would fain set down something besides facts. . . . I would so state facts that they shall be significant, shall be myths or mythologic, facts which the mind perceived, thoughts which the body thought,' and then as if his conscience is not quite clear, he pulls round to the romantic again: 'I cherish vague and misty forms, vaguest when the cloud at which I gaze is dissipated quite, and naught but the skyey depths are seen.' It is fortunate for his art that he avoided these cherished misty forms and that what he calls his 'falsehoods to the common sense' retained a concrete excellence without becoming crude facts.

Thoreau's weakness is that he cannot trust his more concrete concepts or even his own abundant common sense. He feels a need to idealize and intellectualize, and in doing so he is in danger of missing the life he so diligently seeks. The curious thing is that he knows idealism leads inevitably to disappointment—but he persuades himself that it is the real not the ideal which lets him down. 'What right have I to grieve, who have not ceased to wonder?' he asks a married lady for whom he seems to have had a romantic but platonic affection. His friends rarely live up to his illusion of them, so he tries to remember them only as ideals. But it is not so with nature, the nearer he comes 'to an actual and joyful intercourse with her', like a welcome guest, the more content he is. But much as he desires to realize rather than idealize his relations with nature, he has moments when he mistrusts himself, for 'the same must be true of Nature and of man: our ideal is the only real'. The finite and temporal leave him with an 'unsatisfied yearning.' That yearning is relieved by an association with nature which in the last resort is mystical. He wants to escape from himself, to merge his restless self-consciousness in that of the growing and moving things which are the real companions of his rambles.

6

Thoreau is a field-naturalist and a philosopher rather than a scientist, belonging to the curious and fascinating tribe of John Burroughs and W. H. Hudson, not to that of Agassiz or Darwin. Nature is not for him the raw material of research but a means of getting nearer to life, and of finding inspiration for a fuller and better life. At the same time his knowledge of the local wild-life is remarkable. 'He knew the country like a fox or bird,' says Emerson, 'and passed through it as freely by paths of his own. He knew every track in the snow or on the ground, and what creature had taken this path before him.' Wild creatures know and trust him: 'Snakes coiled round his leg; the fishes swam into his hand, and he took them out of the water; he pulled the woodchuck out of its hole by the tail and took the foxes under his protection from the hunters.' Thoreau might have sat to George Meredith for the picture of Melampus:

> *For him the woods were a home and gave him the key*
> *Of knowledge, thirst for their treasures in herbs and flowers*
> *The secrets held by the creatures nearer than we*
> *To earth he sought, and the link of their life with ours.*

He is a nature-liver as well as a nature-lover: a cultured man trying to shed his culture for something nearer the bone of life, an ideal wildness, 'a nature which I cannot put my foot through . . . a New Hampshire everlasting and unfallen'. Yet he is neither a mere enthusiast of nature-study nor a propagandist of the return to nature. Those who follow him even as observers are moved by a desire to imitate rather than from conviction. Emerson and Channing doubtless gain something from closer observation of natural sights and sounds, even though they only see what Thoreau saw, never anything for the first time, as he did. Bird-watching is for them a recreation, for him a communion. He is not in pursuit of nature but in flight from civilization, and his books are written to encourage himself in the enterprise. His desire is to 'get away from men' who 'very rarely affect' him as 'grand or beautiful', enough that there is a 'sunrise and sunset every day'. Emerson and Whitman, on the other hand, are gregarious. They have no fundamental complaint against mankind, and never doubt that preaching and progress will ultimately improve the quality of the race so that eventually there will be no need to run away from it.

Thoreau's philosophy, like his life, is more direct than that of Emerson. If Emerson is a scholar bourgeois, Thoreau is a scholar gipsy. He is influenced by the more sophisticated of the Emersonian formulae, but he is more realistic than the Master, less inclined to be satisfied with a theory, and, in the end, his philosophy seems to be a criticism of Emerson. The vice of the intellectual is inaction, which Thoreau fears and condemns and Emerson fears and condones. The difference is summed up in a famous interrogatory when Emerson visits Thoreau, who is in prison for refusing to pay a tax which went to support slavery. Emerson calls at the prison. 'Henry, why are you here?' he asks. Thoreau replies, 'Why are you *not* here?'[1] Thoreau practises where Emerson preaches and it is for that reason that we turn to him for a conception of individual action.

7

Thoreau is the complete individualist. 'When will the world learn that a million men are of no importance compared with one man.' He thinks that the sight of 'herds of men' has a 'very bad influence on children'. Carlyle would put and keep the masses in their place because he fears

---

[1] 'Under a government which imprisons any injustly, the true place of a just man is also a prison.' Thoreau, 'Civil Disobedience'.

them. Thoreau does not fear the masses, he disdains them. He is repelled by intimacies, they offend his sense of chastity, and the intimacies of the herd disgust him. 'The gregariousness of men is their most contemptible and discouraging aspect.' In 'Civil Disobedience' he repudiates all democratic claims, and he does not scruple to attribute his belief to God —as both Carlyle and Emerson are fond of doing. 'God', he announces, 'does not sympathize with the popular movements.' He denies the existence of virtue in the actions of masses of men. 'What man calls social virtues, good fellowship, is commonly the virtue of pigs in a litter which lie close together to keep each other warm. It brings men together in crowds and mobs in bar-rooms and elsewhere, but it does not deserve the name of virtue.' He has no sympathy with the various ideas of Socialism which are becoming current, and suspects 'any enterprise in which two are engaged together'. Even his neighbours in the mass are 'barbarians with their committees and gregariousness'.

It is obvious that Thoreau is not a democrat, neither is he a supporter of autocracy. His philosophy, in so far as it has any doctrinal form, resembles the anarchism of Bakunin or of Tolstoy. Pushed to its logical conclusion that philosophy means doing what you want to do, come what may, holding yourself indifferently towards everything that obtrudes between you and your desires, whether you call them intuitions, ideals, or instincts. Thoreau is most himself when furthest from the morality which he believes is paralysing the society into which he was thrown by accident of birth. Freedom is the right and the will to choose your own lot, and choice is inadequate unless guided by desire. Good resolutions even about writing are not to be encouraged. You must discipline yourself to yield only to love. 'Suffer yourself to be attracted.' His pose is amoral. 'Strictly speaking,' he says, 'morality is not healthy. The undeserved joys which come uncalled, and make us more pleased than grateful, are they that sing.'

His method would eliminate from life all but what is characteristic of and essential to the individual. For that reason

Thoreau has been welcomed as the revivalist of the Simple Life. But such simplicity is relative and packed with implications which might dishearten the professional simplifier, and fill the luxurious with consternation. The easy way has no attractions for Thoreau. He is convinced that luxury, not simplicity, is the line of least resistance. Luxury is shallow and common, simplicity is as profound as it is rare, and anything like an advantage is a disadvantage.

8

He is as sincere as Emerson and as profound, but he has not always been credited with these qualities in equal degree, because he is less patient. He is inclined to snap at fools and his rebukes are rarely gloved. And since he has a keen eye for character, lights his wisdom with humour, and reprieves his sentences from solemnity by surprising contexts and antitheses, his sincerity is sometimes questioned. He is a witty Stoic: Marcus Aurelius with a sense of humour. And if he never allows that dangerous sense to laugh him into stupidity or indifference, he escapes the charge of frivolity from those numerous people who find it difficult to associate seriousness with laughter, but towards the end of his life he doubts his own 'levity' and tries to remove the more humorous passages from his essays. His humour, however, is not of the popular sort. Jokes are not in his line and he will tolerate none of those familiar quips about sex which are as ancient as mankind. 'We do not respect the mind that can jest on this subject', he says, in the manner of Queen Victoria or Mr. Gladstone. Yet he can be merry enough on occasion, although his remarks rarely evoke more than a smile. He lacks Emerson's cleverness and his prose does not dazzle one out of judgment. It has a quieter glow relieved by sly or pert paradox and flash of wit, recalling the puckish technique of Samuel Butler. His masterpieces are sentences or at best paragraphs and, whether aphoristic or descriptive, the best of them have a gem-like perfection. In this lapidary excellence he achieves his aim which is to write sentences as 'durable as a Roman aqueduct', sentences which 'suggest far more than they say'.

9

His method of interpreting life is such that one is not so much dominated by his personality as put into closer relation with one's own, which is Thoreau's intention. He is a touchstone by which you may test your own metal, as he tests his. He is inclined to repudiate any tendency to proselytize, and even goes so far as to emphasize this distaste by disclaiming any power to influence others. 'I could', he says, 'tame a hyena more easily than my friend.' Few of the readers of *Walden* want to become hermits, but it is conceivable that after sauntering beside the pond with so wise a companion you may want to embark on the most romantic of all adventures—the discovery of yourself. Thoreau does not promise to be your guide. His idea of a man is one who 'takes his own way, or stands still in his own place'; and standing still often suffices. But whether you stand still or move on you must find your own way, and live your own life. All he can do, and grumble as he may, all he wishes to do, is to indicate a path by telling you about his method of living and his own ideas of life.

He demands a margin to his days, and endeavours to reduce drudgery to a minimum by simplifying social equipment and possessions. He strives to revert to a more primitive state, but this effort, which he likes to advertise, must not be exaggerated, any more than we should exaggerate his amoral poses. It is not so much a case of atavism as a process

of the art of living, with a protesting glance at those who
are inclined to depend overmuch upon material encumbrances. Thoreau throws back to step forward, but he is not
averse from a little admonitory boasting. He is proud of his
ability to do without those goods and chattels which are
supposed to be necessities, because he believes he is more and
not less civilized without them. And, finally, these abnega-
tions are not for bravado or for morality so much as for
proficiency. He sheds possessions as an athlete strips for the
contest. Life is short, shorter for him even than he imagined,
there is much to be observed, thought, experienced, and
nothing eradicable must be allowed to stand in his way—not
even himself: 'as long as a man stands in his own way, everything seems to be in his way.'

I O

He poses also as an idler before those who set material
pursuits above spiritual. But his records convict him
both of inexhaustible powers of application and faith in effort
as 'the prerogative of virtue'. There is, nevertheless, something of the odd-job man in his bones. 'I have as many trades
as fingers', he brags; and well he may for besides being a
tutor, author, and lecturer, he was at different times a pencil-
maker, a surveyor, a carpenter, a gardener, and it is on record
that he once, like Tom Sawyer, turned an honest penny by
whitewashing a fence. He can be useful at household tasks,
and has some skill even as an amateur mechanic, and he is
always willing to do a little gardening, or to look after the
family pets, or to entertain his circle with conversation, or a
song, or a tune on the flute, an instrument he mastered early
and played well. His objection is to routine, not to work: to
'all who are engaged in any routine . . . the whole earth is a
treadmill'. He knows precisely where he stands and has

stated his real business very clearly. He is determined not to waste his time earning a living. 'Better go without your dinner than be everlasting fishing for it like a cormorant.' Yet he works hard at his chosen job. 'For many years', he says, 'I was self-appointed inspector of snowstorms and rainstorms, and did my duty faithfully; surveyor, if not of highways, then of forest paths and all across-lot routes, keeping them open, and ravines bridged and passable at all seasons, where the public heel has testified to their utility.' The country-side is a possession and a trust: 'Almost, I believe the Concord would not rise and overflow its banks again, were I not here.'

He is not, like Walt Whitman, an inspired loafer, though Emerson calls him 'the only man of leisure in the Town'; and so he is but not through idleness. He buys his leisure with labour dredged of its superfluities. This excellent economics is summed up in a typical paradox: 'I have been maintaining myself entirely by manual labour', and 'this toil has occupied so few days,—perhaps a single month, spring and fall each,—so that I must have had more leisure than any of my brethren for study and literature'. Moreover he is convinced that working as a labourer is the best way of earning a living.

Work, however, and here he differs from Carlyle and the more conventional moralists, is not an end in itself, nor merely good for one. 'It is not enough to be industrious; so are the ants.' He enjoys only self-imposed jobs. It is 'more amusing' to collect his own firewood, to carry it on his own back from his boat on the river and to chop it himself rather than to buy it. 'Each stick I deal with has a history, and I read it as I am handling it, and last of all, I remember my adventures in getting it, while it is burning in the winter evening. . . . Thus one half the value of my wood is enjoyed before it is housed. . . .' And so he resolves other reputed drudgeries to his own delight: 'I enjoy more, drinking water at a clear spring, than out of a goblet at a gentleman's table. I like best the bread which I have baked, the garment which I have made, the shelter I have constructed, the fuel I have gathered.'

He likes also to sit and stare. There are days when idleness is 'the most attractive and productive industry', and others when he feels that he would be 'content to sit at the back-door . . . under the poplar trees, henceforth forever'. If, therefore, he repudiates business as 'a negation of life' he himself is ever busy. He is always on the move, poking his nose into the affairs of all manner of wild creatures and growing things, yet rarely wandering far from his base. He has in fact, as he knows, 'a real genius for staying at home'. New England is the universe, Concord its centre, and, 'what a fool he must be who thinks that his El Dorado is anywhere but where he lives'. Compared with him Emerson is a citizen of the world both in thought and habit.

I I

He is also an open-air man by preference and on principle. 'We must go out and re-ally ourselves to Nature every day. We must make root, send out some little fibre at least even every winter day. I am sensible that I am imbibing health when I open my mouth to the wind. Staying in the house breeds a sort of insanity always.' He walks in all weathers and at all hours of the day or night; rows on the Concord River in summer and skates on it in winter. He is adept at such exercises, but they are not sports, they are the means by which he indulges the perpetual exploration which for him is life. His curiosity never sleeps. 'No method nor discipline can supersede the necessity of being forever on the alert.' He likes to imagine that his predilection for nature is a sort of animal atonement, and his happiness 'is a good deal like that of the woodchucks', and like many animals he enjoys being out in the dark.

He is proud and austere but that does not destroy his sympathy, any more than his self-sufficiency, hard though it can be, prevents him from showing the utmost consideration for the concerns and feelings of wild creatures. 'He neither killed nor imprisoned any animal,' says Channing, 'unless driven by acute needs.' He will not even injure a plant unnecessarily. Observation takes the place of hunting, binoculars and microscopes, of traps and guns. Once he 'brought home a flying squirrel to study its mode of flight', but after he had satisfied his curiosity he carried it back to the wood again. One winter's day he finds a caterpillar frozen and 'rolled up into a ball like a woodchuck', and thaws it by placing it in his hat. On another occasion he enforces an armistice between two quarrelling woodchucks by pulling one of them out of its burrow by the tail and preventing it with his foot from returning to the charge. Yet his innate kindness to animals is never sentimental and rarely even squeamish. The ruthlessness of nature has its place. His attitude is protective. The threatened extermination of a species arouses him to anger. He has the utmost contempt for those neighbours who would kill the last surviving pair of hen-hawks to save a few chickens! 'Such economy', he says, 'is narrow and grovelling.' He would rather 'never taste chicken's meat nor hens' eggs than never to see a hawk sailing through the upper air'.

12

His desire is to be on friendly terms with animals. They are very much his fellow creatures and he is never so complimented as when they recognize it by some show of confidence. Mice eat from his hand, sparrows perch on his shoulders, and he makes a pet of a mole. All his energy, his eternal rambling, in all weathers and at all hours, is a quest for animal contacts and confidences. The scientific naturalist conducts research, Thoreau pays visits. He goes out at three o'clock in the morning to observe the lilies opening, but he is only interested in natural phenomena as the expression of life in relation to himself. He has nothing but contempt for material possessions, but sets a high value upon the commonplaces of nature. 'We are rained and snowed on with gems', he says. He is the devotee of flowers and notes them tenderly in their moments of beauty and of ugliness. *Smilex herbacea* may smell 'exactly like a dead rat in a wall', but it has its place no less than his favourite wild rose 'glancing half-concealed from its own green bowers', with a 'noble and delicate civility about it, not wildness'. He believes that 'the man is blessed who every day is permitted to behold anything so pure and serene as the western sky at sunset, while revolutions vex the world'. He is under no illusions about his methods or his objects, and believes that he is acting socially when he visits flowers and fishes, birds' nests, and rat holes. The fishes in Concord River honour him with their trust. The birds are his musical performers and he would rather hear an owl hooting 'than the most eloquent man of the age'. He opens up communications with bream and pout as well as with water-rat, bull-frog, and turtle, and he shows the same interest in their domestic affairs, in the spawn, eggs, or young, as a village gossip in the season's crop of babies.

13

Deeply imbued with the spirit of discipline, he inclines towards the austerities, takes the hard path, flagellates himself with difficulties. 'Thunder and lightening are remarkable accompaniments to our life, as if', he adds, 'to remind us that there is or should be a kind of battle raging.' Both he and Emerson are enamoured of Carlyle's love of duty, but

Thoreau gives the idea a new and characteristic turn. It
suffices Carlyle and Emerson that you do the duty which lies
nearest; Thoreau, on the other hand, adds difficulty to the
task. Effort is the 'virtuous soul's relaxation'. You must not
only follow the Emersonian gleam of genius, plus the Carlylean dutiful behaviour, you must 'do the things which lie
nearest to you, but which are difficult to do'. Cold and solitude are his friends and he comes to his 'solitary woodland
walk as the homesick go home'. Like Emerson, he has to
fight low spirits. The best way to keep your spirits up is to
'take long walks in stormy weather, or through deep snows.
Deal with brute nature. Be cold and hungry and weary.'
Emerson likes calm weather and sunshine, Thoreau any
weather that kicks and bites, and he prefers a nation of 'snow-
men' to one of 'fair-weather men', just as he prefers sour
fruits, acid flavours, and the coarser smells, as the 'strong,
rank scent of ferns', and his favourite music is the crowing
of cocks and the whistling of wind through telegraph wires.
    He flouts niceness and preciosity, especially in feeding.
Asked at table which dish he preferred, he replies, 'the nearest!' He enjoys the harsh flavours of wild berries, and the
acrid taste of acorns, and once confesses that he 'could eat a
fried rat with relish'. The cushioned life and the garden
enclosed are anathema. 'It is better to warm ourselves with
ice than with fire.' Exhortations to Spartan living are commonplaces in his essays and journals. He never wearies of
ringing the changes upon the theme that 'that aim in life is
highest which requires the highest and finest discipline'.
And although he means what he says there is something
deeper than advocacy in these passages. Thoreau is spartan-
izing himself, but not for love of hardness. He is protecting
a delicate physique and a sensitive mind from the perils and
affronts of the outer world. He is so tender-hearted that he
cannot face the world without a coat of mail, so he disciplines
himself with hardship and fastidiousness. He craves sympathy and is saddened by unsympathetic persons, so disapproves of sympathy: 'look at our literature what a poor, puny,

social thing, seeking sympathy.' Yet though he specializes
in resisting the overtures of civilization, his refusals are not
fantastic. He is on occasion both prig and poseur, but he is
genuinely out to live his own life and to exalt it above its
common level, believing that to be the best way of adding to
the common lot.

He minds his own business in an interfering world and
among a nation of busybodies. 'What a foul subject is this
doing good; instead of minding one's own life, which should
be his business . . . instead of taking care to flourish, and smell
and taste sweet, and refresh all mankind to the extent of our
capacity and quality.' That is the quintessence of him. You
may search all through his writings and sift all his axioms
and you will find no more concise statement of what he
means.

The doctrine is propagated mainly by personal example.
His books are not sermons so much as comments on his own
experiments in spartan living. The bulk of them are diaries
and letters, the remainder organized extracts from his
diaries. This is no accident, neither is it the result of literary
frustration. He desires to become known to himself, and
ultimately has as much fame as he needs. The method is
natural to him and becomes deliberate. He consciously sets
down 'choice experiences' that his 'own writings' may inspire him, and at last he 'may make wholes of parts'. The
contemplation alone of 'the unfinished picture may suggest
its harmonious completion'. Further 'each thought that is
welcomed and recorded is a nest-egg by the side of which
more will be laid', and although he pretends that his journals
are a stock-pot for future enterprises, the raw material of
essays, he knows also that they are finally an extension of
himself and sufficient in themselves, ever growing and depending for their charm upon 'a certain greenness and not
in maturity'. His notebooks are always with him. He posts
them up on the spot, in his boat, under trees whilst 'nooning'
in rain or frost, and even by the light of the moon. No man
ever got more fun out of note-making. 'My thoughts are my

company,' he writes, 'they have a certain individuality and separate existence, aye, personality.' So although he publishes a book or so and a few essays in periodicals he remains an amateur.

14

His trade is living: he has no time for anything else. 'Life is so short that it is not wise to take roundabout ways, nor can be spent much time in waiting.' His love of solitude is not misanthropic but a condition of his vital economy. 'Society or encounter' may 'yield a fruit', but he cannot help feeling that he 'should have spent those hours more profitably alone'. When friends invite themselves to go with him on one of his interminable walks, he hesitates, there is nothing so important to him as his walk; he has 'no walks to throw away on company'. But he does not always object to company even on his rambles, in fact, he prefers to take his friends for a walk than to entertain them indoors where they are a waste of valuable time: 'In the midst of the most glorious Indian summer afternoon, there they sit, breaking your chairs and wearing out the house, with their backs to the light, taking no note of the lapse of time.'

On the same principle he writes little and talks little, meaning 'always to spend only words enough to purchase silence with'. Silence and solitude are his subterfuges for prolonging time. Even his limited career as a lecturer, which might have added to his small means, is curtailed. He cannot afford to be telling his experiences to people who might take no interest in them. 'Whatever succeeds with an audience', he says, is 'bad'. His real business is 'getting experience', and as for the 'lecture-goers', what he thinks is none of their business—doubtless an oblique hit at Emerson and his highbrow audiences. He eventually becomes a lecturer, so must have modified his opinion which at one time goes so far as to look upon lecturing as 'impertinent and unprofitable'. He has never chanced to meet any man 'so cheering and elevating and encouraging, so infinitely suggestive as the stillness and solitude of the Well Meadow Field'. And when men think him odd and perverse because he does not 'prefer their society to this Nymph or Wood God' his reply is that he has tried them and they did not inspire him. He has even gone so far as to sit down with a dozen of them in a club with no success. He demands of his companion not that he can tell a good story, but that he can 'keep a good silence'.

15

Yet, in spite of his austerity, this grumpy philosopher, who thrives best on solitude, and who finds that companions depreciate the value of his time, is no curmudgeon at heart, except to the pretentious. At the same time he is always unapproachable even to his intimates. Only the creatures of the woods dare risk familiarity with Henry Thoreau. A chipmunk has no fear of nestling in his hand, but Emerson would no more take his arm than he would think of taking the arm of an elm-tree; and he makes the significant confession that he loves Thoreau, but 'cannot like him'. Friendship between the two philosophers tends to cool off into regard, and there are indications of incompatibility. Nathaniel Hawthorne records that 'Mr. Emerson appears to have suffered some inconveniency from his experience of Mr. Thoreau as an inmate'; and, he adds, that 'it may well be that such a sturdy and uncompromising person is fitter to meet occasionally in the open air, than to have as a permanent guest at table and fireside'. Emerson is doubtless troubled also by his young friend's intellectual audacity. He loves him as Wordsworth loved Charles Lamb, but is always a little

shocked by the humorous irreverence which Thoreau shares
with Lamb, though otherwise so little alike. There is more
than a suspicion not only that Thoreau enjoys a little 'leg-
pulling', that he even goes so far as to pull the august leg of
the Sage of Concord. He may have been tempted to do so as a
sly protest against Emerson's Olympian pose. His fire-
works are all squibs, and he 'will come as near to lying as you
can drive a coach and four'. Emerson cannot fail to observe
this contrariness but may not have entirely divined its cause
although his suspicions must have been aroused as he compares Thoreau in conversation to a boy who 'from universal
snow lying on the earth, gathers up a little in his hand, rolls
it into a ball, and flings it at me'. He realizes, however, that
although his friend is 'stubborn and implacable' he is always
'manly and wise' if 'rarely sweet'. Thoreau needs an antagonist. He 'wants a fallacy to expose, a blunder to pillory, requires a little sense of victory, a roll of the drums, to call his
powers into full existence'. This is all very admirable, but
Emerson has reached the age when men of Olympian tem-
perament prefer disciples to critics.

Apart from his quixotism, Thoreau loves an intellectual
set-to for its own sake, and, at times, reveals a grammarian's
liking for nice shades and subtle meanings. It would have
surprised him to be told that he was something of a pedant,
yet we must remember that he is a scholar as well as a saun-
terer and odd-job man. He is not only a student of Eastern literature, but well-read in the classics, especially Greek,
and in English poetry. In one of his poses he seems to resent
these learned experiences, but cannot escape from them.[1]
He is a bookman in spite of himself, even when he tries to
go native; but he never really succeeds in slipping his
Harvard cables.

Thoreau's cussedness smells of midnight oil and the 'cam-
pus'. It is blood-brother and a forerunner of that art of
shocking the middle classes which was the signature of a cult

[1] 'Scholars are wont to sell their birthright for a mess of learning.' *A Week
on the Concord*, 81.

in the eighteen nineties, whose chief demonstrators were Oscar Wilde and Bernard Shaw.[1] Emerson notes and suspects it early in their friendship. It is first 'the old fault of unlimited contradiction', and then an easy rhetorical trick consisting of the substitution for 'the obvious word and thought its diametrical antagonist'. Thus Thoreau 'praises wild mountains and winter forests for their domestic air; snow and ice for their warmth; villagers and wood-choppers for their urbanity, and the wilderness for resembling Rome and Paris.' But however much Emerson may doubt the wisdom of this love of advertising ideas and images by spotlighting them with unusual adjectives or startling contexts, he believes that the instinct to controvert a proposition at sight is finally due to impatience of the limitations of contemporary thought. Excuses, however, are no longer necessary. Thoreau has made up his mind to be what he is, and he sticks to his guns. 'If I am not I,' he asks, 'who am I?' It is easier now to understand him as we see him in perspective and to realize that the idiosyncrasies which disturb Emerson are as earnest as even that sedate mentor could have wished. Time has ripened Thoreau as wine is ripened, and even his paradoxes, designed as many of them were to disturb local smugness, have a vintage mellowness, and he startles us only as we are startled by the familiar and recurrent aspects of the Nature he loved and courted.

16

The year 1845 ought to be remembered in the history of the United States of America, for it was then that

---

[1] His studied indifference to personal appearance may have been a craving for distinction, like Wilde's velvet breeches and Shaw's Jaeger suit. But at Harvard he tried the opposite method of being different, wearing a green coat 'because the authorities required black'. Marston Watson Qt. Sanborn, *Familiar Letters of Thoreau* (1894), 364.

Henry Thoreau, aged twenty-eight years, began his experimental renunciation of the conveniences of civilization. The decision to take the step which produced one of the most fascinating books in the English language and a classic of American literature, answered a challenge from Ellery Channing. Amiably irritated by so much talk of being oneself and living on oneself, this candid friend advises the grumbling philosopher to prove his worth by breaking away from society and eating himself up, for he prophesies, 'you will eat nobody else, nor anything else'. Under this spur, the experiment begins, and Thoreau moves 'confidently in the direction of his dreams'. The dreamland is the wood by Walden Pond within walking distance of Concord, and there he lives for two years in a hut which he has had the satisfaction of building for himself from timber felled by himself with a borrowed axe which he returns to its owner 'sharper than he received it'.

The experiment in hermitage is a demonstration of self-sufficiency. Thoreau has no illusions about it, he knows what he is doing. He has more than the usual stock of common-sense, and he never tricks himself into believing that he is to be taken literally. That he had been thinking of some such experiment for years, proves that it is necessary to his salvation. 'I want to go soon and live away by the pond where I shall hear only the wind whispering among the reeds.' He writes in his journal in 1841: 'It will be a success if I shall have left myself behind.' This resistance of himself is coincident with his self-curiosity. Some three years before the Walden adventure he laments that he has been living too near himself. 'I have tripped myself up,' he writes, 'so that there is no progress for my own narrowness.' Such nearness seems almost profane. 'I cannot walk conveniently and pleasantly but when I hold myself far off in the horizon, and when the soul dilutes the body and makes it passable. My soul and body have tottered along together . . . tripping and hindering one another, like unpractical Siamese twins. The two should walk as one that no obstacle may be nearer than the firmament.'

His retreat is thus an escape, as much from himself as from the world. Individualist though he is he shudders a little at his individuality: 'I am under the awful necessity to be what I am.' And yet not even nature interests him so much as himself. Nothing is so 'unfamiliar and startling' to him as his own thoughts. 'I never waited but for myself to come round', he says, and he is convinced that the 'secret charm of Nature's demeanour towards us' is 'strict conscientiousness, and disregard of us when we have ceased to have regard for ourselves'. The interplay of his thought is always from and to nature: himself apropos of nature and nature apropos of himself. But nature has the last word, for he may get tired of himself, but never of her. He believes that his happiness is a good deal like that of the woodchuck.

17

Probably he knows instinctively that his reaching after the 'tonic wildness of Nature' is partially inspired by his own physical weakness. For the valiant spirit of Thoreau has to endure imprisonment in a consumptive body. When he says that to be well you must 'see that you are attuned to each mood of nature',[1] he is thinking of his own need for physical fitness. Modern science would now admit that his desire for the fields and woods was sound. Again the experiment, in spite of its divorce from comfortable habits, is not divorced from the only sort of social life which appeals to him. It is staged before the intelligentsia of Concord, whose inquisitiveness threatens to wreck the whole business. He is plagued by a procession of visitors, and at one time there are

---

[1] *Journal: Autumn*, 441. The idea of health appears throughout his works in a large variety of contexts. Thus, 'Sympathy with nature is an evidence of perfect health.' Ib., 296. 'To speak or do anything for mankind, one must speak and act as if well, or from that grain of health which he has left.' *Familiar Letters* (1894), 141. 'Poetry is nothing but healthy speech', Ib., 350.

as many as 'twenty-five souls, with their bodies, at once' under his roof. In Channing's irreverent words 'the little Yankee squatting by Walden Pond', becomes one of the sights of Concord. Thoreau's irritation is not very deep for, after all, he is no more than a temporary and partial hermit. He seeks no moody solitude, but a life without material impedimenta with a wider margin between himself and his kind, for 'individuals, like nations, must have suitable bread and natural boundaries, even a considerable neutral ground, between them'. He is neither a misanthrope nor an anchorite and is not above considering the risks of loneliness. These he soon learns are unnecessarily reduced during the day by visitors and domestic duties; and at night he consoles himself with the companionable thought that 'our planet is in the Milky Way'.

18

The centre of his philosophic system is a desire to meet life without encumbrances, seeking no other reward than an inward enrichment, which those who live sheltered lives rarely acquire. This desire quickens also his suspicion of conformity and finally prompts him to leave the woods, as he truly says, for as good a reason as he went to them. 'I had not lived there a week before my feet wore a path from my door to the pond side; and though it is five or six years since I trod it, it is still quite distinct. It is true, I fear, that others may have fallen into, and so helped to keep it open. The surface of the earth is soft, and impressible by the feet of men; and so the paths which the mind travels. How worn and dusty, then, must be the highways of the world—how deep the ruts of tradition and conformity! I did not wish to make a cabin passage, but rather to go before the mast and on the deck of the world, for there I could best see the moonlight amid the mountains. I do not wish to go below now.'

19

The experiment is a natural stage in a life which is a continuous experiment in the art of living. His method is always tentative; he does not seek finality or repose. The Promised Land is not at the end of his journey, but in every step of the pilgrimage, for Thoreau being a romantic, looks beyond and courts surprise. Yet he never loses his affection for Walden. He lives there only for two years, but keeps an eye on it at all seasons and in all weathers for the rest of his life. So although he would not like to have been forced to live there for ever—'one would think twice before he accepted heaven on such terms'—he never resists an opportunity of revisiting the scene of his great adventure.

He is inquisitive about Nature, but so indifferent towards social events, even to those which might reasonably interest intelligent people, that he might be suspected of posing. He would not, he says, 'run round the corner to see the world blow up', but he will not miss an appointment with the sun and is 'eager to report the glory of the universe'. When asked how he will occupy the time at Walden, he replies, 'Will it not be employment enough to watch the seasons?' He will not read the foreign news because nothing has happened in England since 1649, but the leaves of the green-briar excite him to 'a sort of autumnal madness'. If he makes few concessions to convention, he is naturally gracious, sometimes even courtly in his rough way, and rude only by design. Respectability is a private affair. It is only 'worth while to live respectably to ourselves'. And in spite of a spiritual impetus which urges him to reduce the needs of life to the bone, he is not particularly concerned about the hereafter, although he has a Platonic affection for immortality. The recurrences of Nature help him to argue himself into faith in some sort of a future life. The rebirth of the white lily out of stagnant water, looking and smelling of purity, is 'the resurrection of virtue', and it is such 'sights and sounds and fragrances that convince us of our immortality'. But, actually, he prefers his immortality here and now, in the quality of his daily life. 'One world at a time!' thus he rebukes the friend who seeks to console him at the close of his life with talk of a Better Land. He does not fear death but death in life, for 'who knows but he is dead already?' He is willing to admit that 'it is hard to part with one's body', but, 'it is easy enough to do without it once it is gone'. And when the end is in sight, he admits that he has enjoyed life and regrets nothing.

'Let us spend the day as deliberately as Nature,' he says, 'and not be thrown off the track by every nutshell and mosquito's wing that falls on the rails. Let us rise early and fast, or break fast, gently and without perturbation; let company come and let company go, let the bells ring and the children cry—determined to make a day of it. Why should we knock under and go with the stream? Let us not be upset and overwhelmed in that terrible rapid and whirlpool called a dinner, situated in the meridian shallows. Weather this danger and you are safe, for the rest of the way is downhill. With unrelaxed nerves, with morning vigour, sail by it, looking another way, tied to the mast like Ulysses. If the engine whistles, let it whistle till it is hoarse for its pains. If the bell rings, why should we run? We will consider what kind of music they are like. Let us settle ourselves, and work and wedge our feet downward through the mud and slush of opinion, and prejudice, and tradition, and delusion, and appearance, that alluvion which covers the globe, through Paris and London, through New York and Boston and Concord, through church and state, through poetry and philosophy and religion till we come to a hard bottom and rocks in place, which we can call *reality*, and say, This is, and no mistake; and then begin, having a *point d'appui*, below freshet and frost and fire, a place where you might found a wall or a state, or set a lamp-post safely, or perhaps a gauge, not a Nilometer, but a Realometer, that future ages might know how deep a freshet of shams and appearance had gathered from time to time. . . .

Be it life or death, we crave only reality. If we are really dying, let us hear the rattle in our throats and feel cold in the extremities; if we are alive, let us go about our business.'

20

Transcendentalism is for him no pose. It is a genuine effort of practical imagination, a mode of living, the art of packing each moment with the utmost life. 'To affect the quality of the day, that is the highest of the arts.' He is not interested in getting, or even in doing, but in being; the reward lies in what you are. He is thus more artist than philosopher. Where Emerson teaches ethics, Thoreau teaches aesthetics. Life for him is an affair of taste. It is real when individuality rules circumstance, and draws sustenance from its surroundings by the exercise of fastidious selection. Appetite and taste ought to be related. 'We live too fast and coarsely,' he says, 'just as we eat too fast, and do not know the savour of our food.' Yet he wishes to live so as to derive his 'satisfactions and inspirations from the commonest events'. He can live without the aid of a 'furnishing warehouse', most of our troubles being 'house-bred', the house being 'the very haunt and lair of vice'. He stands, in fact, for a free and independent soul stripped of doctrinal upholstery. Doctrines, dogmas, theories, and shibboleths, are no better than material possessions.

He possesses the spirit of a boy and the wisdom of the ages, and he above all his contemporaries has learned how to taste all the stars and all the heavens in a crust of bread, a doctrine which had been revived by Goethe and annexed by Carlyle in England and Emerson in America. Thoreau pust it in his own fantastic way: 'If a man does not believe he can thrive on board-nails, I will not talk to him.' He and Emerson meet on common ground at this point. 'Man is an analogist,' says Emerson, 'and therefore no man loses any time or any means who studies that one thing that is before him, though a log or a snail.' But, again, Thoreau is not content with ideas for their own sake. 'That man is richest whose pleasures are the cheapest' is no mere sentiment as it is with most of those who make such statements. He is talking from experience. He has 'thriven on poverty and solitude', and he never tires of telling us that, no matter what our conditions, where we are is heaven. 'It makes no odds where a man goes or stays, if he is only about his business.' It is wise not to go too far: 'staying at home is the heavenly way.'

This insistence upon going about one's business is fundamental, but the interpretation is peculiar, especially when related to himself, for it must not be forgotten that, like each of the dreamers examined in this work, he is not primarily engaged in saving anyone but himself. His wish is to 'love and revere' himself 'above all the gods that man has ever invented'. His method is a sensitive alacrity both mental and physical before the phenomena of Nature; a desire to live profoundly and vividly. He believes that life is experimental and that the laboratory is oneself. His aim is to make himself 'the thoroughfare of thrilling thoughts', so that he can live all that can be lived. 'My desire is to know *what* I have lived, that I may know *how* to live henceforth.' He is continually testing his powers of perception and endurance, for you must 'build yourself up to the height of your conceptions'. And in the process he discovers that seeing is a chief adjunct of being. His conceptions are never far from perception. He lives largely by sight and is fond of setting observation on a pedestal. 'How to observe is how to behave' and 'we are as much as we see.'

2 1

It may be argued that, since he admits that he sees with more integrity than he feels, he is doing no more than justifying, after the Emersonian manner, his own limitations That, however, would not be true. He is not deficient in feeling, and although he sees more than most men it is because he insists upon seeing more. 'No one', he says, 'has observed the minute differences of the seasons. Hardly two nights are alike.' Seeing is a conscious operation in the technique of living, closely associated with feeling: 'a man has not seen a thing who has not felt it.' 'Men talk about travelling this way and that,' he writes, 'as if seeing were all the eyes, and a man could sufficiently report what he stood bodily before, when seeing depends ever on being. All report of travel is the report of victory or defeat, of a contest with every event and phenomenon, and how you came out of it.' He feels with his eyes and his ears. Life is being alert, penetrating, absorbing:

> *I hearing get, who had but ears,*
> *And sight, who had but eyes before;*
> *I moments live, who lived but years,*
> *And truth discern, who had but learning's lore.*

The condition that best suits him is that of Nature, even Nature in her less comfortable moods, and as we have seen, in some of his own moods the more uncomfortable she is the better he is pleased. Comfort is defeat. He enjoys the stimulus of battling with cold and stormy weather and would emulate the 'wrecker' he saw on the beach at Cape Cod who 'looked as if he sometimes saw a doughnut, but never descended to comfort; too grave to laugh, too tough to cry; as indifferent as a clam.' Further he neither expects nor requests Nature to be bountiful: 'You must love the crust of the earth on which you dwell more than the sweet crust of any bread or cake; you must be able to extract nutriment out of a sand heap.'

Efforts of the kind also flatter his spartan sense of virtue, effort being the relaxation of the virtuous soul.

Thoreau, however, differs from his fellow transcendentalists in not elaborating this idea. He loves Nature for several reasons, one of them that 'she is not man, but a retreat from him'. Man taints what he touches and barricades us against the goodness of life with rules, definitions and moralizings. 'If this world were all man,' he says, 'I could not stretch myself. I should lose all hope. He is constraint; she is freedom to me. He makes me wish for a better world; she makes me content with this . . . the joy which Nature yields is like that afforded by the frank words of one we love.' He likes to think that he is less human than he proves himself to be, and less dependent on men than he is. 'I feel myself not so vitally related to my fellowmen. I impinge on them by a point on one side. It is not a Siamese-twin ligature that binds me to them.' So it is ever his object to get closer to Nature, not for love only, but for recreation and sustenance: 'I milk the sky and the earth.' The scent of the gale wafted over the naked wintry ground fills him with 'real vigor' and makes him realize again how 'man is the pensioner of nature'. If he has been occupying himself with some duties in the village it delights him to 'withdraw out of the wearying and unprofitable world of affairs', and to wade once again through the woods and fields, 'conversing with the sane snow'. The woods are his bath where he is 'cleansed of all social impurities'. There also he becomes 'a witness with unprejudiced senses to the order of the universe', is more 'cognisant of wit' than in a 'society of wits', and there he gets his 'underpinnings laid and repaired, cemented, levelled'.

22

Nowhere is there so confident a reliance upon Nature, except perhaps in Wordsworth, and, even then, Wordsworth prefers a tameness and a convenience which Thoreau does not demand. Each, however, finds in nature consolations for the unrest of human society. Both, as Thoreau puts it, believe that 'Nature must be viewed humanly to be viewed at all, that is, her scenes must be associated with humane affections, such as are associated with one's native place. . . . She is most significant to a lover. If I have no friend, what is Nature to me? She ceases to be morally significant. . . .' Not even Wordsworth read into Nature so many moral concepts. In some moods Thoreau can see nothing but sermons in stones and books in running brooks. He moralizes everything from the mould which is 'the flower of humid darkness and ignorance', to the rainbow which is 'a faint vision of God's face'. And although he seems at times to be teaching aesthetics rather than ethics, he is too much of a child of his age to ignore the opportunity of associating the two. His attitude recalls that of Ruskin. Good taste is good manners for both of them. Ruskin would not have quarrelled with Thoreau's conviction that 'the perception of beauty is a moral test', nor with his assertion that 'men are great in proportion as they are moral'. But such statements reflect Thoreau's social and intellectual background rather than himself, revealing as they do the influence of Emerson and Carlyle whose moral ideas dominated so much of the thought of the period.

Thoreau is also a devout lover of Nature for her own sake, and often so passionate in his attachment that he can rebuke Wordsworth for speaking of some natural scene coldly. Yet he is as temperate as Wordsworth and as prim, but he does not share Wordsworth's love of the picturesque. Where the English poet needs a Lake District, the American philosopher is content with a pond. The repudiation of the picturesque is deliberate. He produces a readable book out of the dismal coast of Cape Cod, and confesses that if a landscape is 'dreary enough' it has beauty. His spirits rise in proportion to the outward dreariness. Like many lovers, he sometimes doubts, but not for long. If Nature looks 'shallow all at once' so that he does not know what has attracted him all his life, he blames himself, and is rewarded by being 'unexpectedly struck by the beauty of an apple-tree'. She may be rough and he will love her none the less. He will not return her roughness. She may snap and snarl, but not he. She may be opulent, but he will keep his head and his heart, for he is convinced that, in spite of occasional appearance to the contrary, she is innately moderate. If, therefore, he aspire to such a nymph, he must be like her, moderate and more. The conditions of such aspiration are an uprightness of the senses which will tolerate neither languors nor lapses: 'Beauty, fragrance, music, sweetness, and joy of all kinds are for the virtuous.' Thoreau is a Spartan in loving as well as in living. Life for him is a pilgrimage with no goal. To reach any place is a sign to push on. Even when close to Nature he feels that he may be missing the advantages of some supernatural contact. Contentment of any kind is taboo because he fears that it will encourage him to exact less of himself, to get used to his 'meanness', to accept his 'low estate'. 'Oh,' he cries, in such a mood, 'if I could be discontented with myself! if I could feel anguish at each descent.'

23

The ideal which governs Thoreau's opinions is chastity, not as an abstraction but as a practical guide to the art of life. 'The glory of the world is seen only by a chaste mind. To whomsoever this fact is not an awful, but a beautiful mystery, there are no flowers in Nature.' It is customary to relate chastity and sex, but with Thoreau chastity neither begins nor ends with sex, although it is not likely that so human a philosopher should avoid the subject. Sexual inquisitiveness, however, does not dominate him as it dominates so many of the thinkers of his own time and ours. There are other matters equally, and perhaps for him, even more interesting. But he neither burkes the subject nor tolerates any nonsense about it. If he were not conditioned by transcendentalism he might content himself with a frankly biological interpretation of sex without admixture of idealism and its hand-maiden modesty. As it is he weaves the theme into that aesthetic idea of chastity which governs all his thoughts. 'If I would preserve my relation with Nature, I must make my life more moral, pure, and innocent.'

The purity he demands for these relations demands also a delicacy of approach which almost amounts to negation. If this were mere chivalry it might be passed as but one more symptom of recurrent romanticism. But, in spite of much lip homage to instinct, he fears the heart and all its work. 'The heart', says Thoreau, 'is only for rare occasions, the intellect affords the most unfailing entertainment.' There is an echo of Emerson here, but New England puritanism is not so much at the root of it as egoism. Thoreau has a fear of being possessed by anybody or anything but himself. Emerson wished to write over his door the word 'Whim', Thoreau should have written over his 'Trespassers will be Prosecuted'. He might give himself but he will not be owned by circumstances, conventions, or passions. So love is scrapped: 'Let us love by refusing, not accepting one another.' To a lady who sends him a proposal of marriage, 'I sent back', he tells Emerson, 'as distinct a *no* as I have learned to pronounce after considerable practice', and he wishes 'it will burst like hollow shot. . . . *There was no other way.* I really had anticipated no such foe as this in my career.'[1] There are rumours that he loved and lost and the fact or legend has been used to explain his coldness, when it should be fairly clear that such a man holding such ideas must have lost wherever he loved. He is too fastidious for love. In moments of quiet and leisure his thoughts 'are more apt to revert to some natural than to any human relation'. It might be argued from this that he is inhuman, but the opposite conclusion would again be wiser. It is only human beings who reflect themselves into lovelessness.

[1] *Familiar Letters*, 166. The *italics* are his. Thoreau was thirty at the time.

24

The foregoing opinions, taken from his journals, are so near his real attitude that he turns some of them into two rather fragmentary essays, one on 'Love' and the other on 'Chastity and Sensuality'. In form they have none of the polish or sparkle of Emerson's essays, though they often reflect Emersonian idealism; but in addition they flash with a self-expression which reveals a man who is half-conscious that his idealization of love is not quite normal. The letter enclosing the fragments to his friend, Harrison Blake, makes this certain. 'I send you the thoughts on Chastity and Sensuality', he writes, 'with diffidence and shame, not knowing how far I speak to the condition of men generally, or how far I betray my peculiar defects.' Thoreau is nowhere so bewildered as here, and nowhere else does he doubt his own judgment or think that his own opinion might be due to a personal defect. The letter to Harrison Blake was written in 1852, when Thoreau was thirty-five years old, but some seven years earlier, his friend Ellery Channing refers to the implied defect in a quizzing letter in which he adopts the style of Teufelsdröckh. 'That fellow Thoreau might be something, if he would only take a journey through the Everlasting No, thence for the North Pole. . . . He needs the Blumine flower business; that would be his salvation. He is too dry, too composed, too chalky, too concrete.'[1]

Stripped of this transcendentalism the notes on love and chastity reveal, indeed, a defective lover, or would-be lover. The naturalist who, despite his frequent moralizings over nature, often accepts her for what she is cannot face the predominant fact in nature with equal courage and frank-

---

[1] Qt. Sanborn, *Thoreau* (1882), 210. Blumine represents the love motive in Carlyle's *Sartor Resartus* which brought colour and music into the heart of Teufelsdröckh: 'Thus did soft melodies flow through his heart; tones of an infinite gratitude; sweetest intimations that he also was a man, that for him also unutterable joys had been provided.' *Sartor Resartus*, chap. v, 'Romance'.

ness. He prefers the company of women who do not remind him of their sex. Love for him is not enough, he bargains for something better. He will separate the ethereal from the earthly, the refined from the coarse, the ideal from the real, love from lust. He believes that love is fundamentally good, but at the same time not always reliable unless met 'on the ascending path', for without 'discernment, the behaviour even of the purest soul may in effect amount to coarseness'. And 'it is not a true apology for any coarseness to say that it is natural. The grim words can afford to be very delicate and perfect in the details.'

The heart, apparently, is not an infallible instrument of love: 'the heart is blind; but love is not blind. None of the gods is so discriminating.' The best guides are perceptions refined and sharpened by imagination. Sensuality is to be sweated out of passion. 'If it is the result of pure love, there can be nothing sensual in marriage. Chastity is something positive, not negative. It is the virtue of the married especially. All lusts or base pleasures must give place to loftier delights. They who meet as superior beings cannot perform the deed of inferior ones.' It is not surprising that such an ideal should end in denial. Thoreau is a monk at large not for the sake of devotion but because he cannot endure the intimacies of love. He shrinks from them as he shrinks from all close contacts. He remains a bachelor for the same reason as he became a hermit.

25

His attitude to friendship has the same reserve and, in addition, an exalted sense of loyalty. Friendship should be both real and austere: so real that it lasts 'for good, for evil', so austere that it needs no mutual sign or service. It is a pure and inexpressible affinity, which is so certain of itself that it is able and willing to recognize differences. 'My friend is one who takes me for what I am. A stranger takes me for something else than what I am. . . . I cannot abet any man in misapprehending myself.' Friendship cannot be based upon mutual admiration: 'A lie is not worse between traders than a compliment between friends. I would not, I cannot speak. I will let you feel my thoughts, my feeling.' It is not surprising to learn that such friendship is best when most remote. He prefers to 'postpone all active intercourse' with his friends 'to a certain real intercourse which takes place when we are actually at a distance from one another'.[1] In this lack of heartiness he is akin to Emerson, and recalls the shyness of the master. 'In the presence of my friend I am ashamed of my fingers and toes. . . . There is more than maiden modesty between us. . . . We should sooner blot out the sun than disturb friendship.' There is an innate and admitted chilliness at the heart, neither mean nor unkind, a shrinking rather than a denial. 'I am too cold for human friendships', he laments and hopes he may not 'soon be too cold for natural influences'.

He says many things which do not bear examination, for they carry on the face of them that intellectual persiflage which is the jargon of the transcendentalists of Concord and scarcely intended for literal consumption. Yet he has fewer of these tricks than Emerson, who loves to wallow in a warm bath of rhetoric. Verbal flourishes never deceive Thoreau, even when he is author of them. He is never overcome with the exuberance of his own verbosity, but as he tries to match his thoughts with his acts, believing that 'what can be expressed in words can be expressed in life', he makes his sentences lean and active as the life he admires. He wants his words to be as 'verdurous and sempiternal as the hills'. There was every reason why he should be particular, for is he not primarily hammering out guidance for himself?

[1] *Journal: Summer*, 143. It may be remembered that distance lent enchantment to Carlyle's affection for his wife.

26

Thoreau is always mixing himself a verbal cocktail. He shrinks from normal life and justifies himself by charging his fellows to imitate him, and they might do worse, especially in those moments when he is most himself, for then, perhaps inevitably, he is most humane and most universal: 'Pursue, keep up with, circle round and round your life, as a dog does his master's chaise. Do what you love. Know your own bone; gnaw at it, bury it, unearth it, and gnaw it still. Do not be too moral. You may cheat yourself out of much of life so. Aim above morality. Be not simply good; be good for something. All fables, indeed, have their morals; but the innocent enjoy the story. Let nothing come between you and the light. Respect men and brothers only. When you travel to the Celestial City, carry no letter of introduction. When you knock, ask to see God—none of the servants. In what concerns you much, do not think that you have companions: know that you are alone in the world.'

Whatever there was of quaintness or abnormality in his life or letters, the outstanding assumption is that by becoming himself (which more than most men he does) and by risking freakishness, he becomes what many men entangled in the world would like to be, but which, lacking even his negative courage, they can never be.

WHITMAN

---

*A world primal again, vistas of glory incessant and
   branching,*
*A new race dominating previous ones and grander
   far, with new contests,*
*New politics, new literatures and religions, new in-
   ventions and arts.*
*These my voice announcing—I will sleep no more but
   arise,*
*You oceans that have been calm within me! how I feel
   you, fathomless, stirring, preparing unprecedented
   waves and storms.*

WALT WHITMAN

I

Most American writers are American because they happen to have been born in America; even though they use an American idiom or write with an American accent about American things or ideas, they might have produced the same work in any other country. Walt Whitman is autochthonous. He is not exaggerating when he says that *Leaves of Grass* 'could not possibly have emerged or been fashioned or completed, from any other era than the latter half of the Nineteenth Century, nor any land than democratic America'. He is no literary Autolycus peddling European ideas. America is the only raw material upon which his art can thrive. He is American in attitude and idea: the quintessence of the United States; more American than the Declaration of Independence, more characteristic than Abraham Lincoln, more western than Mark Twain: as American as a Sky Scraper or a Wisecrack. And if his voice is still a voice crying in the wilderness, if as yet he is neither appreciated nor comprehended by the majority of his compatriots,[1] and may never be, he is none the less American, and *Leaves of Grass*, nearly a hundred years after its birth, is still America's most native literary production.

Whitman is the personal focus of American idealism. He not only 'reports' everything from a local point of view, but he wishes to become the embodiment of an American folk. In the last resort Emerson and Thoreau dislike their country and are either running away from it or trying to make staying at home a virtue. Whitman prefers to stay at home, is an American, rare in his day, who finds in America all the material and spiritual comforts of a home. He is thus something more than a literary phenomenon; more even than a writer of peculiar and original genius; he is a symbol and a

[1] 'We care nothing for Walt Whitman.' Edgar Ansel Mowrer, *This American World* (1928), 22.

portent. His expression combines all that is eventful and enduring in a complex and cosmopolitan community, and although the *English Bible* inspires somewhat the form of his poetry, his is less affected by foreign influences than any of his contemporaries or by almost any of his compatriots. He is finally unaffected by the American variant of Transcendentalism, and he is in open revolt against the imported puritanism which inhibited both Emerson and Thoreau.

2

By the example of his life no less than by his poetry he seeks to be the interpreter and saviour of his land and its people. He is as emphatic and direct as an Old Testament prophet. There is something prophetic even in the lounge of his self-confidence. In a world already obsessed by haste he believes there is no hurry: in a land already committed to success, he thinks that what is showy and shallow will pass, and that the worship of dollars will pass, so he 'loafs and invites his soul', as if this Now were eternity, and all were well, and he goes singing into a future which for him holds no mystery.

He comes as one having something to say, something real, urgent: 'Whoever you are, to you endless announcements!' He proclaims, with superb confidence, that he is blazing a trail, not singing a song. He democratizes not only mankind but ideas, thoughts, spirit, the whole universe. *Leaves of Grass* is a fanfare of affirmations. No poet has voiced such unqualified approval of life, if not since *Genesis* was written and the work of creation declared to be good, at least since the canticle *Benedicite, omnia Opera* rejoiced in the splendour of the world. Whitman is Nature's 'Yes man', the personification of the Everlasting Yea.

To accept him as a poet and reject him as a thinker, or to

accept him as a thinker and reject him as a poet, is to refuse to meet him unless he pretends, or lets you pretend, that he is what he is not. And it is not always clear what he is. Sometimes he seems to be deliberately elusive, just as he is often tiresome and occasionally disconcerting. At first his frankness is so foreign to the puritanical reticences of America that *Leaves of Grass* is looked upon as a bawdy book. Emerson, impressed by its 'buffalo strength' and disturbed by its frankness, seeks consolation by showing it to a few trusted friends, only to have his favourable impressions further undermined. Whittier throws it on the fire, and Whitman himself loses his job as a Civil Servant for publishing it. To this day few who read these now familiar chants remain unmoved, they either attract or repel, rarely leaving the reader indifferent. This is what Whitman intended. He discourages half measures and will tolerate no glib acceptance. You must take him, complete, without expurgations, or reject him entirely.

No other poet makes so sweeping or so personal a demand, not because no other poet expresses so much of himself, but because no other poet expresses so much of himself in terms of moral propaganda. He does not 'give lectures or a little charity'. When he gives he gives himself. You must be as inquisitive about him as he is. Other poetry springs from selected moods: Whitman's, from every mood. Who touches his book, he says, touches a man.

3

His poetry has other peculiarities. Most books of poetry are collections of detached or detachable pieces which express or pretend to express the unique experience of exceptional persons. Whitman's poems are as nearly as possible the reverse of this. They are interpretations and records of a distinct and peculiar personality, but also of a personality which claims to be the average of all personalities. Whitman is unique without desiring to be unique. He desires to become Everyman by expressing a kind of life which he believes to be common to all human beings, and in doing so, this singer of the 'divine average' becomes unique, for no other poet has tried to become something which does not exist. Whitman is distinguished in spite of himself, but he is unique by deliberation. Before a line of *Leaves of Grass* was written, he had 'presupposed something different from any other, and as it stands' it is the 'result of such presupposition'.

The voice heard in *Leaves of Grass*, although the work takes the form of separate chants and rhapsodies, is continuous and indivisible, a continuum of moods with a will to live and grow. Once Whitman projects and defines his poetic self, which he does without apparent effort, he keeps close to his own pattern, adding, altering, from time to time, and brooding over it from day to day. *Leaves of Grass* is as personal and intimate as a private diary, but Whitman does not hesitate to make a public show of what the most flagrant of diarists keep to themselves, and he is as unreserved about his aims as he is about his person. He announces himself as the epitome of American life and his book as 'the song of a great composite democratic individual, male or female'. The excessive frankness of pronouncements of this kind are kin to the innate showmanship of the nation which gave Barnum to the world, and although they and others like them are obvious symptoms of exhibitionism Whitman turns them into a fanfare for Utopia. Such patriotism and such egoism are as rare as they are disconcerting, for never before have they received such confiding and confident expression. They are saved from effrontery and grotesque eccentricity by their sincerity.

4

Whitman's patriotic philosophy is as grandiose and as accommodating as his democratic ideal. It is 'to help put the United States (even if only in imagination) hand in hand, in one unbroken circle in a chant—to rouse them to the unprecedented grandeur of the part they are to play, and are even now playing—to the thought of their great future, and the attitude conform'd to it—especially their great esthetic moral, scientific future: of which their vulgar material political present is but as the preparatory tuning of instruments by an orchestra.' There would seem to be nothing very revolutionary in such an idea, but underlying its platitudinous surface is a revolutionary idea—the idea of patriotism consciously and logically practised. Whitman is unusual even among idealists because he believes that the average man is normally susceptible to heroic patriotism in thought and deed, when history proves that only unusual people, like Whitman himself, are capable of more than a sentimental attachment to their country, unless moved to deeper and more immediate fervour by the catastrophic persuasion of war or revolution.[1] Fear, not devotion, is as yet the only cure for national disintegration.

But Whitman's patriotism is no narrow and fanatical love of his own country. Thoreau's romanticism looks inwards and finds a cosmos in a grain of sand. Whitman adopts the opposite procedure for, 'starting from fish-shaped Paumanok', he does not rest until he has embraced the world, and even then sighs, like some cosmic Alexander, for fresh universes to conquer. Not content with an American continent 'indissoluble by the love of comrades', he dreams of an America, sprung from the seed of all the elder lands rejuvenating the world, first politically, next materially, and then spiritually.

[1] H. G. Wells invariably uses catastrophe as the prelude to social upheaval in his utopian romances. See particularly *In the Days of the Comet*.

He visualizes the New World progressing by cosmic stages. Two of these have already passed. 'Two grand stages of preparation-strata.' The first, 'the planning and putting on record the political foundation rights of immense masses of people'; the second 'relates to material prosperity'; and the third, 'rising out of the previous ones', seeks 'to make them illustrious', by means of 'a native expression'.

Behind this conception, Whitman postulates mystical forces which must ultimately create a new and still greater people. Up to his time few had thought seriously of doing more than graft European culture upon America. Emerson and Thoreau were among the first to demand an American culture for America. Whitman goes much further; like Lenin and Hitler, and the Roman Catholic Church, he is a cultural imperialist. He demands that America shall not only evolve a culture of her own, but that she shall impose it on the rest of the world.

That is the broad generalization behind the varied modes and complexities of *Leaves of Grass*. It is not sufficiently remarkable in itself to require more than passing notice, and had it not been for the peculiar methods of propagation as well as presentation, the Whitman democratic ideology might have been long since forgotten. The various characteristics and implications of the idea will be considered later, it is necessary first to glance at the method proposed and in some measure practised by Whitman. He is a convinced believer in propaganda by personal example and hopes by being democratic to aid and abet the coming of a great democratic nation. He knows that without national self-consciousness there can be no nationhood; he is as convinced as Nietzsche and Spengler that the soul of a people is in its culture, and he hopes to awaken the dormant soul of America by anticipating that awakening in himself.

5

Whitman's appearance and manner of living are thus more than usually important. They are still more important when it is recalled that if his poetry is frankly a distillation of himself—an essay in poetic and propagandist portraiture, his personality is equally an extension of his poetry. Walt Whitman is as much the child of *Leaves of Grass* as *Leaves of Grass* is the child of Walt Whitman. He would have us think of himself as a large, easy-going, friendly personality; healthy, sun and wind-tanned; owning no property, giving himself freely without distinction of class, race, or creed; respecting all callings, and whilst allowing no convention or tradition to stand in his way, showing infinite tolerance and good temper towards all men and every honestly held opinion. This character survives comparison with the original model.

In appearance he is large, loose-limbed, hairy; his face is weathered to a rosy-tan, and he exudes the clean smell of a healthy animal. In his prime he looks like a fine specimen of stevedore, or backwoodsman. A conspicuous figure even in a crowd. 'Well, he looks like a man!' In those words Abraham Lincoln paints his portrait. Not even those who are inimical to his poetry and its implications escape being impressed by his presence. Moncure D. Conway, a cautious admirer, becomes enthusiastic when he sees the bard of democracy bathing on Staten Island. Conway is 'impressed by a certain grandeur about the man', and remembers 'the picture of Bacchus on the wall of his (Whitman's) room', and he recalls that the sun has put a 'red mask on his face and neck, and that his body was a ruddy blond, pure and noble, his form being remarkable for fine curves and for that grace of movement which is the flower of shapely and well-knit bones'. All personal records of Whitman strike the same enthusiastic note.

6

As the years pass the backwoodsman changes into the bard. Hair which turns grey early now whitens, and is allowed bardic freedom. This is the familiar figure in the later phase, often seen weighing heavily upon the arm of Mrs. Davis, his devoted and self-sacrificing friend and house-keeper, as he hobbles to the waterfront at Camden, New Jersey, for his daily revel in the busy scene. This is the figure which is cheered on public platforms in Philadelphia and New York when he recites his lecture on Abraham Lincoln; this is the figure known to that procession of admiring and inquisitive visitors who gratify and weary his declining years; this is the figure which drives in the carriage given him by friends, to the cemetery where he contemplates with satis-faction the grandiose tomb of rough-hewn granite he has built for himself; and, later, this is the figure of the bard, older still, but still imposing in his weakness, as he is wheeled in his bath-chair by one of his 'lovers', through the streets of Camden, receiving the salutations of ordinary and extra-ordinary people alike as the homage due to the 'friendly and flowing' personality of the 'Good Gray Poet'.

As decrepitude increases, Whitman's burly form, wrapped in a robelike overcoat of grey cloth, is 'anchored' in a massive armchair, over the back of which is thrown a wolf skin. Thus enthroned, the Bard of Democracy spends his last decade in the small house in Mickle Street, Camden, New Jersey, seated mostly at the window where he greets and is greeted by neighbours, or receiving visitors and disciples in his un-tidy living-room, pleased with his growing fame, enjoying the affection and the curiosity he arouses. He plays the part of the Good Gray Poet with distinction, and, on the whole, with dignity, for, although he seems to have been almost without a sense of humour, he is protected, even from the unconscious booby-traps of his disciples, by a simplicity which has been mistaken for cunning.

7

Much has been made of his English-Dutch descent and the Quaker faith of his family. But such influences can have meant little in the making of the Bard of Democracy. The poetic characteristics of his European forebears are absent from his poetry, nor are his habits specifically English or Dutch—unless his romanticism be derived from England and his personal cleanliness from Holland. There is no trace of Quaker influence, in either his work or his life, unless habitual caution in some matters and readiness to rely for guidance upon intuition rather than intellect are indications. But the recognition of such resemblances are of little value. They throw no light upon the causes of his poetry or the peculiarities of his moral code. It would be easier to relate both to ancient Greece, with which land and culture he had no links, than to England or Holland. Whitman does not encourage attempts to pigeon-hole his line or lines of descent. 'I am partly of Quaker stock', he says, but 'do not make ado about the stock passions.'

8

It is more important to remember that Whitman makes no claim to moral perfection; on the contrary, he rejects all moral exclusions. But he makes no treaties with wrong-doers. 'In so much as thou hast sinned, I forgive thee: go and sin no more' is the height of Christian magnanimity. But Walt Whitman goes further when he says, 'Not till the sun excludes you do I exclude you.' He believes in human perfectibility, but, characteristically, as we shall see, he recognizes the places of imperfection and when and where it is necessary and inevitable. His democratic faith is so wide as to include equality for good and evil.

9

Interpreting him thus one is less surprised to learn that he has feet of clay, or, rather, that his feet sometimes stick in the clay. How can one who announces himself as 'Walt Whitman, liberal, and lusty as Nature', be otherwise, at least, from the conventional point of view? If he is indulgent to humanity at large, and in detail, he is indulgent also to himself. He recognizes and tolerates inconsistencies in others and in himself. He opposes possessions, but clings desperately to his own small affairs. He believes in giving yet sponges on his housekeeper. He is a democrat and a believer in equality yet a poseur. He is homosexual, yet the father (by his own brag) of six illegitimate children. He is robust and masculine yet his voice is high, and he wears shirts trimmed with lace. He is all these things, and more, yet no man evokes so much affection or inspires those who come near him with such feelings of exaltation and happiness. Poets, hitherto, have only revealed themselves indirectly. Whitman exposes himself to attack by revealing all. He has few reservations, according to the limited ideas of self-revelation of his own time. More than any writer, he is the father of modern frankness, and he survives by giving himself away in more senses than one.

In *Leaves of Grass* we have a rough-hewn model of this dreamer. Abandonment of accepted standards of verse is not a pose; his book is no literary freak. Both manner and matter are in tune with his attitude towards all standards and conventions, whether of art, religion, or social affairs. His own life is the sole standard of his prosody. He strives deliberately to fashion his poems as freely as he lives, and as he would have all men live, for there are no exclusions in his Utopia. His 'chants' are different from all other poems because he is different from all other poets; but, unlike his poetic predecessors, he is not, as he sees himself, sharply different from the common people. He wishes to be the poet of a people, rather than the poet of a class, by disestablishing the vulgar idea that poet is 'a sort of male odalisque, singing or piano-playing a kind of spiced ideas, second-hand reminiscences, or toying late hours at entertainments, in rooms stifling with fashionable scent'.

I O

He challenges the value of artificial beauty, and looks with disfavour upon over-niceness or daintiness in the fine arts. 'Who troubles himself about his ornaments or fluency is lost.' The only beauty which he recognizes is that which 'comes from beautiful blood and a beautiful brain'. Beauty is a by-product, and he believes that those men and women who enjoy robust, open-air lives, are its essential perceivers. 'The passionate tenacity of hunters, woodmen, early risers, cultivators of gardens and orchards and fields, the love of healthy women for the manly form, sea-faring persons, drivers of horses, the passion for light and the open air, all is an old varied sign of the unfailing perception of beauty.'

Whitman's ideal of beauty does not end at the glorifications of health and strength, but would blend them with gracious and generous behaviour. He breaks clean away from the standards and abstractions which bemuse Emerson, and comes closer to making concrete proposals than either Emerson or Carlyle ever succeeded in doing. 'This is what you shall do,' he says: 'love the earth and sun and the animals, despise riches, give alms to everyone that asks, stand up for the stupid and crazy, devote your income and labour to others, hate tyrants, argue not concerning God, have patience and indulgence towards the people, take off your hat to nothing known or unknown, or to any man or number of men—go freely with powerful uneducated persons, and with the young, and with the mothers of families—reexamine all you have been told in school or church or in any book, and dismiss whatever insults your own soul; and your very flesh shall be a great poem, and have the richest fluency, not only in its words, but in the silent lines of its lips and face, and between the lashes of your eyes, and in every motion and joint of your body.'

He prophesies that the poet of the future will approximate to such an ideal. He will be neither classic nor romantic, materialist nor spiritualist. His poems will not be art for art's sake, but art for life's sake. He will not hold himself subservient to accepted rhymes and metres, still less to those gods and goddesses which for so long were the chief literary properties of the poets of Europe. Poetic diction is also condemned because it is tainted by convention and ecclesiasticism. All of which is part of his apologia.

Whitman himself has tried out his own principles. For him the day of conventional rhyme is ended, and 'the Muse of the Prairies, of California, Canada, Texas, and of the peaks of Colorado, dismissing the literary, as well as social etiquette of over-sea feudalism and caste, joyfully enlarging, adapting itself to comprehend the size of the whole people, with the free play, emotions, pride, passions, experiences, that belong to them, body and soul . . . to the modern, the busy nineteenth century (as grandly poetic as any, only different) with steamships, railroads, factories, electric telegraphs, cylinder presses—to the thought of the solidarity of nations, the brotherhood and sisterhood of the entire earth—to the dignity and heroism of the practical labour of farms, factories, foundries, workshops, mines or on shipboard, or on lakes and rivers—resumes that other medium of expression, more flexible, more eligible—soars to the freer, vast, diviner heaven of prose'.

He, therefore, makes his songs out of the immediate, common life of America, and he believes those songs are nearer to earth, nearer to the nature of things than has hitherto been tried in America. He 'sounds his barbaric yawp over the roofs of the world' but only in apparently careless measures.

Leaves of Grass is not as sprawling and untidy as it looks. It has form as well as rhythmic beauty, matchless imagery, and primitive forcefulness.

I I

Walt Whitman's pose is that of an honest, healthy, proud yet friendly American citizen, free of European influences and traditions, and though he admits the influence of the past, even to a smug appraisal of his Old World descent from Dutch and English stock, he rarely bends the knee to precedent:

> *I have taken off my hat to nothing known or unknown,*
> *I am for those that have never been mastered.*

He accepts all without reserve; normal and abnormal; strong and weak; good and evil; seeing himself in all, in man as well as woman, in all races and conditions, and seeing all in himself. And what he demands for himself he demands for everyone. 'By God!' he blusters, 'I will accept nothing which all cannot have their counterpart of on the same terms.' He is arrogant and confident; certain that he is right, admitting no poems into his book until they have been tested by the sun and the hills and the sea. He is under no illusions about his mission, and is as frank about his aim as he is about his habits and his person. Yet, confident as he is in his achievement, he holds no finality for his poems. They are but hints, indications for the greater poets to come. 'Poetry (like a grand personality) is a growth of many generations—many rare combinations. To have great poets, there must be great audiences, too.'

The certainty with which he acclaims the essential balance and unity of his poems is equalled only by his rapt faith in the unity of every part of life.

At all times there are men who appear to possess more than

ordinary vision. But so little is known of such phenomena
that it is easy to mistake more for less: it is an easy mistake,
a *naïveté* which surprises by its clarity for a profundity which
surprises by its prescience. Each condition is known to
psychology but the latter is less satisfactorily defined. One
of its characteristics seems to be a temporary but complete
abstraction from self and an apparent merging of the individuality with the whole of life, without loss of the faculty
of self-contemplation. Whitman's egotism is as much a flight
from self as a desire for self-expression, and for that reason
alone the cosmic quality of his poems must be recognized if
his total expression is to be comprehensible. His fundamental
ideas of personality, democracy, and immortality are best
understood in the light of it, and in doing so it will be found
that his ideas of personality, democracy, and immortality are
very different from the popular understanding of those words.

At the same time much of Walt Whitman is common to
all religions:

> *Swiftly arose and spread around me the peace and joy and*
> *knowledge that pass all the art and argument of the man;*
> *And I know that the hand of God is in the elder hand of my*
> *own,*
> *And that all men ever born are also my brothers, and the*
> *women my sisters and lovers,*
> *And that a kelson of the creation is love.*

I 2

Like the mystics, he sees untellable things and hears 'unspeakable words' which he can do no more than indicate:

> *I lie abstracted, and hear beautiful tales of things and the*
> *reasons of things;*
> *They are so beautiful I nudge myself to listen.*

The records of such moments are familiar in mystical writings; but unlike many mystics Whitman does not see in these abstract visions cause for the neglect of earth. He sees in them the fulfilment of the significance of earth and the glory and consummation of material things; for he believes that the world of the senses is no less spiritual than the world of the spirit.

He sees clearly all life evolving into permanency, and he believes that the transient processes towards perfection are no less good than the final perfection itself:

> *And I will show that there is no imperfection in the present,*
> *   and can be none in the future,*
> *And I will show that whatever happens to anybody may be*
> *   turned to beautiful results,*
> *And I will show that nothing can happen more beautiful*
> *   than death.*
> *And I will thread a thread through my poems that time and*
> *   events are compact,*
> *And that all things of the universe are perfect miracles, each*
> *   as profound as any.*
> *I will not make poems with reference to parts,*
> *But I will make poems, songs, thoughts, with reference to*
> *   ensemble,*
> *And I will not sing with reference to a day, but with refer-*
> *   ence to all days,*
> *And I will not make a poem nor the least part of a poem but*
> *   has reference to the soul,*
> *Because having look'd at the objects of the universe, I find*
> *   there is no one nor any particle of one but has reference*
> *   to the soul.*

Thus, without distinction of creed, caste, or colour, he becomes the unusual phenomenon, a yea-saying prophet with a gospel of acceptances, declaring his faith, shouting his news, chanting his glad tidings, sometimes boisterously, sometimes sententiously, sometimes even crudely, but always with inspired seriousness, and often in words and measures which, though they violate the academic traditions of poetry, are so beautiful, that even scholars have admitted him into the hierarchy of the poets. But again, poetry in the literary sense is not his intention. *Belle-lettrists* have accepted him but he is no *belle-lettrist*. If his poetry is great it is great because it is authentic in feeling and idea.

I 3

Whitman does not exclude even death from his benediction. He sees in death not only the prelude to another life, but a necessary, desirable, and healthy part of this life. He is as confident of immortality as the most orthodox of believers, but more courageous than many of them. Poets often try to 'make quick-coming death a little thing', or to luxuriate in lamentations for the evanesence of life ; and even religious exponents of immortality are death's apologists rather than the acceptors of something which is as inevitable as life. It has remained for Walt Whitman to spread the news that 'to die is different from what anyone supposed, and luckier'. And he has reserved for death his richest passion, his most delicate art:

> *Come, lovely and soothing Death,*
> *Undulate round the world, serenely arriving, arriving,*
> *In the day, in the night, to all, to each,*
> *Sooner, or later, delicate Death.*
> *Praised be thy fathomless universe,*
> *For life and joy, and for objects and knowledge curious;*
> *And for love, sweet love—but praise! O praise and praise,*
> *For the sure-enwinding arms of cool-enfolding Death.*

14

To the conception of democracy Whitman applies the cosmic idea which engages his deeper ponderings. The fundamental equality of all things is the keynote of his teaching, and this idea holds good for him throughout every phase of life, in the particular and immediate no less than the universal and remote. The spirit of social equality which, he believes, must be the foundation of modern society and all social systems to come, is not, in his philosophy, inconsistent with individuality. Society is a democratic organism compact of a variety of other organisms, interdependent and independent. 'One's self I sing, a simple separate person, yet utter the word Democratic, the word *En-masse*.' He believes in the essential power of average thought and average emotion. The characteristics which endure, and which spur mankind into a fuller life, are common to all, because what is common is closer to the universal will. Yet, he says, 'produce great persons and the rest follows', and by that injunction he means to strike the balance of a higher average rather than to justify inequality.

His aim is the 'building up of the masses', by 'building up grand individuals'. That, he says, is the 'marrow' of his *Democratic Vistas* and it is even more the marrow of *Leaves of Grass*. In his final *apologia*, 'A Backward Glance o'er Travel'd Roads' (1888) he makes the apparent paradox clearer: 'I have allowed the stress of my poems from beginning to end to bear upon American individuality and assist it—not only because that is a great lesson in Nature, amid all her generalizing laws, but as counterpoise to the levelling tendencies of Democracy . . . I avowedly chant "the great pride of man in himself", and permit it to be more or less a *motif* of nearly all my verse. I think this pride indispensable as an American. I think it is not inconsistent with obedience, humility, deference, and self-questioning.' He is obviously disturbed by the implications of total democracy because he likes individuals and realizes their value, therefore he will have 'a great aggregate Nation . . . enclosing individuals'.

15

His ideal of a great person 'Dear to Democracy, to the very last!' is Abraham Lincoln: 'the grandest figure yet, on all the crowded stage of the Nineteenth Century.' On him Whitman lavishes his greatest poetic fervour. Lincoln inspires that worship which is expressed in Whitman's finest poem and one of the great threnodies of the English language:

When lilacs last in the dooryard bloom'd,
And the great star early droop'd in the western sky in the night,
I mourn'd, and yet shall mourn with ever-returning spring,
Ever-returning spring, trinity sure to me you bring,
Lilac blooming perennial and drooping star in the west,
And thought of him I love.

It is one of his desires to set apart the day of Abraham Lincoln's death for remembrance, and sometimes he reads his lecture on the 'Death of Lincoln' on that anniversary, at others gathers around him a few friends, but he never forgets the day. He sees in the assassination of his hero an incident worthy of Greek tragedy. 'Why, if the old Greeks had had this man, what trilogies of plays—what epics—would have been made out of him.' The death of Lincoln is the final act of American unity: 'a cement to the whole people, subtler, more underlying, than any thing in written constitution, or courts or armies . . . the cement of death identified thoroughly with that people, at its head, and for its sake.' The heroic death of such a Martyr Chief consummates Democracy not only for 'these States' but 'all over the social and political world'.[1]

---

[1] 'Death of Abraham Lincoln.' *Prose Works*, 308–9. Walt Whitman read his lecture on ten or twelve 'successive anniversaries' of the death of Lincoln.

The failure of democracy which the world is now facing, is perhaps due to a shortage of men who have absorbed and epitomized the common life and desired to redistribute themselves, as he might have said, for the common good. It is in the impressiveness of such persons, in the gift of themselves, that he, with Carlyle, looks for social salvation.

This heroic power Whitman will liberate and infuse into everyone until each stands, as he believes he does, 'aplomb in the midst of irrational things'. He has, however, no exalted notions of even the cosmic democrat mingling only with the highest and best, no ambition like Emerson, to hitch his waggon to a star. Lincoln is great because he is the crystallization of the common good and the common evil. Whitman sees himself walking the common way, despising possessions, sharing the common lot:

What is commonest, cheapest, nearest, easiest is Me,
Me going in for my chances, spending for vast returns,
Adorning myself to bestow myself on the first that will take me,
Not asking the sky to come down to my good will,
Scattering it freely for ever.

16

Yet it is not through personalities alone or through the mere consciousness of equality that democracy will be made lifeworthy. There is something else without which all the rest is useless. Come, he sings,

I will make the Continent indissoluble,
I will make the most splendid race the sun ever shone upon,
I will make divine magnetic lands,
    With the love of comrades,
        With the life-long love of comrades.

The idea of comradeship pervades and welds his philosophy. To exclude it is to exclude him. To apologize for it, smooth it down, or attempt to explain it away, is to misrepresent him. Whitman is consciously, almost professionally microcosmic. He will contain everything, even contradictions: 'I am myself as much evil as good.' He is old as well as young, foolish as well as wise, male and female, maternal and paternal, 'stuff'd with the stuff that is coarse and stuff'd with the stuff that is fine'. His various concepts are also microcosmic within their own limits. Love is all forms of love; comradeship is equally heterogeneous, as it was in ancient Greece, as it often is in Western Civilization. Perversion has no meaning for Whitman. His ethical concepts are concerned with living frankly, fearlessly, and disinterestedly so far as possessions or preferments are concerned.

17

Like Thoreau he believes in life without principle. He has faith in impulses rather than in laws, his doctrine, in so far as he has any fixed doctrine, is derived from a belief in the inviolability and invincibility of the instincts. What is instinctive is good. He affirms that comradeship is more necessary than love. It is less exclusive, yet more closely knit by emotion, more intimate, and liberated entirely from distinctions of class and the possessiveness of sex. All souls are equal before Whitman, and all bodies, so long as they are free. He believes that the ultimate solvent of war is not legal enactment any more than force of arms:

Over the carnage rose prophetic a voice,
Be not disheartened, affection shall solve the problems of free-
*   dom yet,*
Those who love each other shall become invincible.

274

In the Civil War he plays the part of comrade to the stricken warriors. His sentiments are with the North but his affection is immune from even a temporary attack of war-hate. For over two years he devotes the whole of his energy to cheering the lives of the wounded soldiers, nursing and comforting the fallen of Northern and Southern States alike. His method is simple, practical, direct. He gives himself, his dominant kindliness, his abounding cheerfulness. He writes letters for the men, reads to them, smooths their pillows, brings them such little luxuries as he can collect, makes the wards gay with flowers. Above all, he sprays the hospitals with the antiseptic of his own health and invincible optimism.

But his ideas of equality and affection are not what we usually understand by such words. His peace carries a sword. 'My call is the call of battle,' he says, 'I nourish active rebellion. He going with me must go well armed.' But this battle is more continuous than the clash of armed forces, it is the war of life, the conflict that does not seek success in peace, but in the realization of a still greater struggle. 'To see nothing anywhere but what you may reach it and pass it', is the aim of his fight, the reward of his victory. The attitude of Whitman is thus linked up with that idea of life which we call romantic. He is as romantic as Byron or Kipling. His ideal blazes with the light of one who does not confine romance to books and art, but of one who believes that romance begins when art and books have been left behind and man has taken himself to the great business of living.

18

Whitman devotes much time and space to the elaboration of his idea of a new literature. He would repudiate the charge of being a bookman or a connoisseur of books, and he is widely rather than deeply read. He has skimmed many books, and has a genius for penetrating rapidly to an author's central idea. It is always the idea rather than the method of expression which interests him. Literature is not ultimately for dalliance, especially in America. 'If America is only for the rule and fashion and small typicality of other lands . . . it is not the land I take it for, and should to-day feel that my literary aim and theory had been blanks and misdirections.' Most modern poems are compared 'to larger or smaller lumps of sugar, or slices of toothsome sweet cake —even the banqueters dwelling on those glucose flavours as a main part of the dishes'. This may lead to 'something' but not to what Whitman wants. 'To have great poetry we need great readers—a heroic appetite and audience.'

He believes that 'great readers' are a spur to the creation of great poetry at any time, but they are all the more necessary in a democratic age if poetry is to express and inspire the masses. But whether America gets her great readers or not, Whitman demands a poetry which shall express the modern, industrialized world as faithfully as Shakespeare and his predecessors and successors expressed the feudal world. He is the first modernist. Wordsworth and Coleridge advocate the abolition of 'poetic diction' and convention and a return to simple observation of nature and human beings who are close to nature. Whitman goes further. He rejects all the old poetic forms, rhyme and metre and verse, and all the old poetical emblems and images which have served poets as 'properties' from Homer downwards. In their place come towns and machines, ships, railways, shops, and farms and factories, and the rough and smooth human masses who attend them. He never forgets the multitudinous character of the modern state. 'Ensemble is the tap-root of National Literature.' He will bring the people into literature for the first time. 'The People! Like our huge earth itself . . . is a constant puzzle and affront to the merely educated classes. The rare, cosmical, artist-mind, lit with the Infinite, alone confronts his manifold and oceanic qualities. Literature, strictly considered, has never recognized the People, and, whatever may be said, does not do to-day.' Even 'great poems, Shakespeare included, are poisonous to the idea of the pride and dignity of the common people, the life blood of democracy.' When he mixes with the 'interminable swarms of alert, turbulent, good-natured, independent citizens, mechanics, clerks, young persons—at the idea of this mass of men, so fresh and free, so loving and so proud, a singular awe' falls upon him and he is filled with 'dejection and amazement', at their neglect by literary geniuses, that so far 'they remain entirely uncelebrated, unexpress'd'.

Whitman designs to remedy the defect by starting a democratic literature that will give the masses, as distinct from the classes a place in the sun. 'Think', he says, 'of the United States to-day—the facts of these thirty eight or forty empires solder'd in one—sixty or seventy millions of equals, with their lives, their passions, their future—these incalculably modern, American, seething multitudes around us of which we are inseparable parts! Think, in comparison, of the petty environage and limited area of the poets of past or present Europe, no matter how great their genius. Think of the absence and ignorance, in all cases hitherto, of the multitudinousness, vitality, and the unprecedented stimulants of to-day and here. It almost seems as if a poetry with cosmic and dynamic features of magnitude and limitlessness suitable to the human soil, were never possible before. It is certain that a poetry of absolute faith and equality for the use of the democratic masses never was.'

His aim is to make such a poetry possible by personal example and by special pleading. But the poetry he has in mind must have a purpose other than entertainment. He has all Carlyle's contempt for dilettantism and none of William Morris's respect for the aesthetic entertainment of leisure. *Leaves of Grass* contains 'nothing for beauty's sake—no legend, or myth or romance, nor euphemism nor rhyme'. To Whitman poetry is a means of implementing and developing the character of men and nations. It is meant to be stimulating and hygienic. In addition, literature must play its part with politics in leading and moulding opinion, but with a sociological and a spiritual rather than a political bias. 'To take expression, to incarnate, to endow a literature with grand and archetypal models—to fill with pride and love the utmost capacity, and to achieve spiritual meanings, and suggest the future—these, and these only, satisfy the soul.'

19

Carlyle and Emerson would sympathize with that object but they would be more cautious about the means to attain it. Both respect and fear books, and Carlyle is frankly and even violently opposed to a popular press. Whitman in America rejoices that history is being made by the printing press, and he visualizes with pride sixty or seventy millions of equals being developed by it, whereas Carlyle in England contemplates with scorn twenty-five millions 'mostly fools', reading or misreading the newspapers. In recent years we have seen these two associated but divergent opinions coalesce and crystallize into organized propaganda and press control. Whitman's idea has become the one and Carlyle's has developed into the other.

Whitman would have found nothing strange or unwholesome in the Communist and Fascist demand that literature should guide as well as express the emotions and thoughts of the State. He does not confuse literature with politics but he has no objections to literature playing its part in politics, or, when politics become illusory or an end in themselves, of supplanting them by 'domestic Sociology'. In his opinion America is 'the great test or trial case for all the problems and promises and speculations of humanity' and literature can help and express the processes by which his country is welding humanity into a new and more enlightened State. 'I think Literature—a new, superb, democratic literature is to be the medicine and lever, and (with Art) the chief influence in modern civilization.'

Walt Whitman's poems are thus intended to be preludes to life, spurs, and inducements to strong and free existence, therefore their literary value can never be the first consideration. 'Literature', he says, 'is big only when used as an aid to the growth of humanity,' and he would have his own work assessed in accordance with that aphorism. 'No one will get at my verses who insists upon viewing them as a literary performance.' Unless that is realized Whitman can never be understood or appreciated. Poems, for him, are tools:

> *The words of all true poems give you more than poems.*
> *They give you to form for yourself poems, religions, politics,*
>   *war, peace, behaviour, histories, essays, daily life, and*
>   *everything else.*
> *They balance ranks, colours, races, creeds, and the sexes,*
> *They do not seek beauty, they are sought.*
> *Forever touching them or close upon them follow beauty,*
>   *longing, faith, love-sick.*
> *They prepare for death, yet they are not the finish, but rather*
>   *the outset,*
> *They bring none to his or her terminus or to be content and full,*
> *Whom they take they take into space to behold the birth of*
>   *stars, to learn one of the meanings,*
> *To launch off with absolute faith, to sweep through the cease-*
>   *less rings and never be quiet again.*

20

That is the character of his romance, and although he has the romantic's faith in personality he has no interest in great persons for themselves. He is neither a lion-hunter nor a supermanian. His romance transcends all boundaries. He is not only the first American writer, but, appropriately, the first romantic universalist, for he would have the miscellaneous and unrelated racial units of the United States find an outlet for their inhibited nostalgia in the brotherhood of man with the world for homeland. Whitman poses himself as the typical citizen of a modern composite state whose main characteristics have developed almost within his own lifetime. And as he is both individualist and democrat so also is he nationalist and internationalist. And just as the individual belongs to and depends upon the mass, so the nation, with its human elements drawn from all lands, belongs to and depends upon all nationals for its spiritual existence. Whitman's nationalism, like his individualism, salutes all men whatever they are and all peoples wherever they are. His ideal of a 'comrade soul' is merged in the larger ideal of a comrade world: 'Below any page of mine, anywhere, ever remains, for seen or unseen basic-phrase, goodwill between the common people of all Nations.'

In spite (or perhaps, because) of this large and generous philosophy, Whitman has never received that acceptance which he desired. The laureate of the average man has been ignored by those for whom he sang and acclaimed by the intellectually exclusive and the emotionally peculiar, much as the productions of William Morris have been accepted largely by connoisseur and collector. He believed he was making a new folk poetry, but nothing could have been further removed from the common taste than the irregularities of *Leaves of Grass*. His tolerances would have been as intolerable to the instincts of the herd as his homosexuality would have been repugnant. The comradeship he upheld would have aroused the suspicion of the ordinary folk he sought to inspire, and those who became his disciples were often peculiar and sometimes perverted. The mania for owning things which he denounced has conquered the whole of the American people and produced a mass-worship of possesions and prosperity such as the world has not hitherto imagined, and mutual mistrust and dislike are as prevalent to-day as they were before Walt Whitman began chanting his gospel of affection and goodwill to all men, over ninety years ago.

INDEX OF AUTHORS
REFERRED TO IN THE TEXT

The names of the six Dreamers themselves are not included in the Index as they occur continually throughout the volume in addition to the chapters devoted specifically to each.

Agassiz, 220
Alcott, Bronson, 16, 215, 217
Amiel, Henri-Frédéric, 38
Anderson, Mary, 130
Angelico, Fra, 116
Angelo, Michael, 116, 162, 190
Argyll, Duke of, 99
Aristophanes, 180
Arnold, Matthew, 30, 150
Aurelius, Marcus, 223

Bacon, Francis, 115, 204
Babbitt, Irving, 50
Ball, John, 159
Ballantyne, Thomas, 12
Bakunin, Michael, 222
Baring, Lady Harriet, 67
Barnum, P. T., 258
Beerbohm, Sir Max, 160
Beaconsfield, Earl of, see under Disraeli
Blake, Harrison, 248
Blake, William, 183 and n.
Boccaccio, 187
Botticelli, 110
Bolingbroke, Henry St. John, Lord, 88
Brown, Dr. John, 100
Brown, John (Harper's Ferry), 37, 215
Browne, Sir Thomas, 52, 76, 200

Browning, Elizabeth Barrett, 125
Browning, Robert, 151, 164
Burne-Jones, Lady, 113
Burne-Jones, Sir Edward, 27, 151, 155, 165
Burroughs, John, 220
Burns, Robert, 90
Butler, Samuel, 67 n., 224
Byron, Lord, 19, 180, 275

Caesar, Julius, 142
Calvin, 88
Carlyle, Jane Welsh, 59, 65, 66 69, 70, 71
Carlyle, John, 65
Carpaccio, Victor, 126, 130
Channing, William Ellery, 28, 215-20, 228, 235, 248
Chaucer, Geoffrey, 145
Cicero, 180
Cockerell, Sir Sidney C., 95 n.
Coleridge, S.T., 29, 74, 276
Conway, Moncure D., 261
Cook, Sir E. T., 105, 108, 123
Correggio, 116
Cromwell, Oliver, 37, 58, 64, 79, 84

Dante, 207
Darwin, Charles, 58, 220
Dickens, Charles, 91

281

Diogenes, 213
Disraeli, Benjamin, 88, 96
Domècq, Adele, 111–12

Eddy, Mary Baker, 50
Eliot, George, 69
Ewing, Joanna Horatia, 107, 109

FitzGerald, Edward, 63
Flaubert, Gustave, 119
Fox, Caroline, 57, 78 n.
Frederick the Great, 37, 64
Froude, James Anthony, 65, 67
Fuller, Margaret, 12, 215

Gaskell, Mrs., 91
Gilfillan, George, 182
Gladstone, W. E., 109, 128, 223
Glynne, Mary, 110, 130
Glasier, J. Bruce, 137 n., 155–7
Goethe, 74, 79, 115, 171, 190,
  207–9, 241
Greenaway, Kate, 110, 130
Gray, Euphemia, 111–12
Grotius, 180

Hallam, Arthur Henry, 114
Harned, Thomas B., 23
Hawthorne, Nathaniel, 171, 201,
  215–16, 233
Hesiod, 130
Hitler, Adolf, 260
Holland, Canon Scott, 108
Homer, 80, 116, 207
Hubbard, Elbert, 50
Hudson, W. H., 31, 185, 220
Huxley, Aldous, 192

Ingersoll, Charles J., 28
Ireland, Alexander, 26

James, William, 50
Jefferies, Richard, 31, 185
Jeffrey, Francis, Lord, 65, 66, 73
Jewsbury, Geraldine, 64, 66
Johnson, Samuel, 71

Keats, John, 74
Kipling, Rudyard, 275
Knox, John, 88

Lamb, Charles, 233
La Touche, Rose, 111, 128
Leighton, Lord, 110
Lenin, 260
Lincoln, Abraham, 37, 255,
  261–2, 272–3
Lyttelton, Alfred, 110
Lodge, Sir Oliver, 105
Lucca, Zita de, 130

Macaulay, T. B., Lord, 90
Marx, Karl, 157
Mazzini, 57
Meynell, Viola, 95 n.
Meredith, George, 91, 220
Mill, John Stuart, 62
Milton, John, 81, 174, 180, 207
Mitford, Mary Russell, 109
Millais, Sir John Everett, 111
Montaigne, 209
Morris & Co., 163
Morris, May, 27, 137 n.
Mowrer, Edgar Ansel, 255 n.

Napoleon, 84, 208–9
Newton, Charles, 113
Nichol, John, 65
Nietzsche, Friedrich, 63, 78, 196,
  260

INDEX

Norton, Charles Eliot, 14, 26, 78 n., 109, 114–15, 117, 130, 175 n.

O'Connor, William, 15

Penn, William, 185 n.
Poe, Edgar Allan, 77
Pope, Alexander, 103
Plato, 180, 204, 208–9
Pulvis, Joe, 37

Reynolds, Sir Joshua, 116
Richter, Jean Paul, 11
Richmond, George, 130
Rossetti, Dante Gabriel, 113, 121, 127, 139, 151
Roosevelt, Theodore, 184
Rousseau, Jean Jacques, 57
Rutherford, Mark, 91, 156

Sand, George, 69
Sanborn, F. B., 187 n., 235 n., 248 n.
Savage, Miss E. M., 67 n.
Scott, Sir Walter, 103, 130
Sedgwick, Anne Douglas, 189 n.
Shaftesbury, Lord, 96
Shakespeare, 80, 116, 174, 204–207, 209, 276
Shaw, Bernard, 35, 235 and n.
Spengler, Oswald, 260
Sterling, John, 179
Shelley, P. B., 74
Street, G. E., 139
Swedenborg, Emanuel, 207–9

Swift, Jonathan, 207

Tennyson, Alfred Lord, 24, 62, 63, 67, 91, 114, 119 n., 151, 164, 207
Tintoretto, 116
Titian, 116, 127
Tolstoy, 81, 222
Traubel, Horace, 24
Turner, J. W. M., 114–17, 128
Twain, Mark, 255

Velazquez, 116
Veronese, Paul, 116, 122
Victoria, Queen, 223
Vinci, Leonardo da, 129, 162

Walker, Sir Emery, 151
Walpole, Horace, 88
Watson, Marston, 235 n.
Webb, Philip, 139, 150
Wells, H. G., 259
Whittier, John Greenleaf, 257
White, Gilbert, 31, 185
Whistler, James A. MacNeil, 118
White, William Hale, *See Under* Mark Rutherford
Wilde, Oscar, 235 and n.
Wordsworth, Dorothy, 217
Wordsworth, William, 29, 41, 74, 190, 217–18, 233, 244–5, 276

Xenophon, 130

Zeno the Stoic, 214
Zola, Emile, 151